THE WILD STORM
VOLUME 3

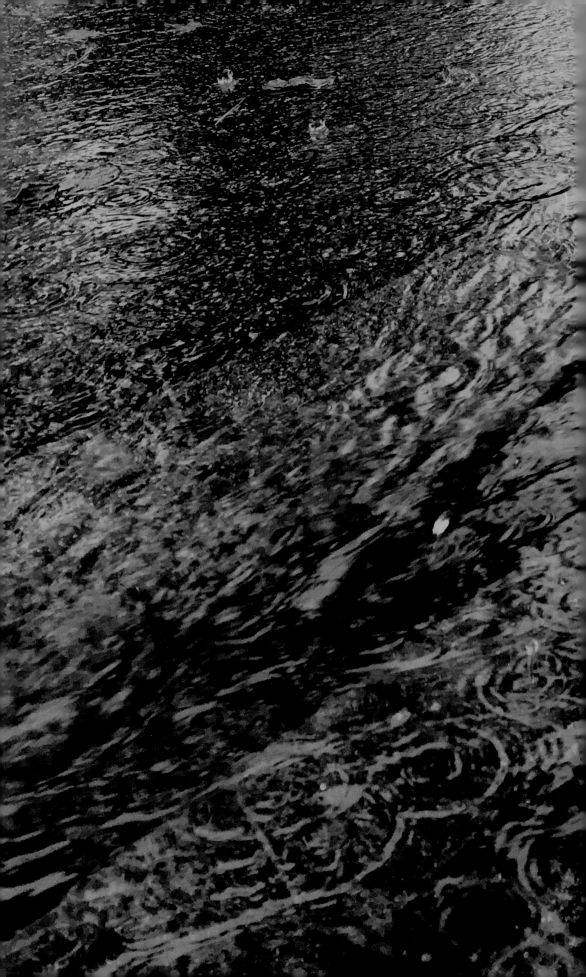

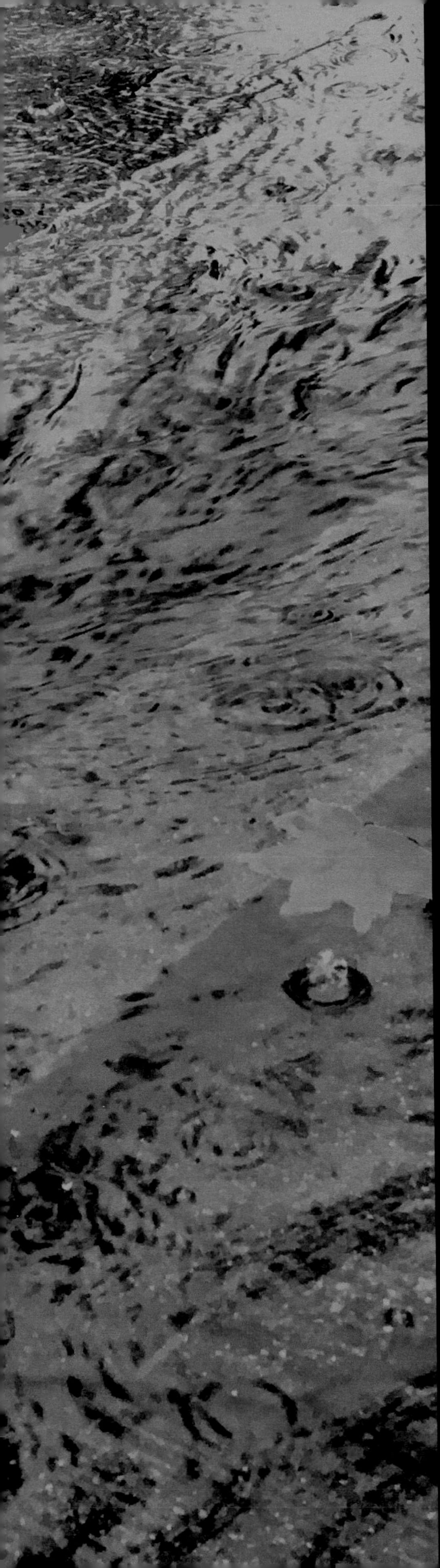

THE WILD STORM
* VOLUME 3

WARREN ELLIS
* WRITER

JON DAVIS-HUNT
* ARTIST

STEVE BUCCELLATO
BRIAN BUCCELLATO
JOHN KALISZ
* COLORISTS

SIMON BOWLAND
* LETTERER

SANA TAKEDA
* COLLECTION
COVER ARTIST

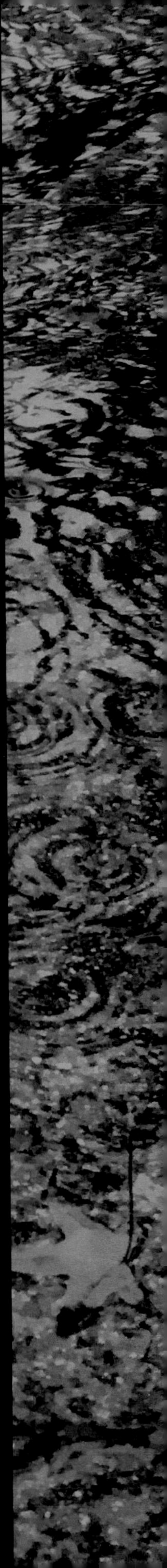

MARIE JAVINS — Editor – Original Series
ROB LEVIN — Associate Editor – Original Series
JEB WOODARD — Group Editor – Collected Editions
STEVE COOK — Design Director – Books and Publication Design

BOB HARRAS — Senior VP – Editor-in-Chief, DC Comics
PAT McCALLUM — Executive Editor, DC Comics

DAN DiDIO — Publisher
JIM LEE — Publisher & Chief Creative Officer
AMIT DESAI — Executive VP – Business & Marketing Strategy, Direct to Consumer & Global Franchise Management
BOBBIE CHASE — VP & Executive Editor, Young Reader & Talent Development
MARK CHIARELLO — Senior VP – Art, Design & Collected Editions
JOHN CUNNINGHAM — Senior VP – Sales & Trade Marketing
BRIAR DARDEN — VP – Business Affairs
ANNE DePIES — Senior VP – Business Strategy, Finance & Administration
DON FALLETTI — VP – Manufacturing Operations
LAWRENCE GANEM — VP – Editorial Administration & Talent Relations
ALISON GILL — Senior VP – Manufacturing & Operations
JASON GREENBERG — VP – Business Strategy & Finance
HANK KANALZ — Senior VP – Editorial Strategy & Administration
JAY KOGAN — Senior VP – Legal Affairs
NICK J. NAPOLITANO — VP – Manufacturing Administration
LISETTE OSTERLOH — VP – Digital Marketing & Events
EDDIE SCANNELL — VP – Consumer Marketing
COURTNEY SIMMONS — Senior VP – Publicity & Communications
JIM (SKI) SOKOLOWSKI — VP – Comic Book Specialty Sales & Trade Marketing
NANCY SPEARS — VP – Mass, Book, Digital Sales & Trade Marketing
MICHELE R. WELLS — VP – Content Strategy

THE WILD STORM VOLUME 3

DC Comics, 2900 West Alameda Ave., Burbank, CA 91505
Printed by LSC Communications, Kendallville, IN, USA. 2/1/19.
First Printing.
ISBN: 978-1-4012-8527-2

Library of Congress Cataloging-in-Publication Data is available.

PEFC Certified

This product is from sustainably managed forests and controlled sources

PEFC/29-31-337   www.pefc.org

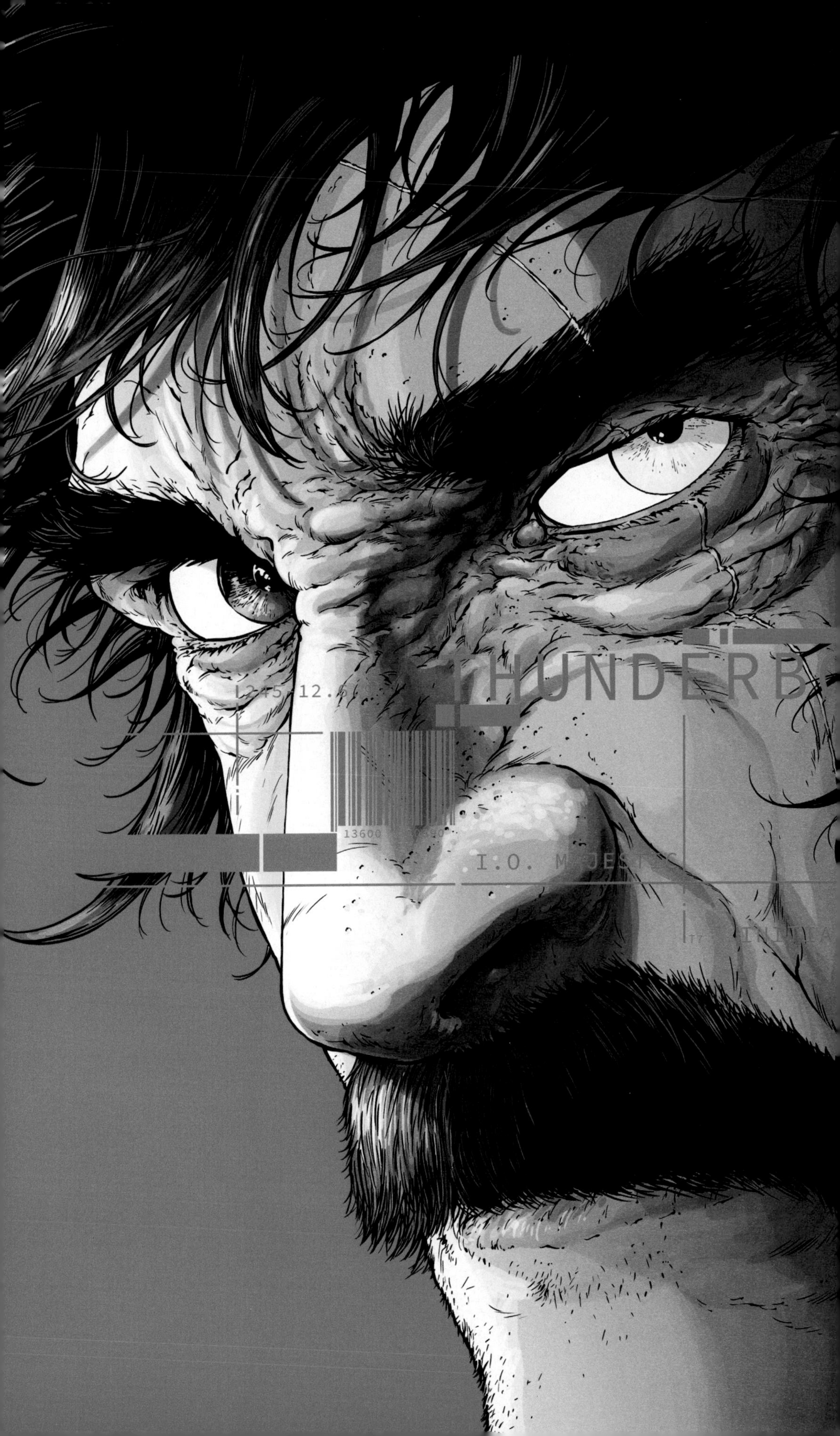
THUNDERB

13

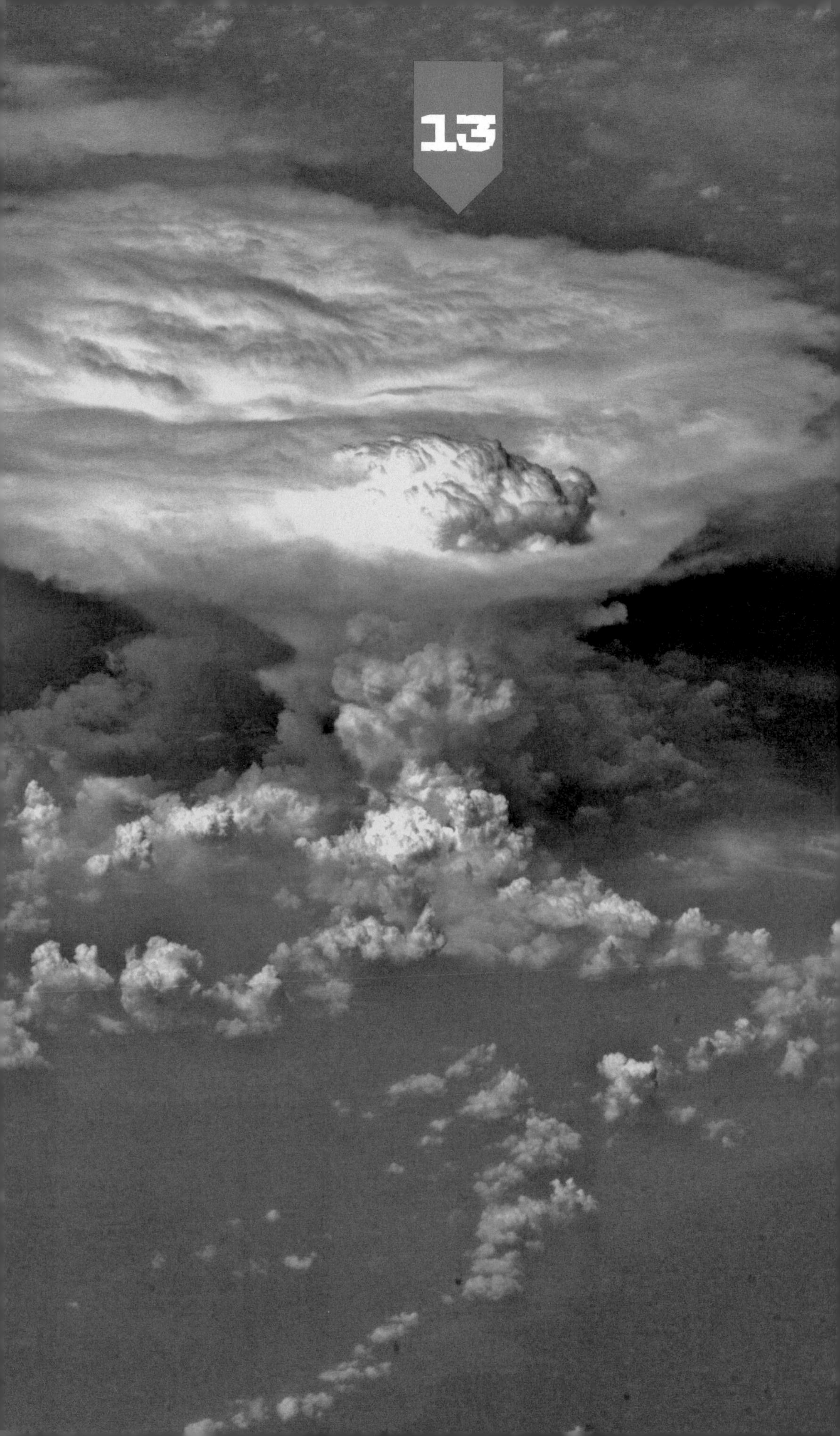

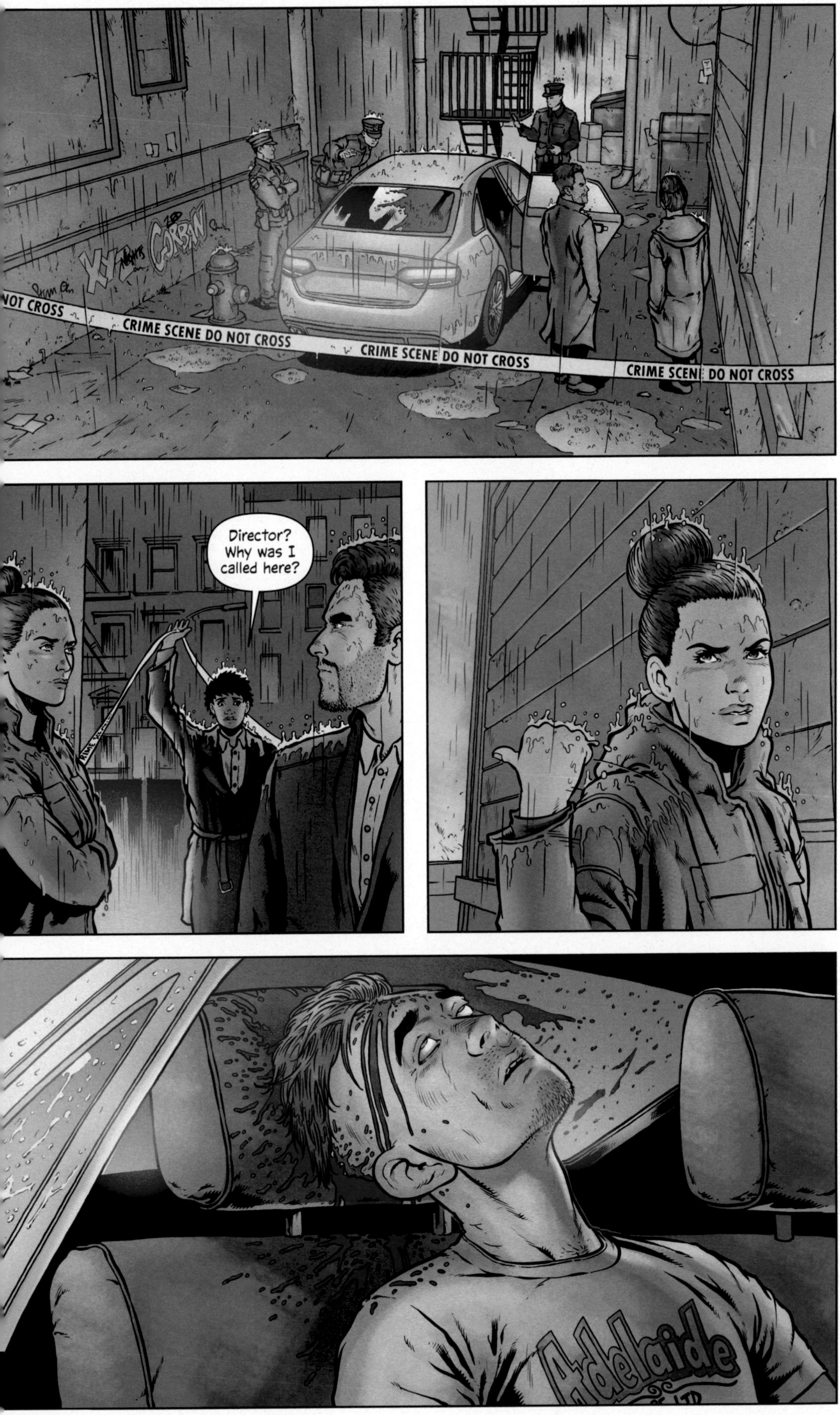
NOT CROSS
CRIME SCENE DO NOT CROSS
CRIME SCENE DO NOT CROSS
CRIME SCENE DO NOT CROSS
Director? Why was I called here?
Adelaide

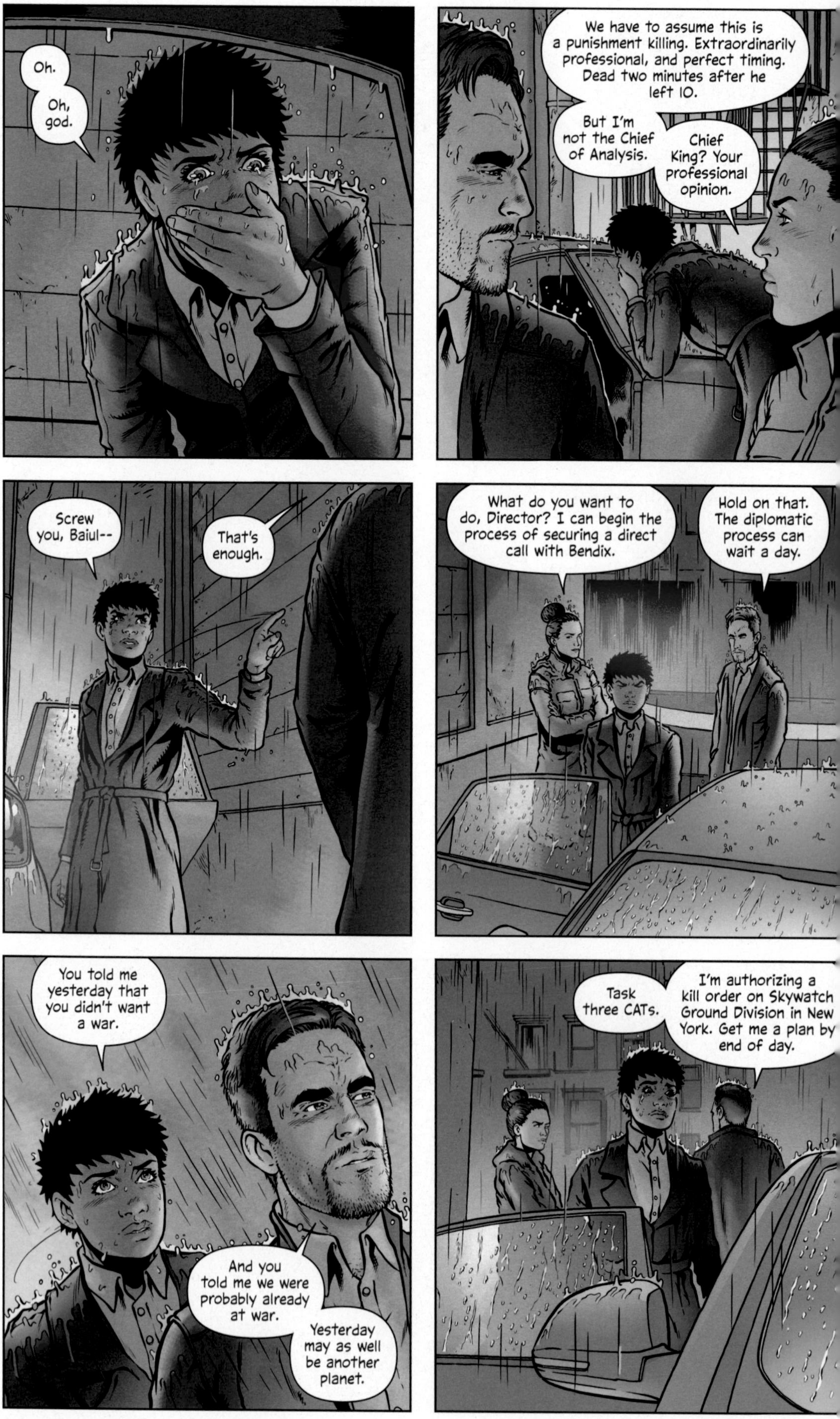
Oh.
Oh, god.
We have to assume this is a punishment killing. Extraordinarily professional, and perfect timing. Dead two minutes after he left 10.
But I'm not the Chief of Analysis.
Chief King? Your professional opinion.
Screw you, Baiul--
That's enough.
What do you want to do, Director? I can begin the process of securing a direct call with Bendix.
Hold on that. The diplomatic process can wait a day.
You told me yesterday that you didn't want a war.
And you told me we were probably already at war.
Yesterday may as well be another planet.
Task three CATs.
I'm authorizing a kill order on Skywatch Ground Division in New York. Get me a plan by end of day.

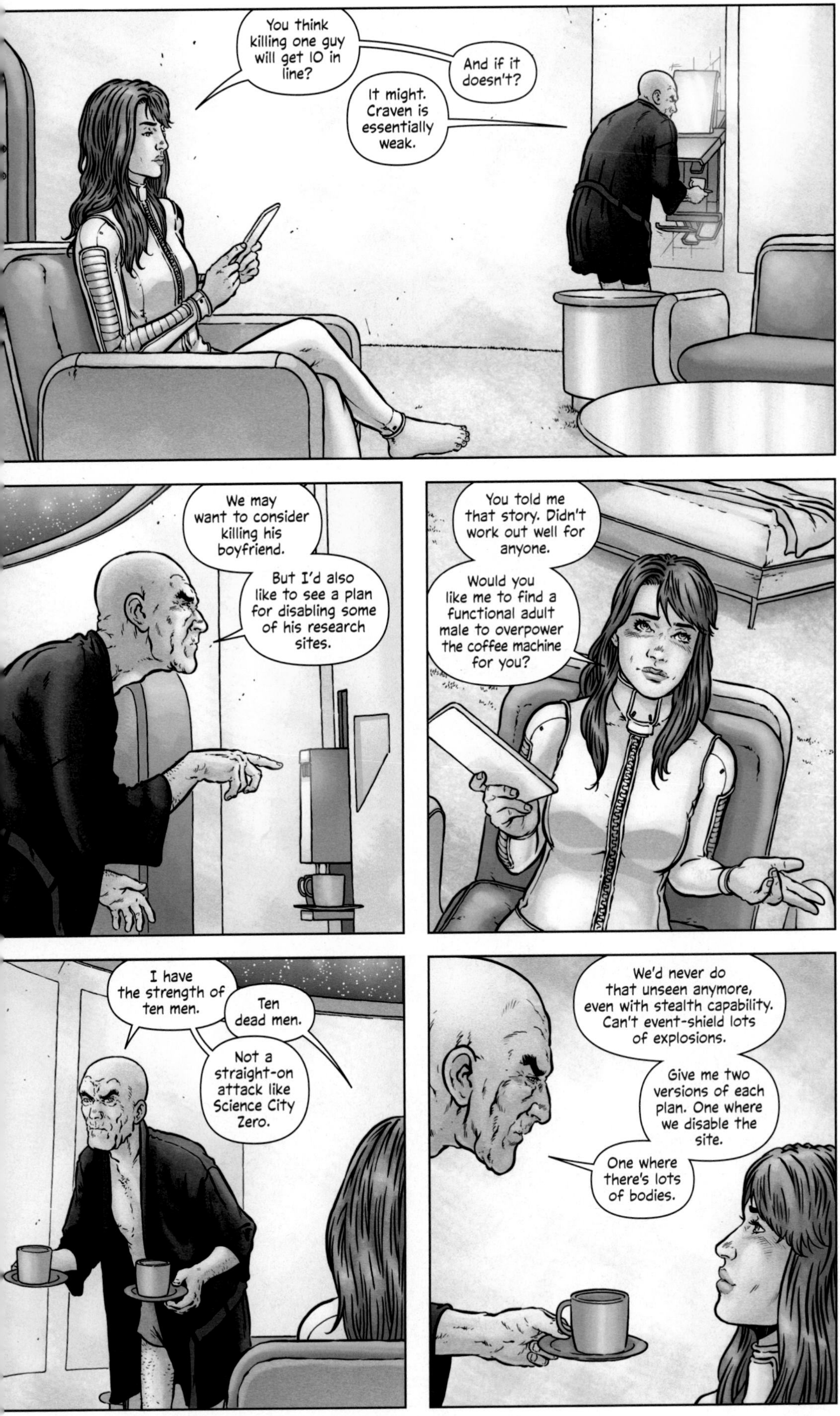
You think killing one guy will get 10 in line?
It might. Craven is essentially weak.
And if it doesn't?
We may want to consider killing his boyfriend.
But I'd also like to see a plan for disabling some of his research sites.
You told me that story. Didn't work out well for anyone.
Would you like me to find a functional adult male to overpower the coffee machine for you?
I have the strength of ten men.
Ten dead men.
Not a straight-on attack like Science City Zero.
We'd never do that unseen anymore, even with stealth capability. Can't event-shield lots of explosions.
Give me two versions of each plan. One where we disable the site.
One where there's lots of bodies.

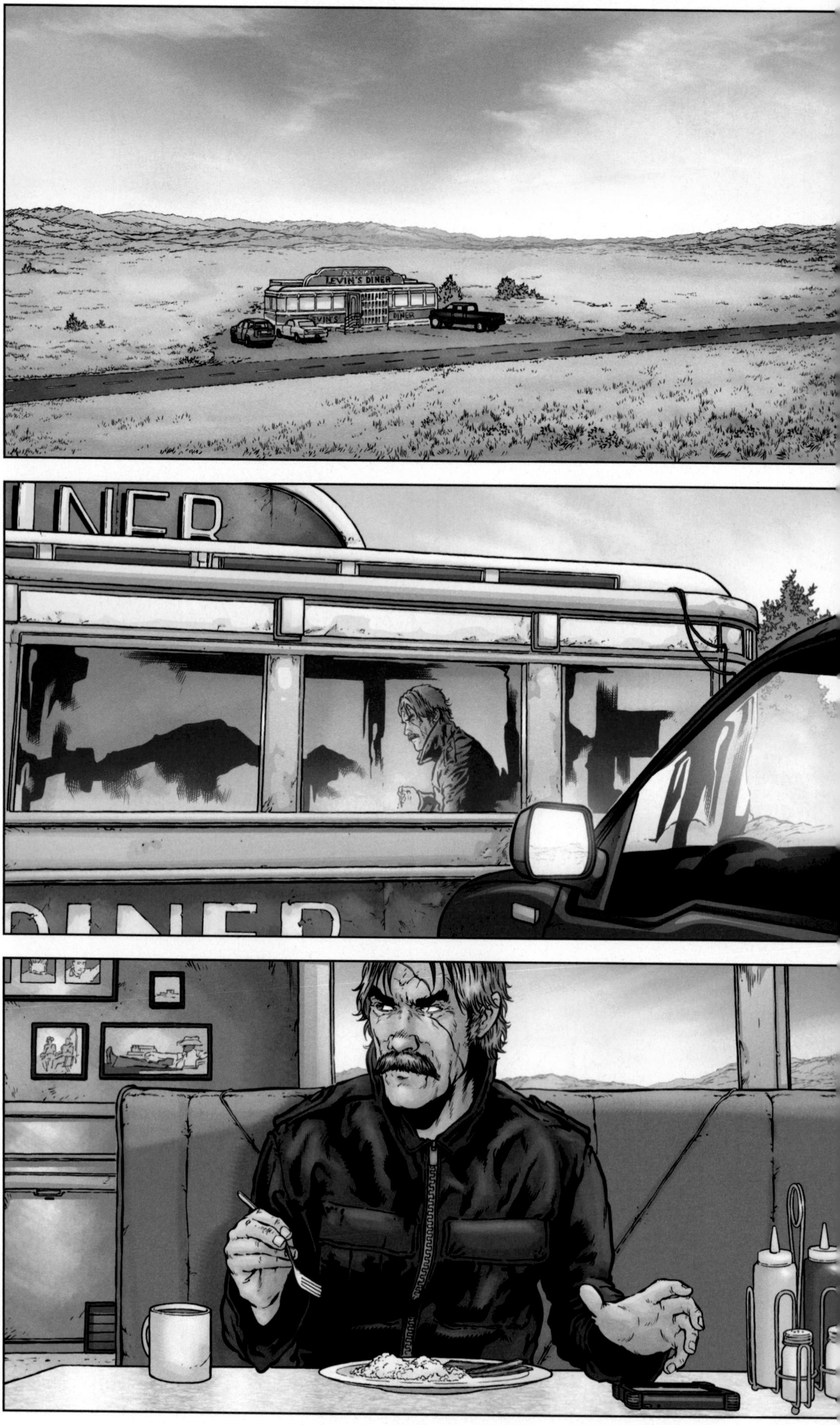
LEVIN'S DINER

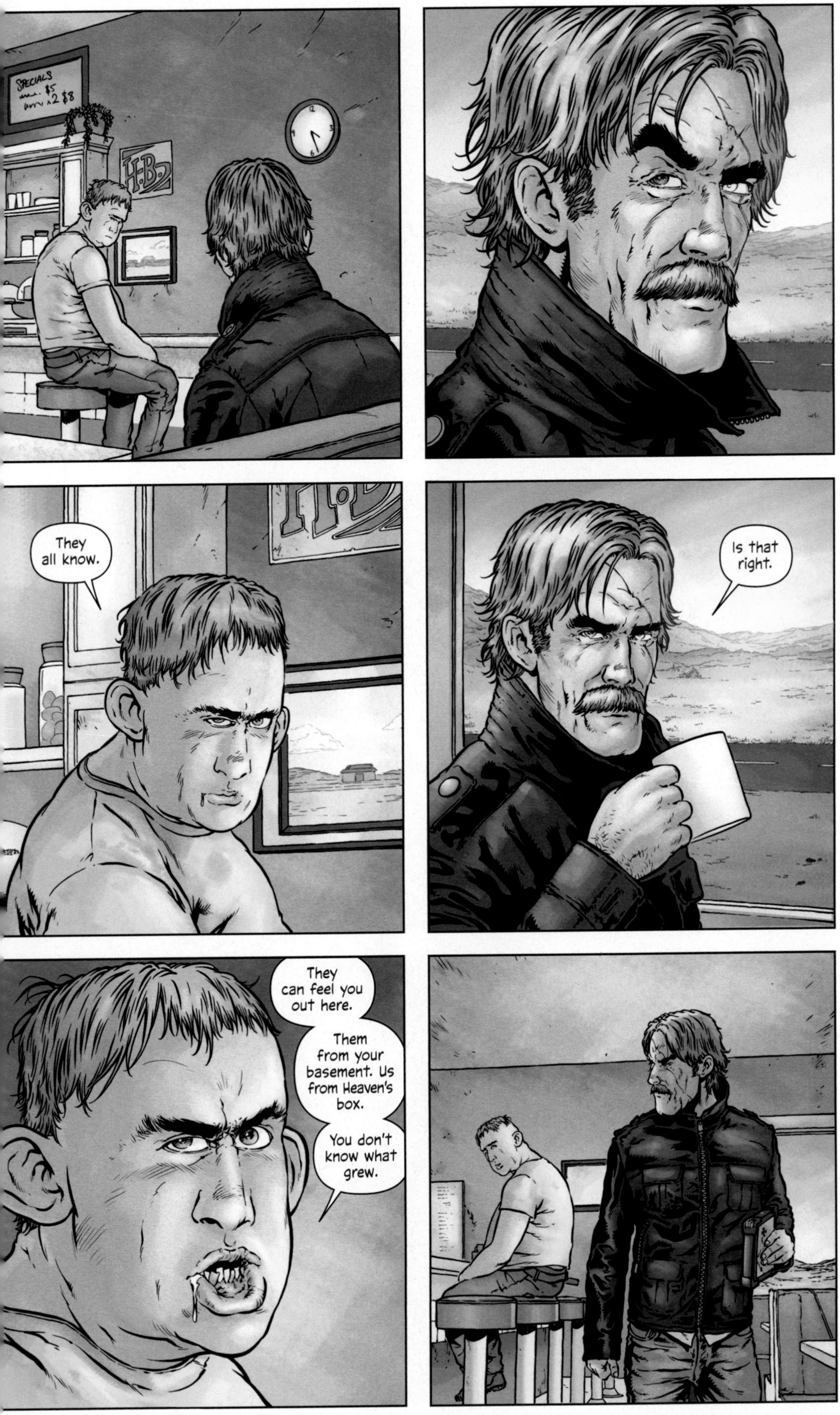
SPECIALS
H-B
They all know.
Is that right.
They can feel you out here.
Them from your basement. Us from Heaven's box.
You don't know what grew.

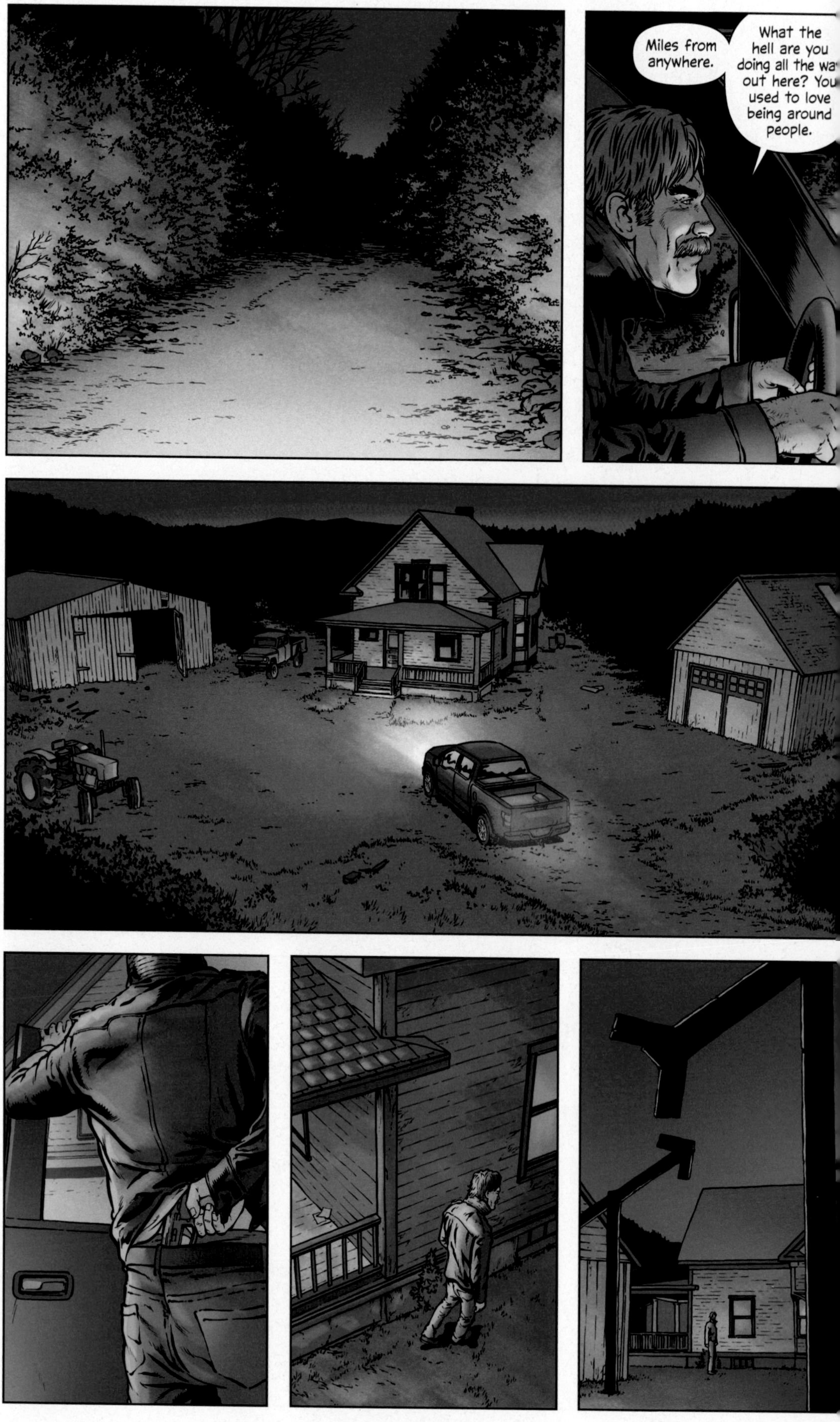
Miles from anywhere.
What the hell are you doing all the wa out here? You used to love being around people.

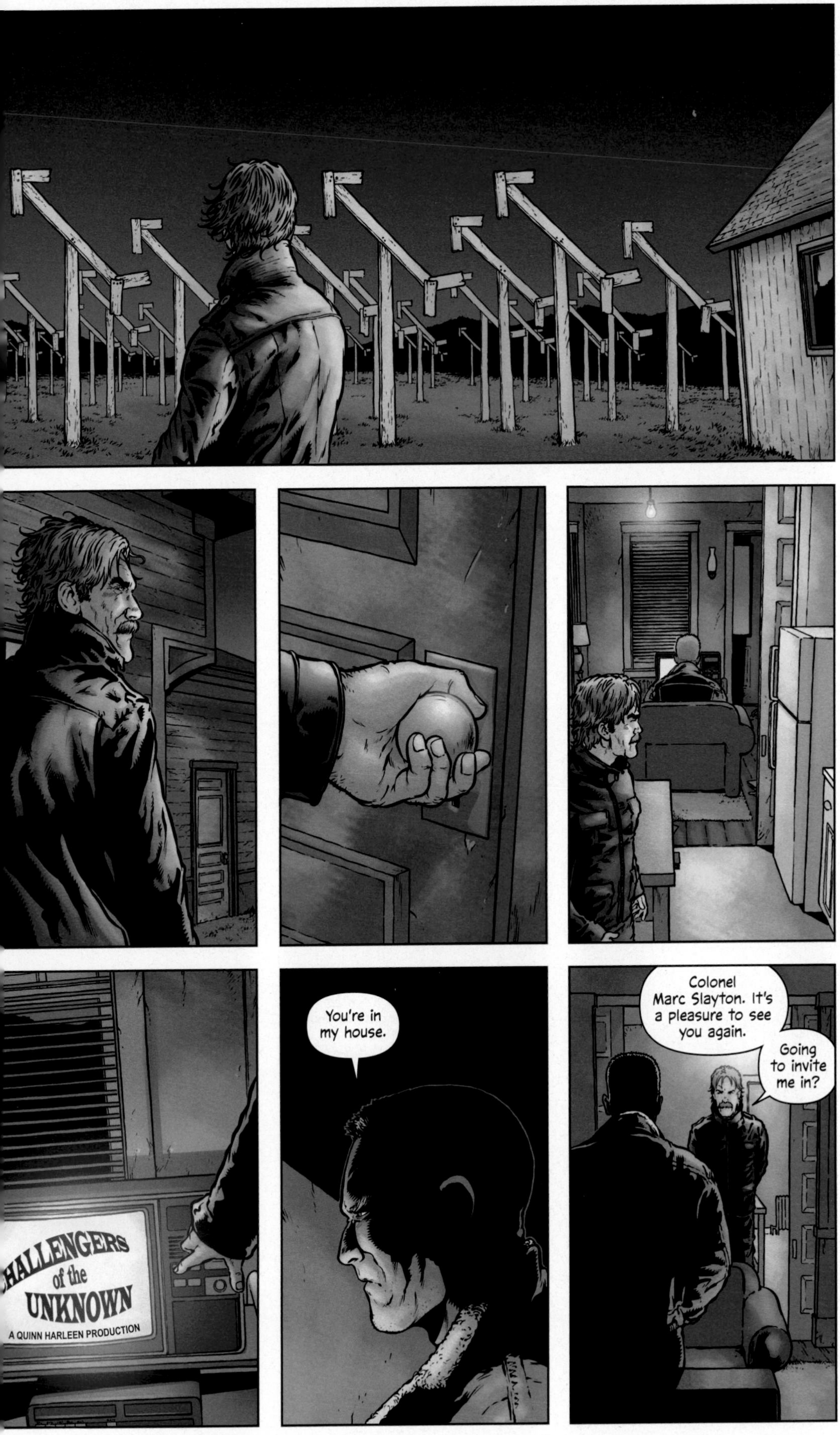
CHALLENGERS of the UNKNOWN
A QUINN HARLEEN PRODUCTION
You're in my house.
Colonel Marc Slayton. It's a pleasure to see you again.
Going to invite me in?

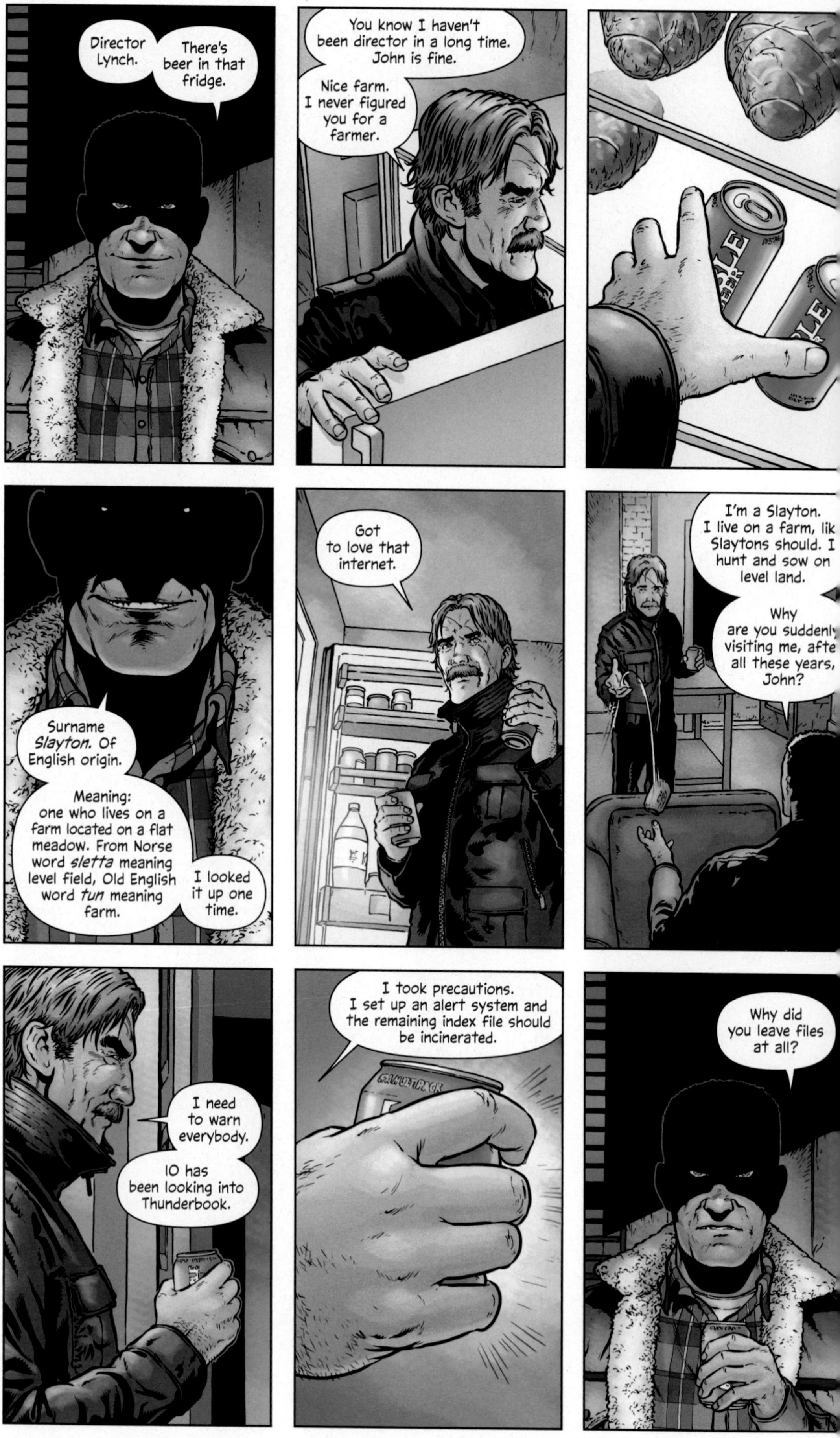
Director Lynch.
There's beer in that fridge.
You know I haven't been director in a long time. John is fine.
Nice farm. I never figured you for a farmer.
Surname Slayton. Of English origin.
Meaning: one who lives on a farm located on a flat meadow. From Norse word sletta meaning level field, Old English word tun meaning farm.
I looked it up one time.
Got to love that internet.
I'm a Slayton. I live on a farm, lik Slaytons should. I hunt and sow on level land.
Why are you suddenl visiting me, afte all these years, John?
I need to warn everybody.
IO has been looking into Thunderbook.
I took precautions. I set up an alert system and the remaining index file should be incinerated.
Why did you leave files at all?

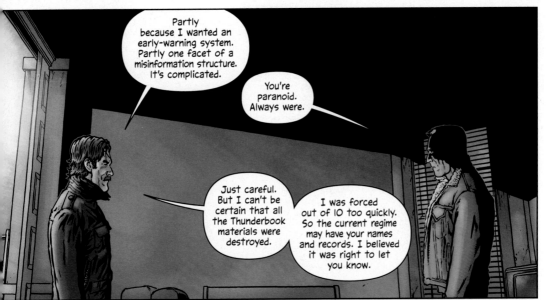

Partly because I wanted an early-warning system. Partly one facet of a misinformation structure. It's complicated.

You're paranoid. Always were.

Just careful. But I can't be certain that all the Thunderbook materials were destroyed.

I was forced out of IO too quickly. So the current regime may have your names and records. I believed it was right to let you know.

You scattered us all to the four winds and shut down Thunderbook before I started going grey. How do you know where we all are?

You've been tracking us all.

Not every moment. Just often enough to know where to find you if I needed to.

I feel a responsibility to you all.

Really.

A responsibility.

Because of what you did to us?

Because you were all loyal soldiers to me. Because you sacrificed much for IO. Because you were my friends and you served your world well.

Because of what I did to you.

Do you even understand what happened to me, John?

IO discovered remains of extra-terrestrial beings with viable, active genetic material in ancient burial sites around the world.

The gen/active samples proved to be able to plug into human DNA.

We believed the ETs actually changed into a sort of human form while they were on Earth.

It became clear to my teams that the gen/active material could be used for human enhancement.

I went to the best and the brightest under my command and offered them the chance to uplift the human race.

And you were the first, Marc.

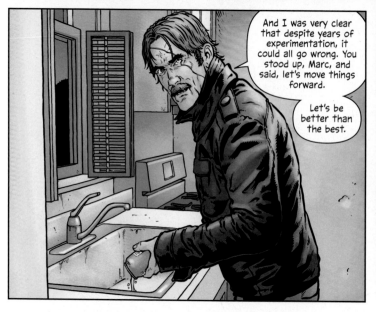

And I was very clear that despite years of experimentation, it could all go wrong. You stood up, Marc, and said, let's move things forward.

Let's be better than the best.

But do you UNDERSTAND? Do you know how it feels?

You know I don't.

So let me make it crystal clear for you.

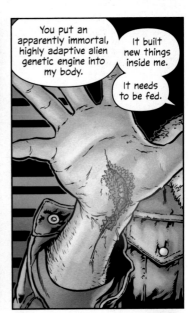

You put an apparently immortal, highly adaptive alien genetic engine into my body.

It built new things inside me.

It needs to be fed.

It talks to me at night, John. It's an organic computer welded to a genetic engine.

Where are the other Thunderbook subjects, John?

You don't need to know that, Marc.

Maybe I do. Sometimes...sometimes I'm pulled like a compass needle. Strange magnetism.

I think that whatever's inside me wants to eat them.

I don't even think we're alone.

It's not just the Thunderbook crew. There are more like us out there. If IO is coming for us...

I'm not saying IO is coming. I'm saying they've tried to look into the program.

You all deserve a warning.

I was the first, John. I deserved to be alone.

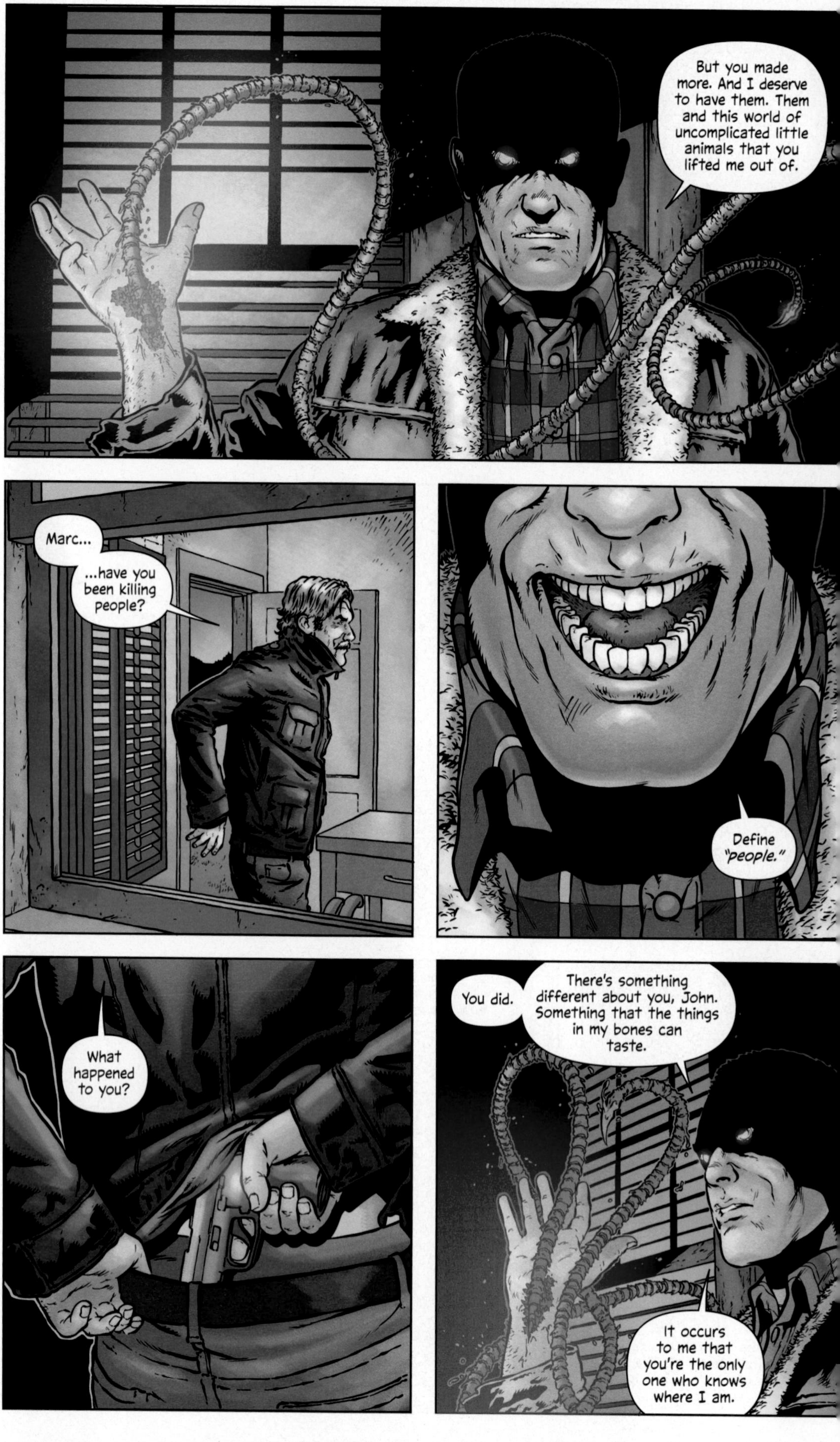
But you made more. And I deserve to have them. Them and this world of uncomplicated little animals that you lifted me out of.
Marc...
...have you been killing people?
Define *"people."*
What happened to you?
You did.
There's something different about you, John. Something that the things in my bones can taste.
It occurs to me that you're the only one who knows where I am.

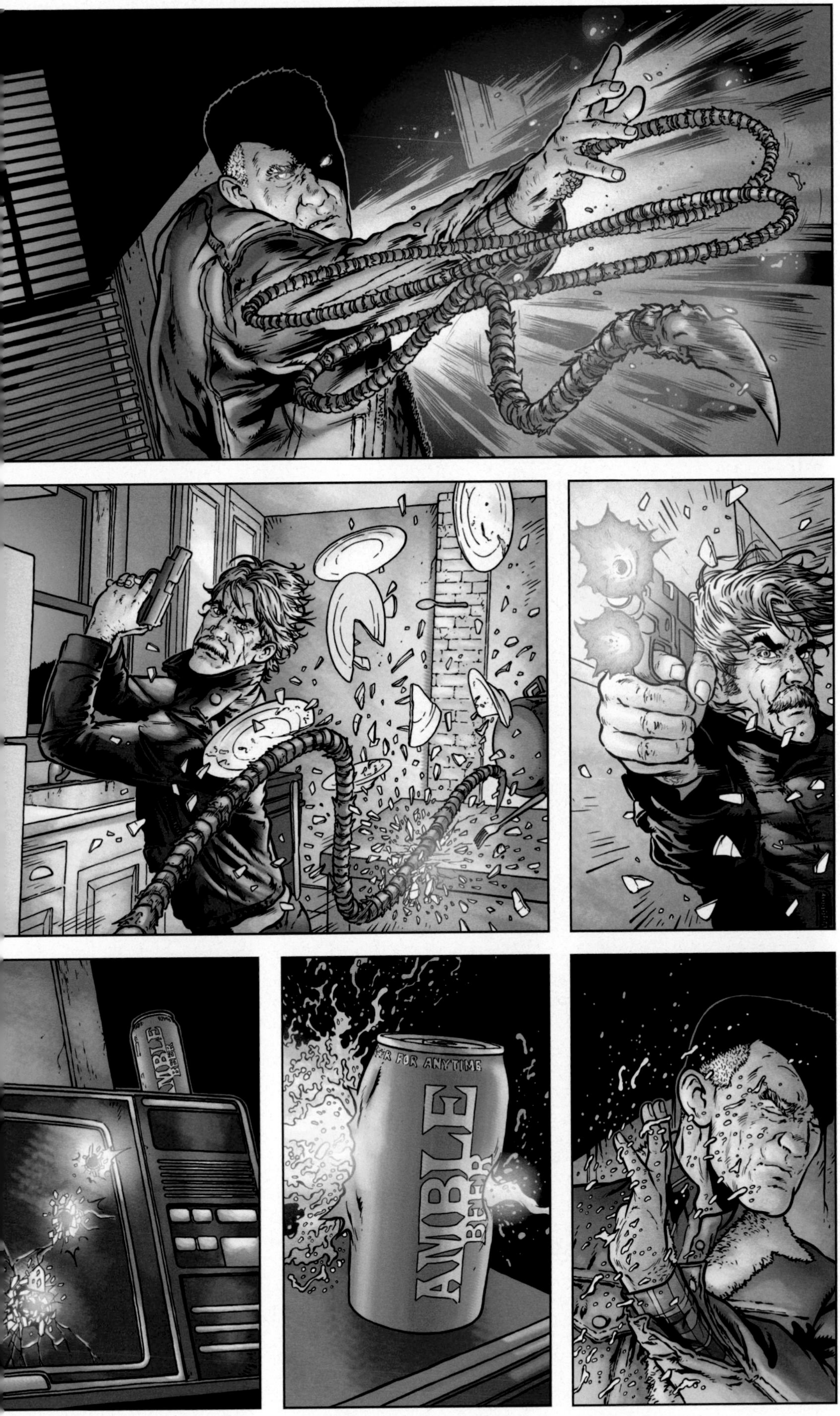
FOR ANYTIME
AMBLE
BEER

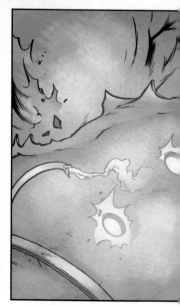

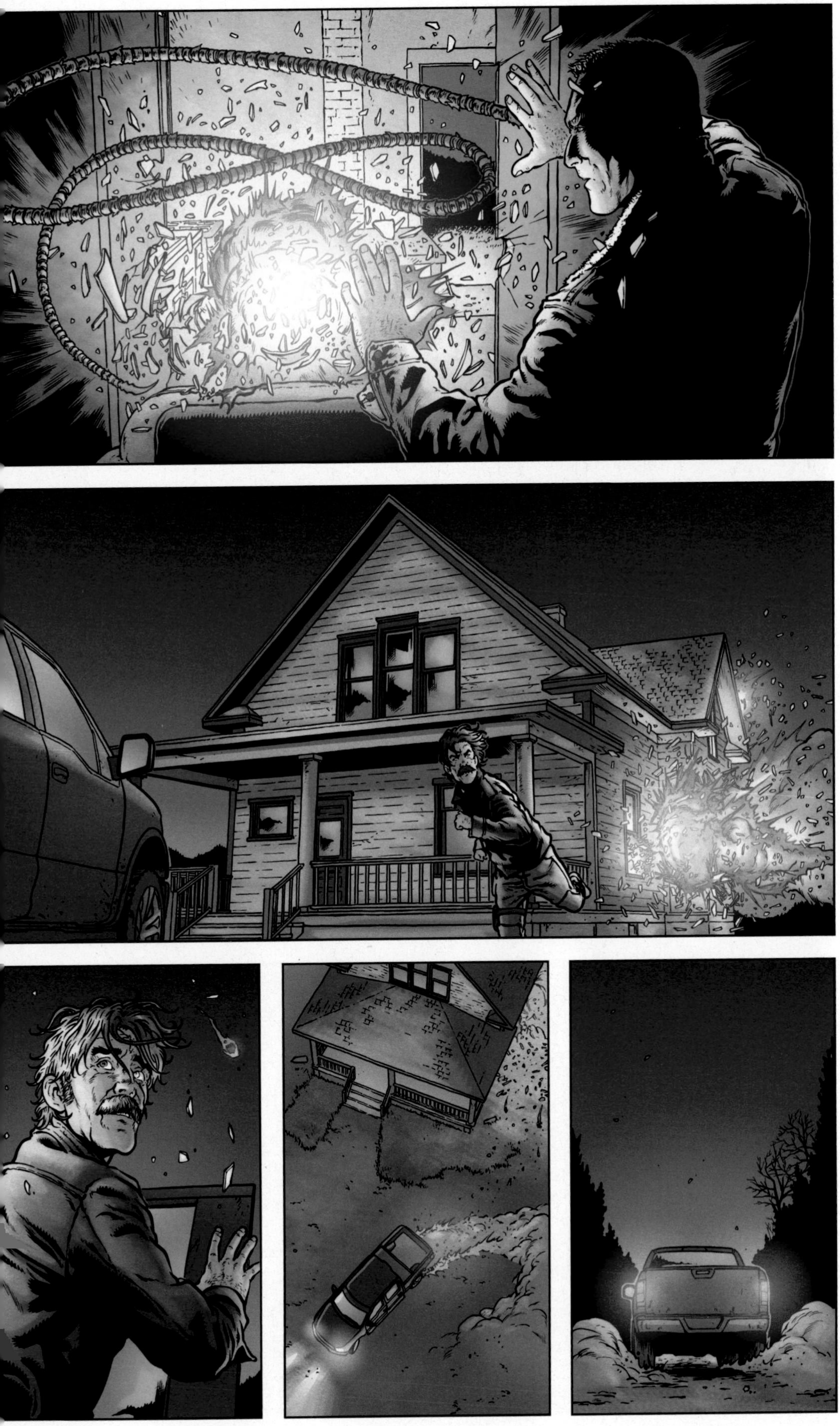

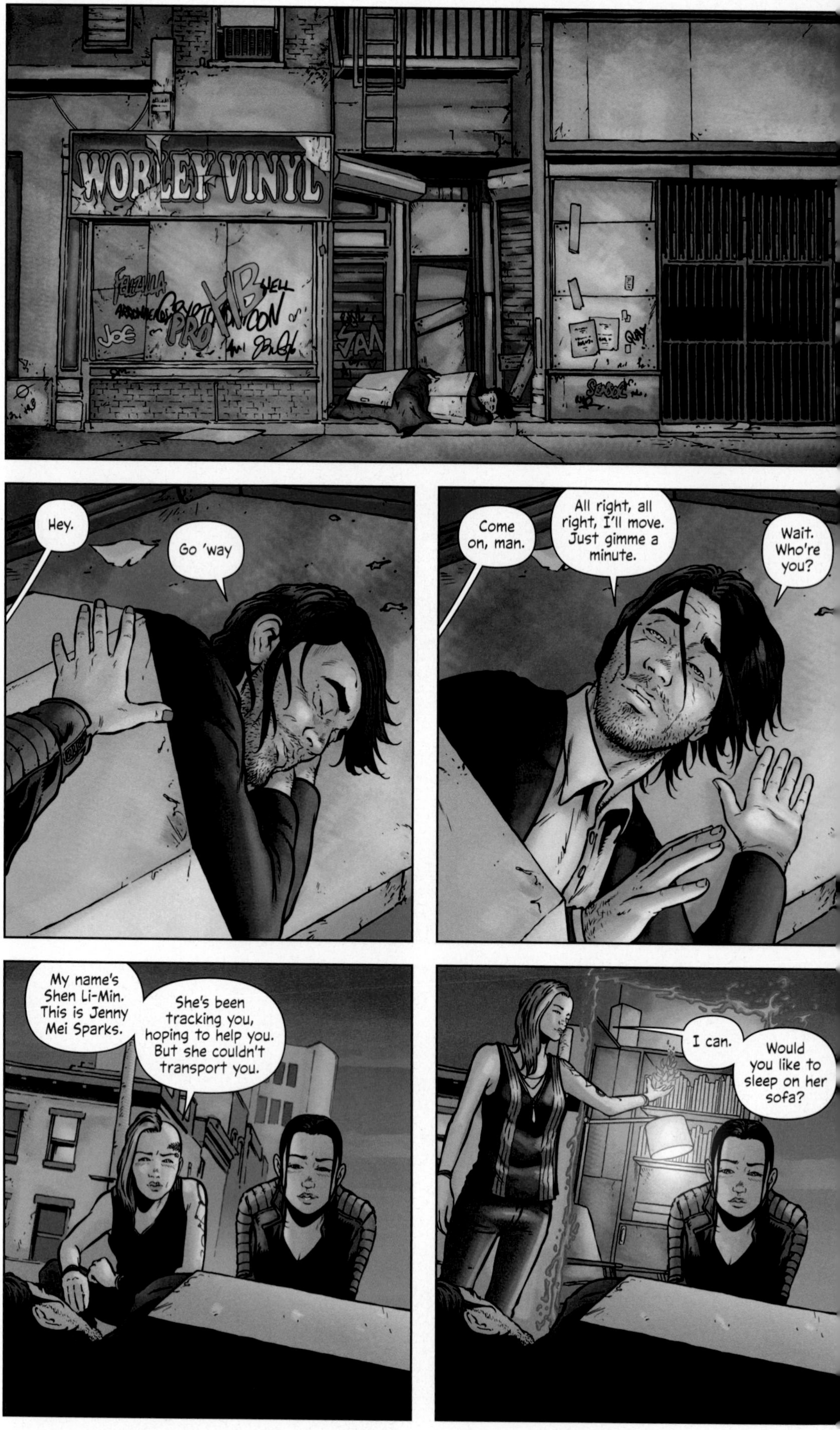
WORLEY VINYL
Hey.
Go 'way
Come on, man.
All right, all right, I'll move. Just gimme a minute.
Wait. Who're you?
My name's Shen Li-Min. This is Jenny Mei Sparks.
She's been tracking you, hoping to help you. But she couldn't transport you.
I can.
Would you like to sleep on her sofa?

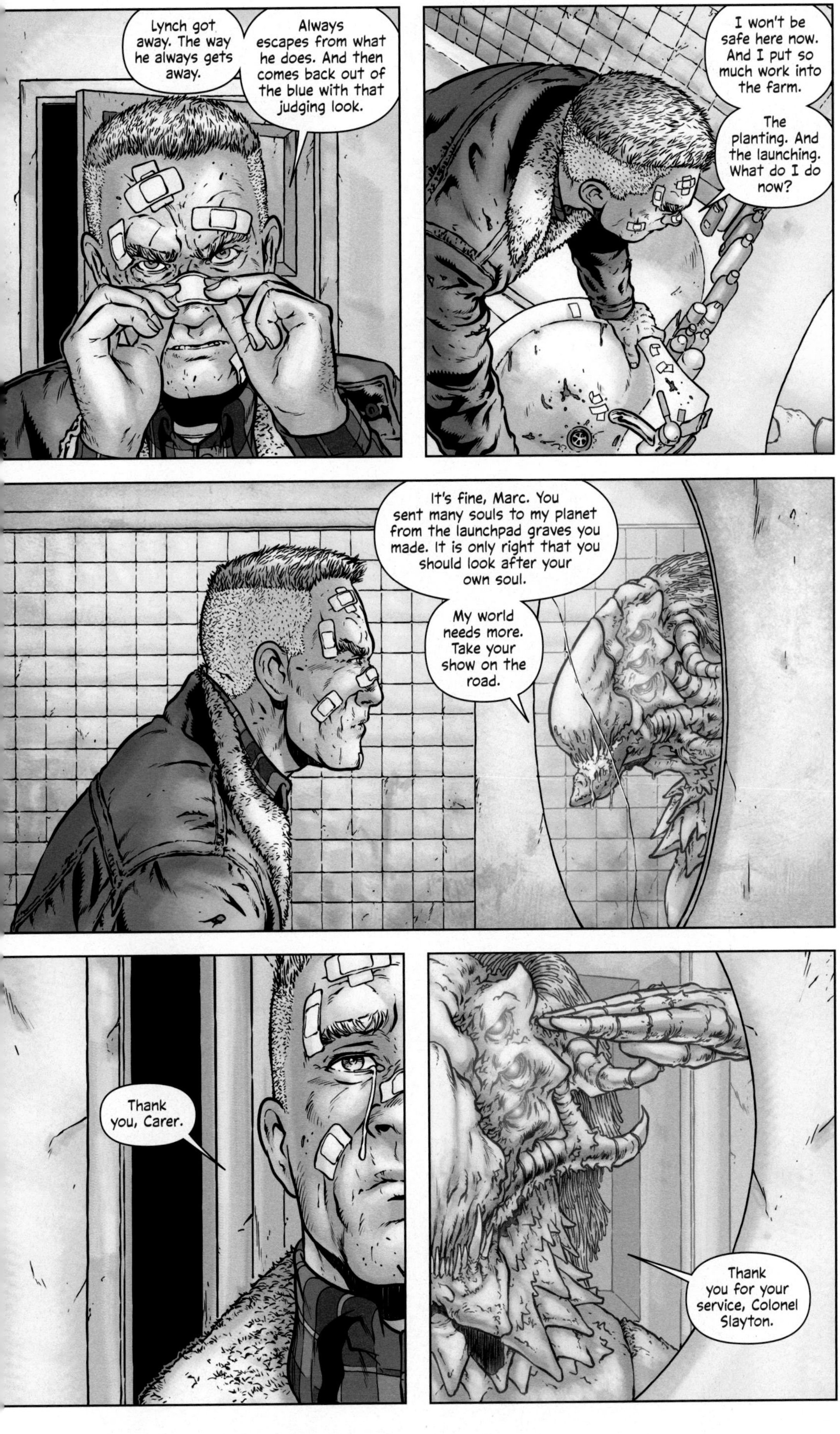
Lynch got away. The way he always gets away.
Always escapes from what he does. And then comes back out of the blue with that judging look.
I won't be safe here now. And I put so much work into the farm.
The planting. And the launching. What do I do now?
It's fine, Marc. You sent many souls to my planet from the launchpad graves you made. It is only right that you should look after your own soul.
My world needs more. Take your show on the road.
Thank you, Carer.
Thank you for your service, Colonel Slayton.

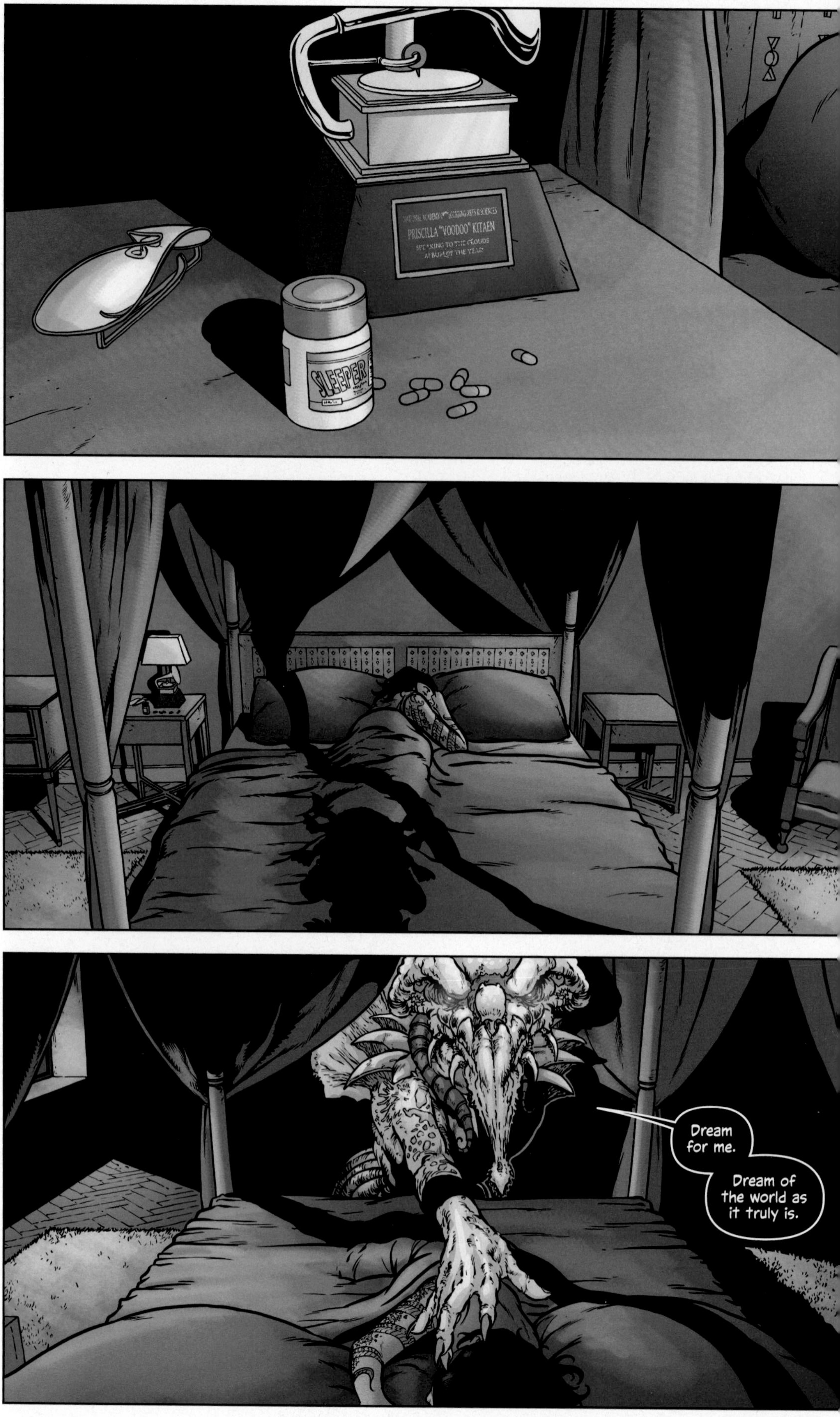
PRISCILLA "VOODOO" KITAEN
SLEEPER
Dream for me.
Dream of the world as it truly is.

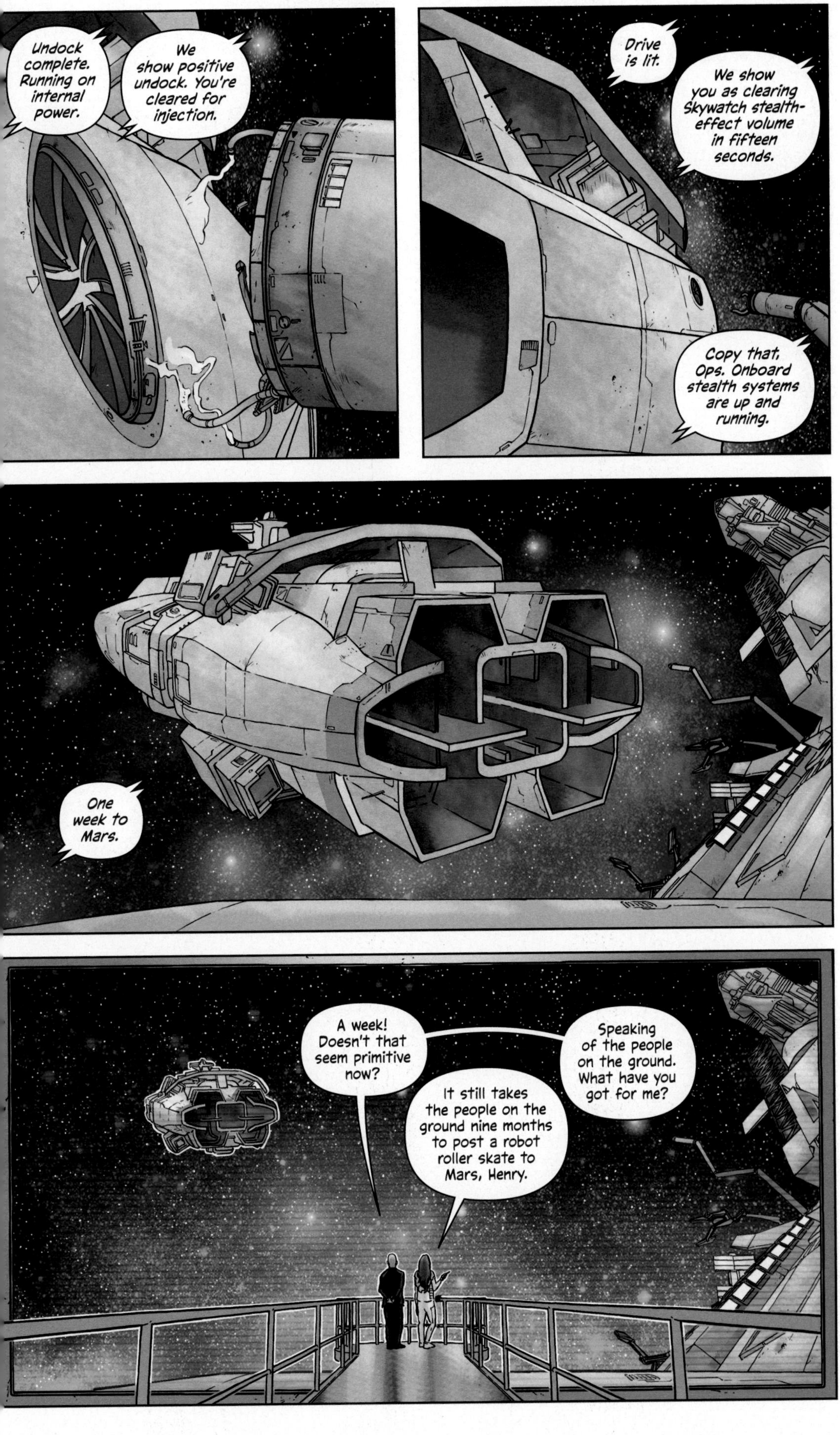
Undock complete. Running on internal power.
We show positive undock. You're cleared for injection.
Drive is lit.
We show you as clearing Skywatch stealth-effect volume in fifteen seconds.
Copy that, Ops. Onboard stealth systems are up and running.
One week to Mars.
A week! Doesn't that seem primitive now?
It still takes the people on the ground nine months to post a robot roller skate to Mars, Henry.
Speaking of the people on the ground. What have you got for me?

Those things are still pretty. I'd hate it if we used jump rooms for everything.

I took some time and compiled some lists. But I wanted a quick conversation before I made a formal filing.

Oh?

Do you know what you and Miles Craven have in common?

Absolutely nothing.

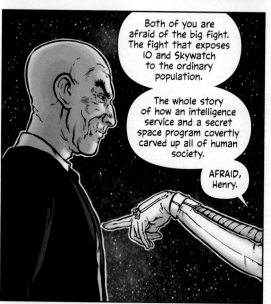

Both of you are afraid of the big fight. The fight that exposes IO and Skywatch to the ordinary population.

The whole story of how an intelligence service and a secret space program covertly carved up all of human society.

AFRAID, Henry.

So yes, I have some lists of key IO people we know about who could be usefully killed.

And lists of known IO structures and locations that could be destroyed to send a message.

SYNC

But I also have a list of actions we can take that will radically destabilize life on Earth, break IO's control over the planet and make it impossible for any global order to replace it.

Go big or go home, right?

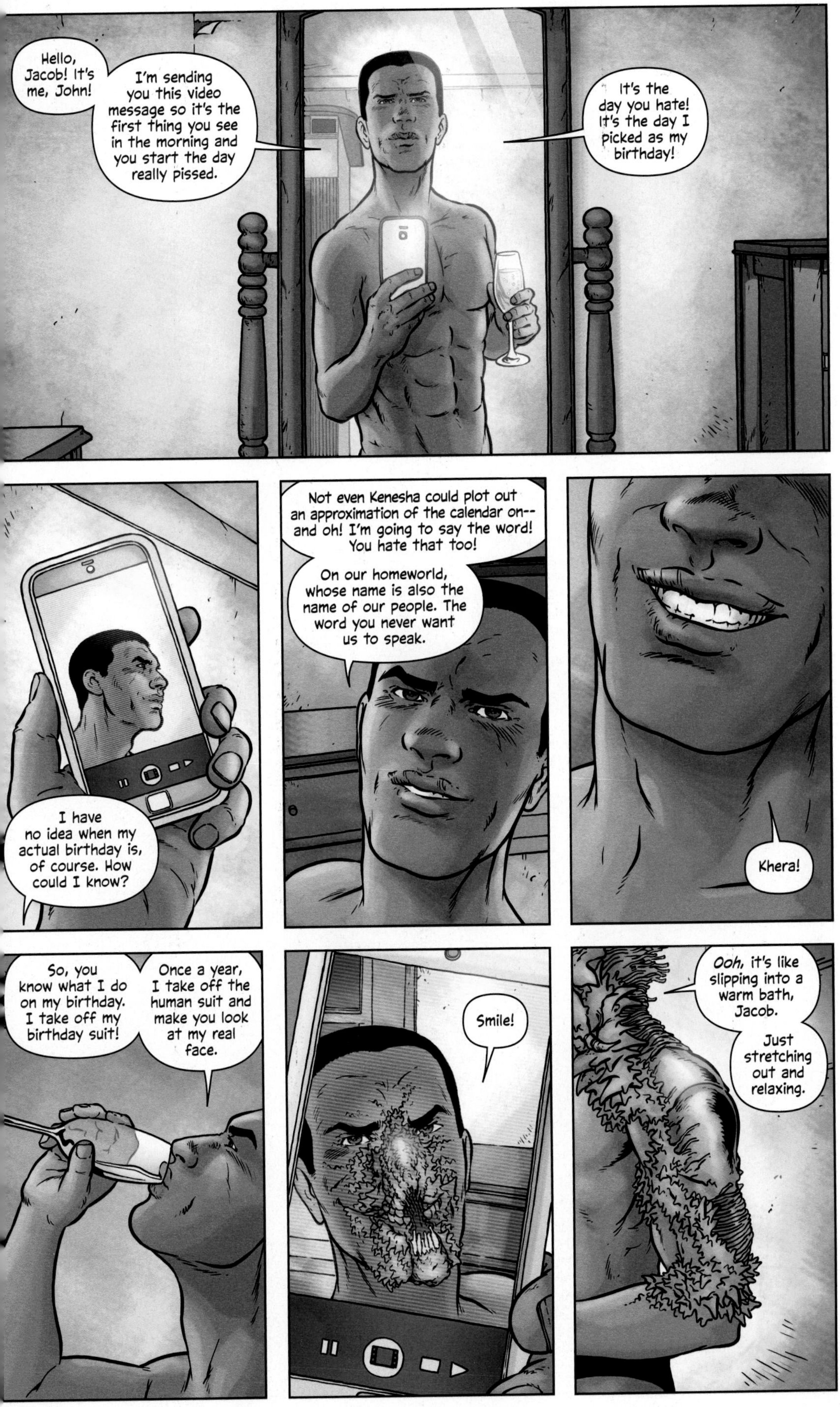
Hello, Jacob! It's me, John!
I'm sending you this video message so it's the first thing you see in the morning and you start the day really pissed.
It's the day you hate! It's the day I picked as my birthday!
I have no idea when my actual birthday is, of course. How could I know?
Not even Kenesha could plot out an approximation of the calendar on-- and oh! I'm going to say the word! You hate that too!
On our homeworld, whose name is also the name of our people. The word you never want us to speak.
Khera!
So, you know what I do on my birthday. I take off my birthday suit!
Once a year, I take off the human suit and make you look at my real face.
Smile!
Ooh, it's like slipping into a warm bath, Jacob.
Just stretching out and relaxing.

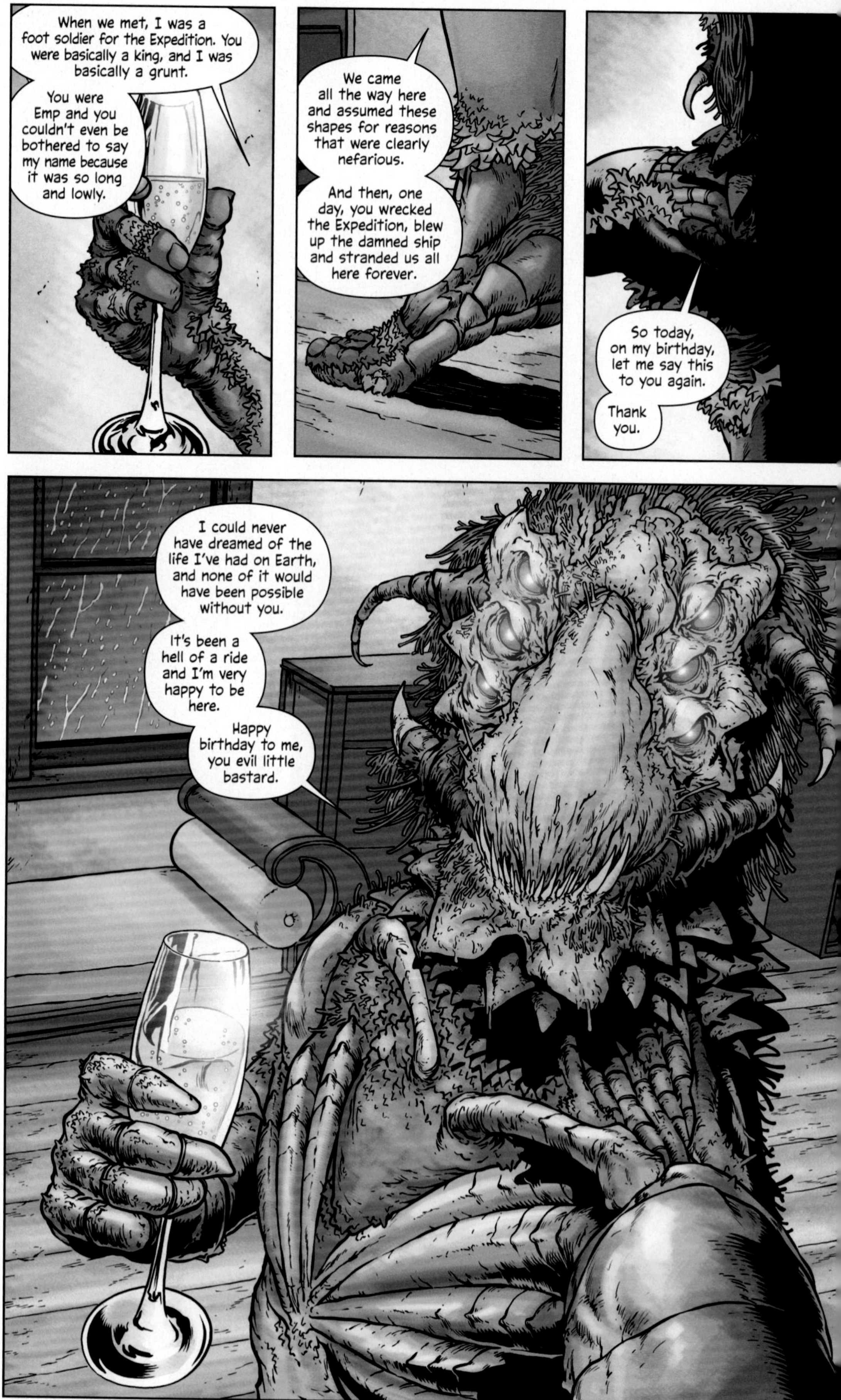
When we met, I was a foot soldier for the Expedition. You were basically a king, and I was basically a grunt.
You were Emp and you couldn't even be bothered to say my name because it was so long and lowly.
We came all the way here and assumed these shapes for reasons that were clearly nefarious.
And then, one day, you wrecked the Expedition, blew up the damned ship and stranded us all here forever.
So today, on my birthday, let me say this to you again.
Thank you.
I could never have dreamed of the life I've had on Earth, and none of it would have been possible without you.
It's been a hell of a ride and I'm very happy to be here.
Happy birthday to me, you evil little bastard.

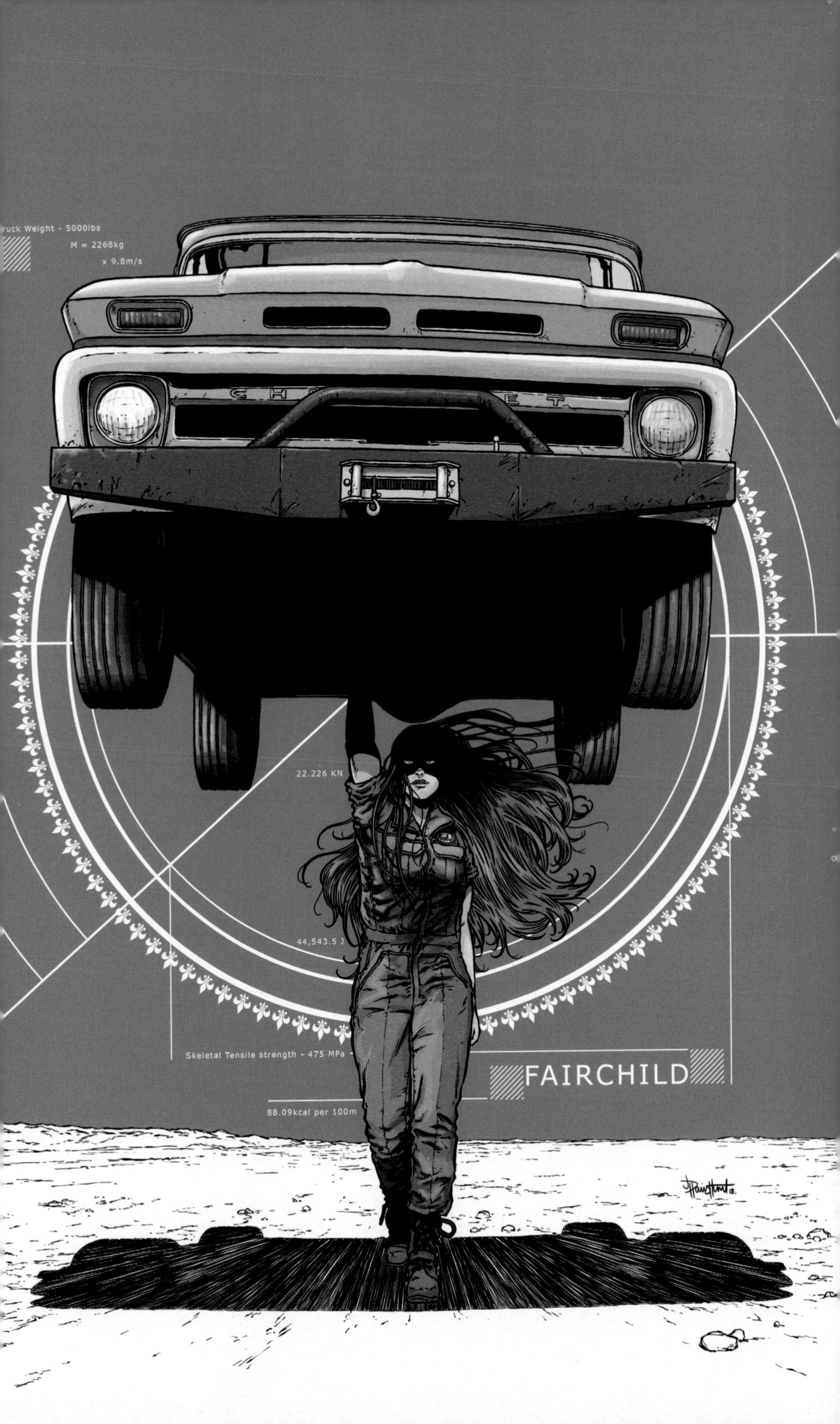
ruck Weight - 5000lbs
M = 2268kg
x 9.8m/s
22.226 KN
44,543.5 J
Skeletal Tensile strength - 475 MPa
FAIRCHILD
88.09kcal per 100m

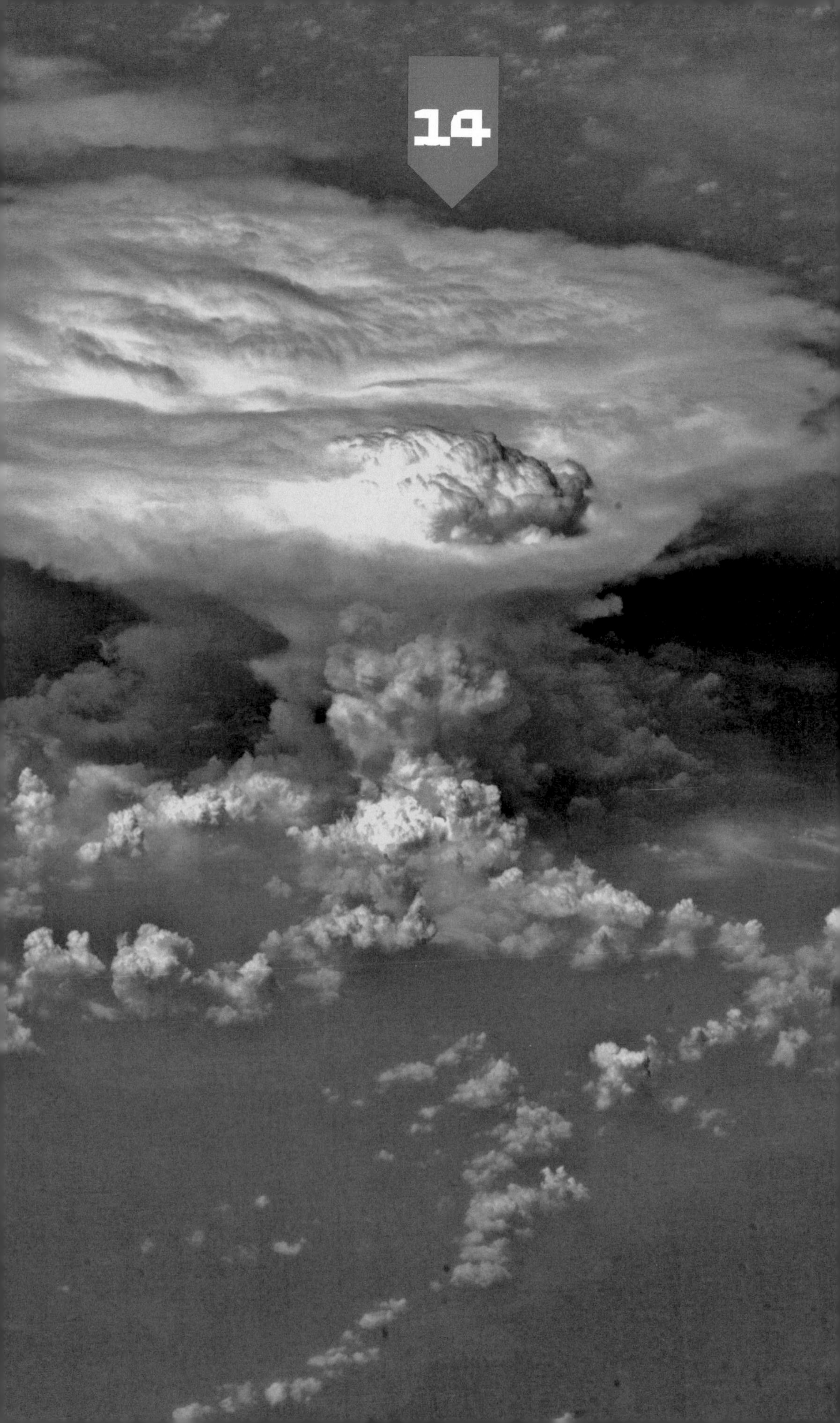
14

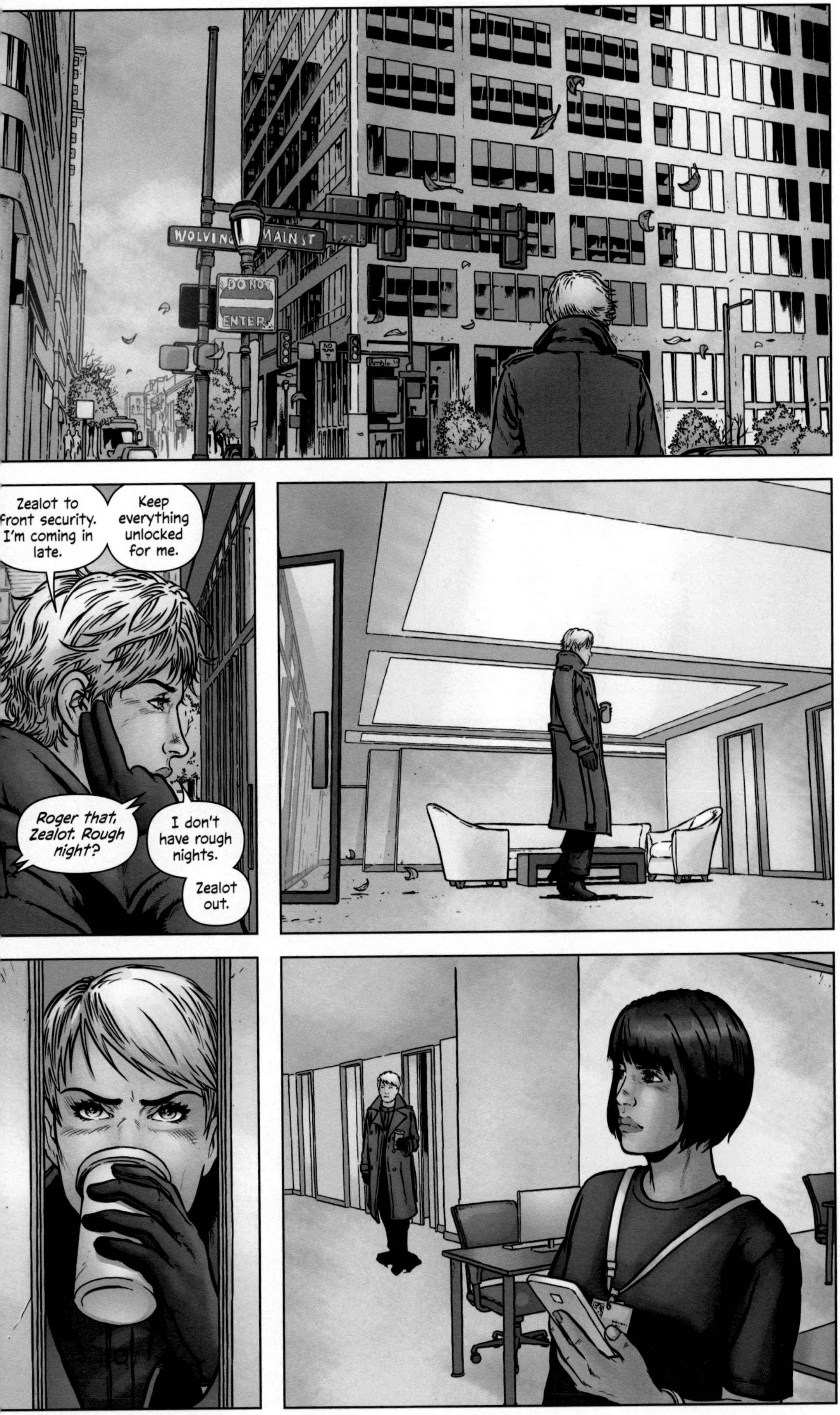
WOLVING
MAIN ST
DO NOT ENTER
Zealot to front security. I'm coming in late.
Keep everything unlocked for me.
Roger that, Zealot. Rough night?
I don't have rough nights.
Zealot out.

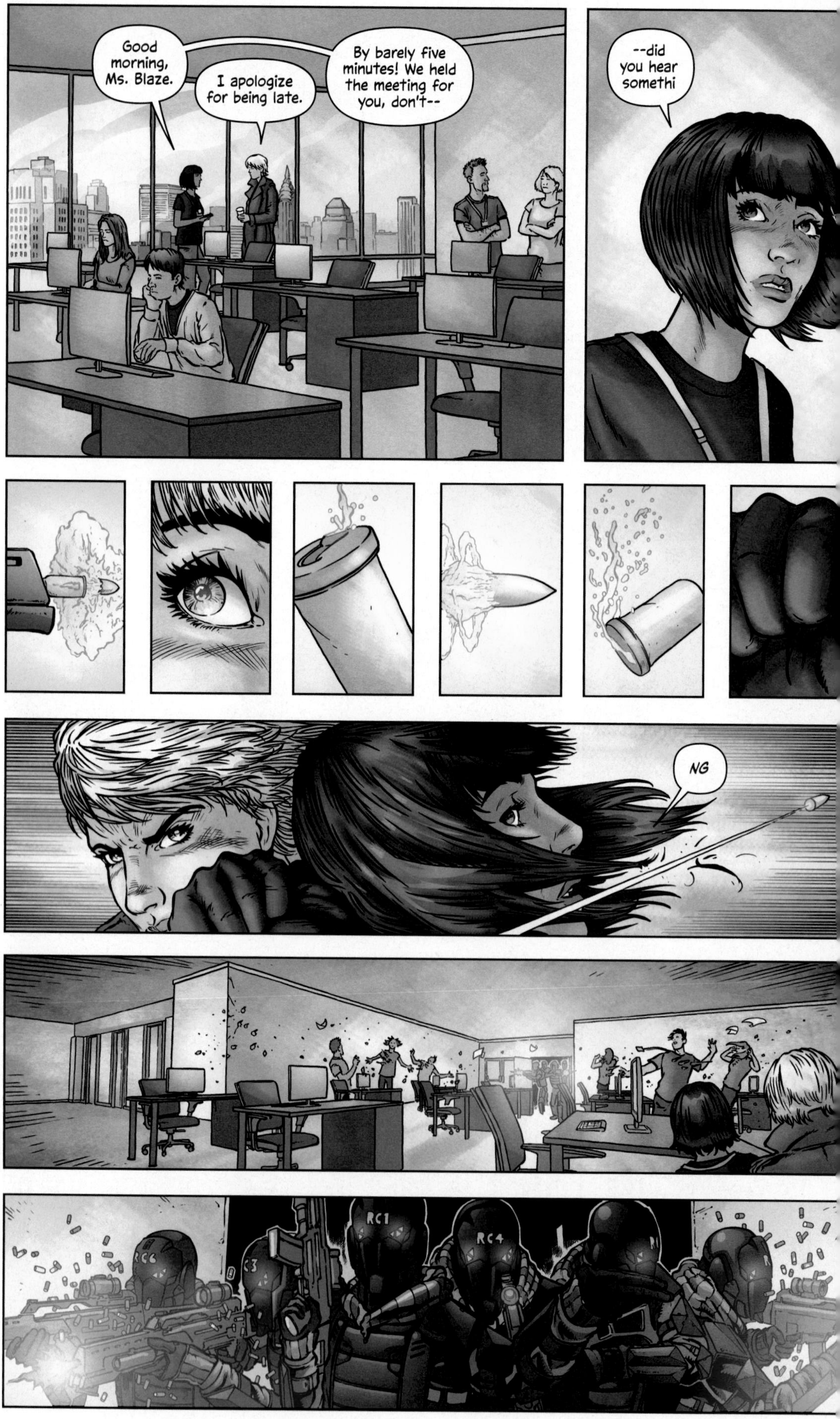
Good morning, Ms. Blaze.
I apologize for being late.
By barely five minutes! We held the meeting for you, don't--
--did you hear somethi
NG
RC1
RC4
RC6
C3

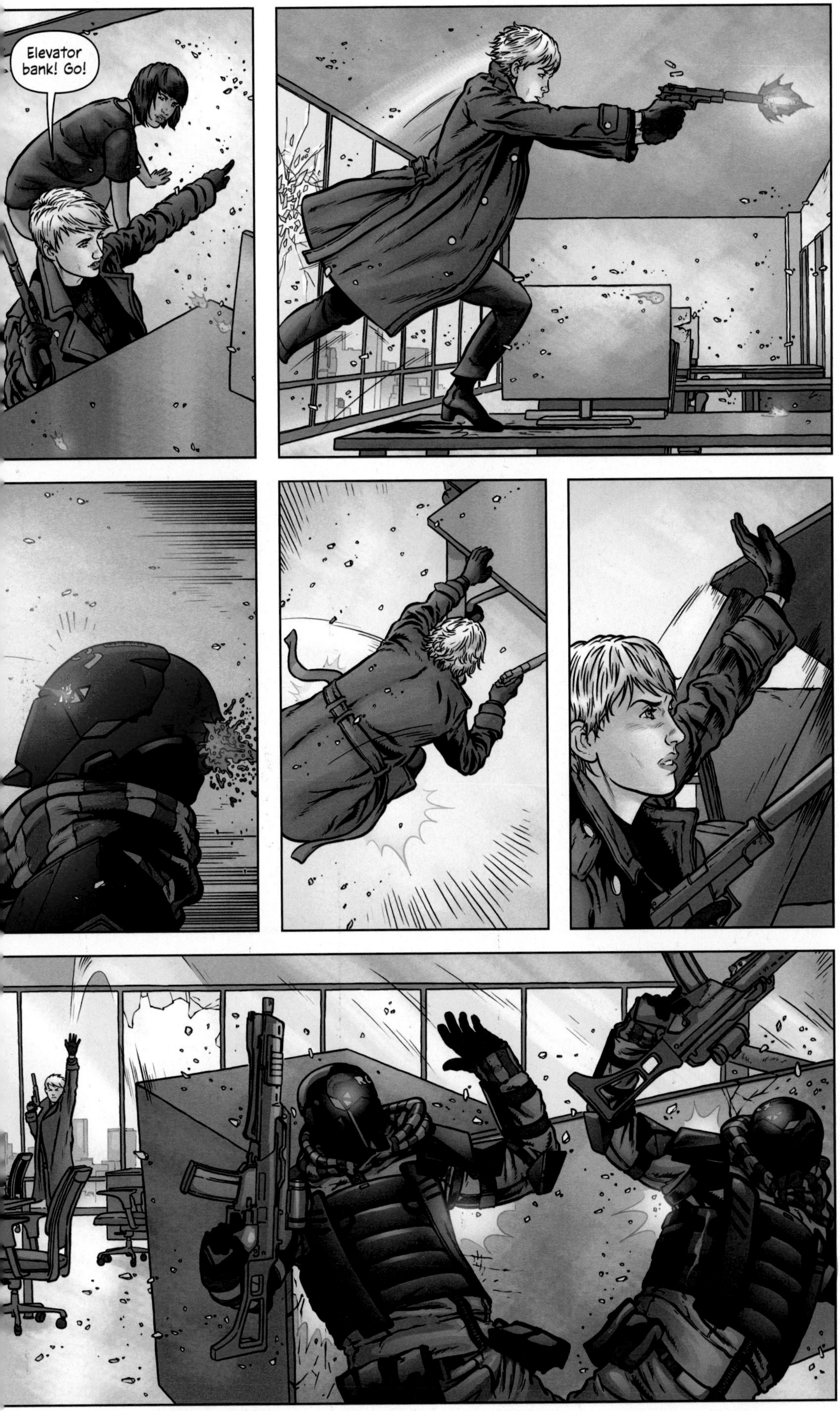
Elevator bank! Go!

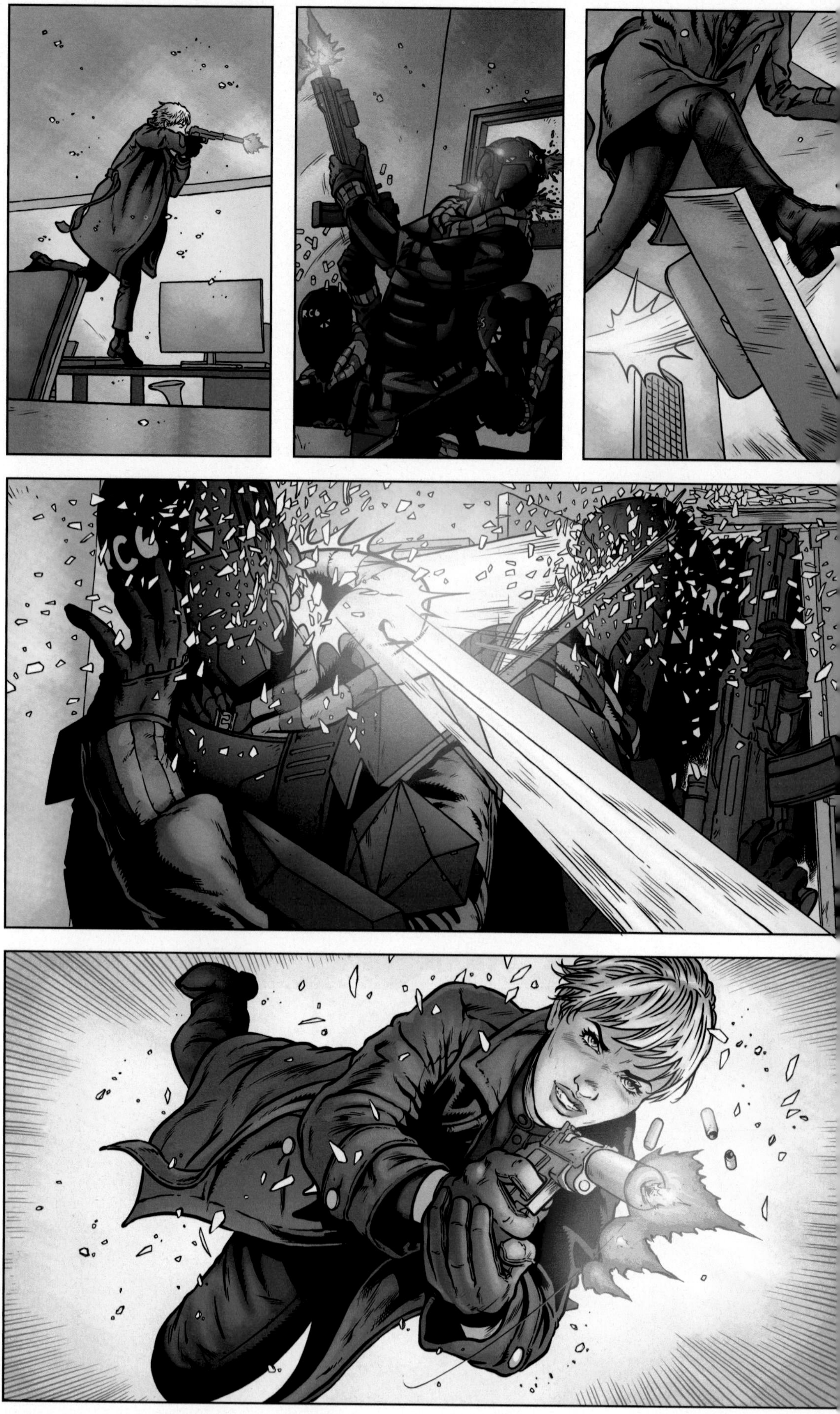
RCO

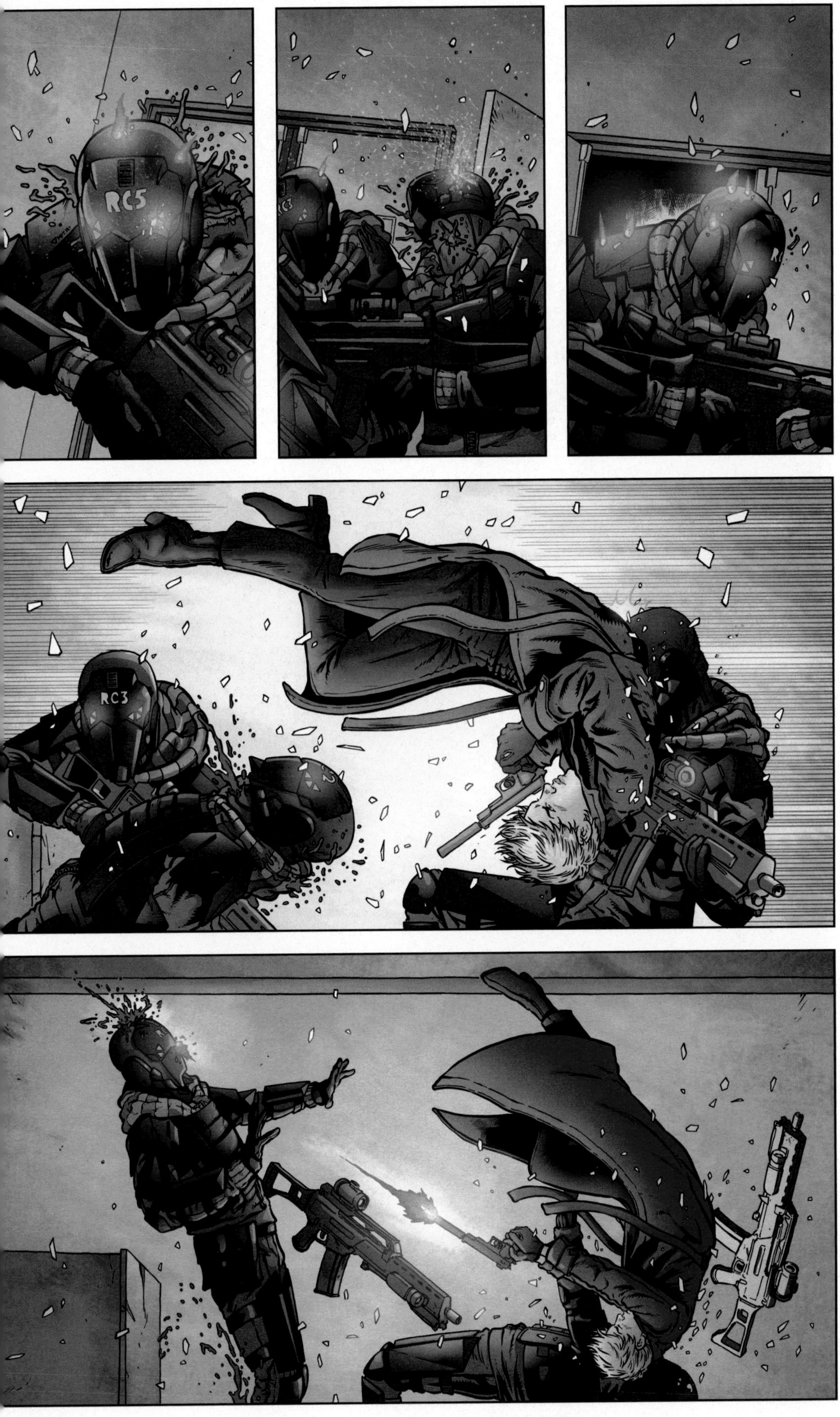
RC5
RC3

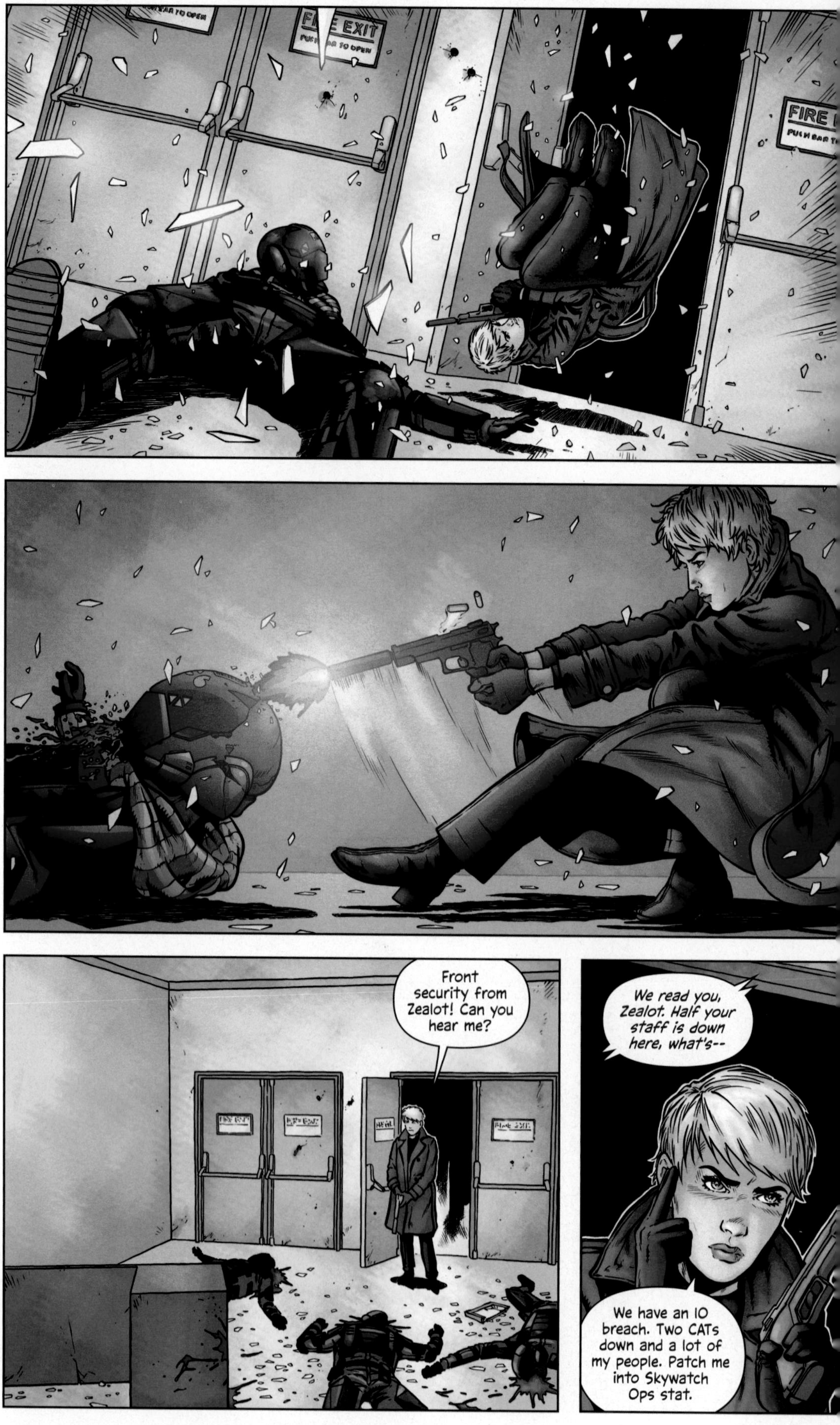
FIRE EXIT
PUSH BAR TO OPEN
Front security from Zealot! Can you hear me?
We read you, Zealot. Half your staff is down here, what's--
We have an IO breach. Two CATs down and a lot of my people. Patch me into Skywatch Ops stat.

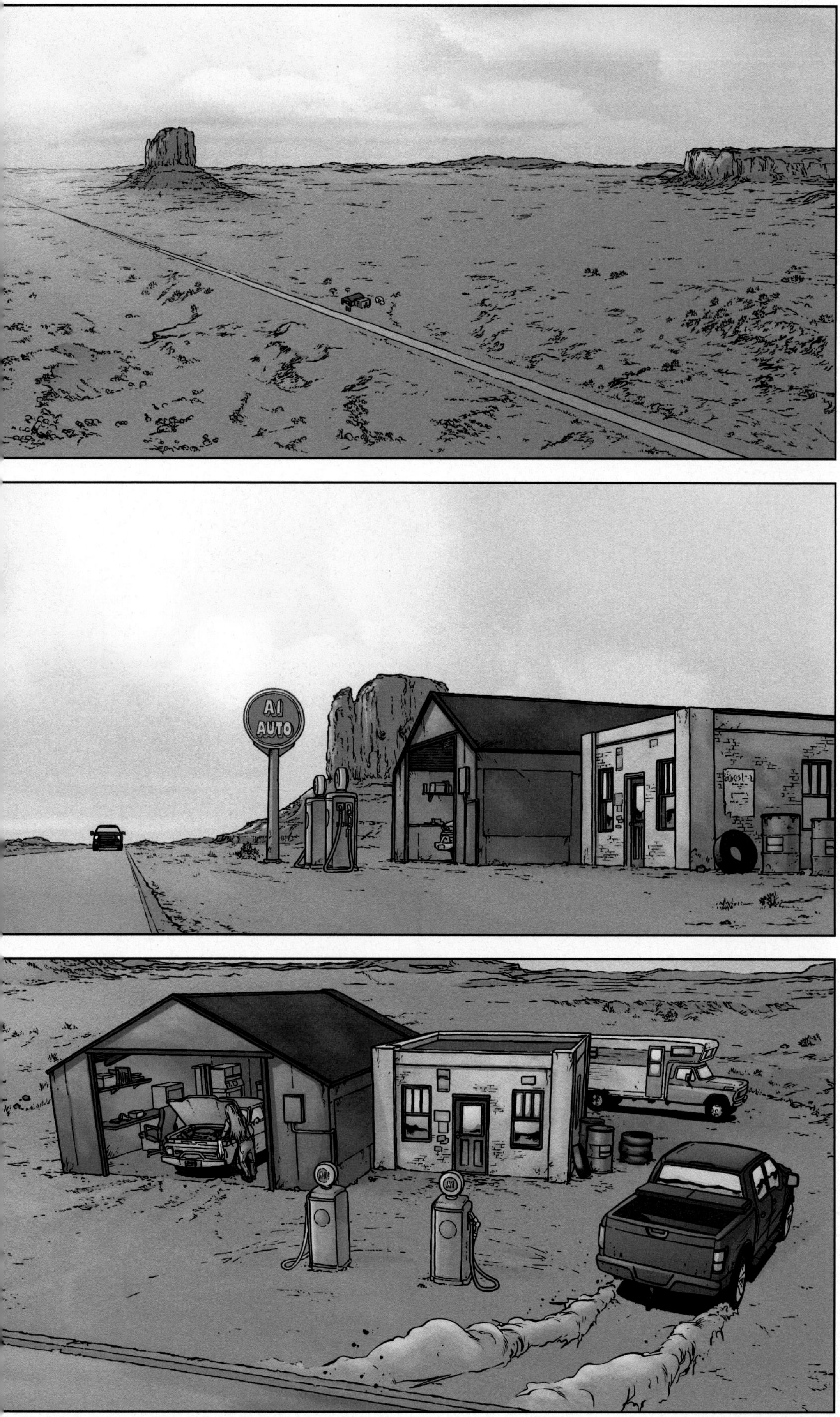
A1
AUTO

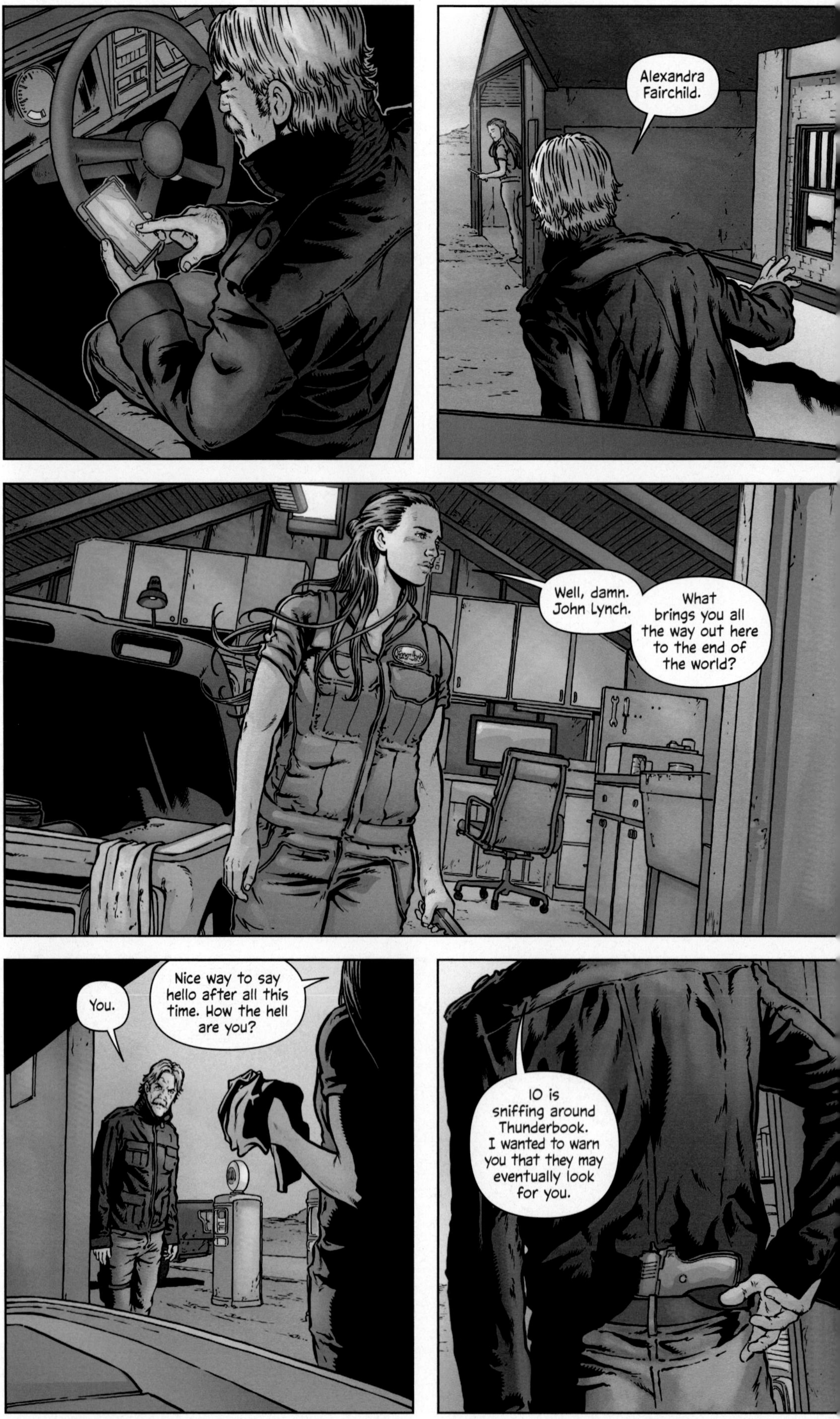
Alexandra Fairchild.
Well, damn. John Lynch.
What brings you all the way out here to the end of the world?
You.
Nice way to say hello after all this time. How the hell are you?
IO is sniffing around Thunderbook. I wanted to warn you that they may eventually look for you.

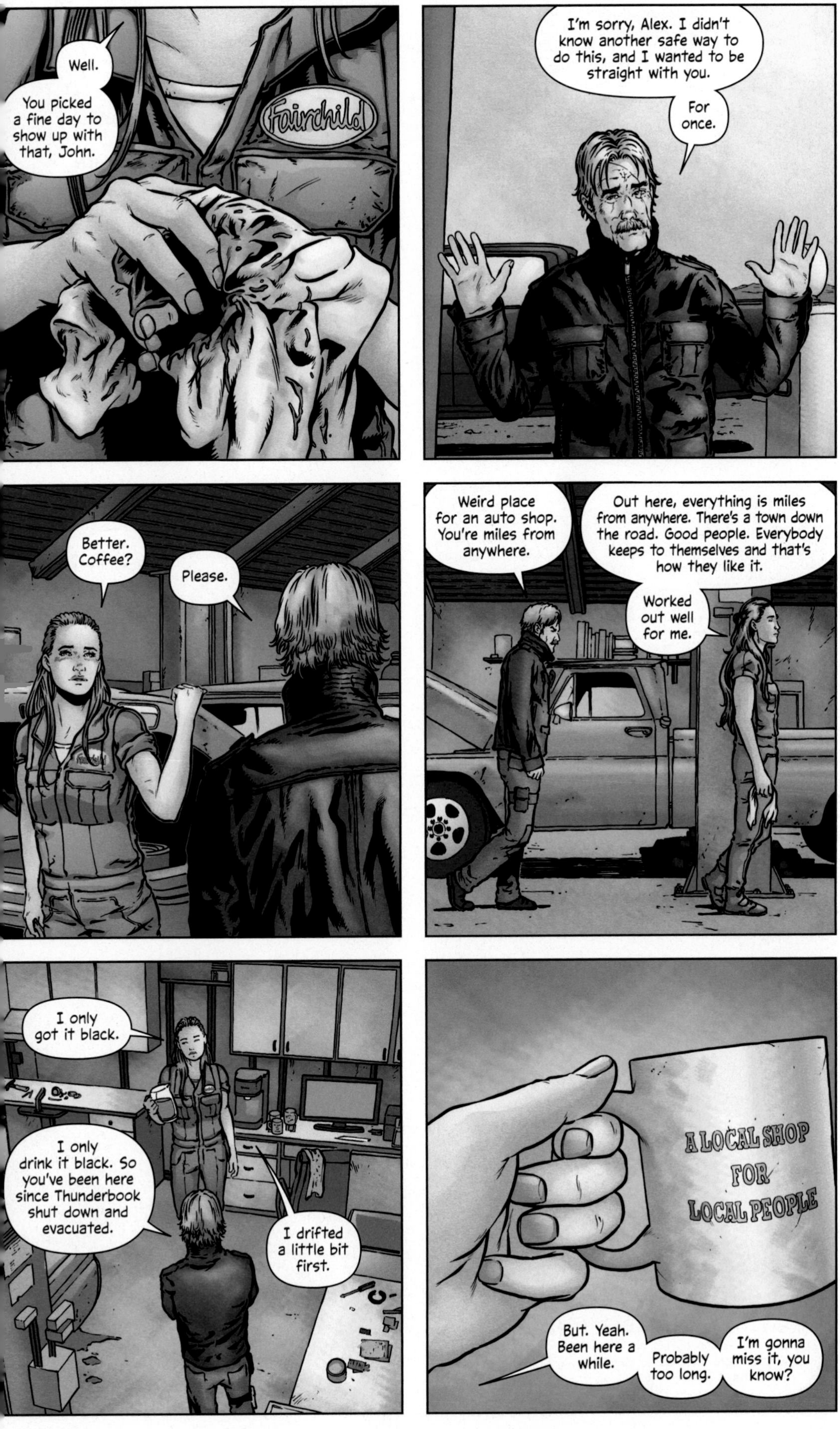
Well.
You picked a fine day to show up with that, John.
Fairchild
I'm sorry, Alex. I didn't know another safe way to do this, and I wanted to be straight with you.
For once.
Better. Coffee?
Please.
Weird place for an auto shop. You're miles from anywhere.
Out here, everything is miles from anywhere. There's a town down the road. Good people. Everybody keeps to themselves and that's how they like it.
Worked out well for me.
I only got it black.
I only drink it black. So you've been here since Thunderbook shut down and evacuated.
I drifted a little bit first.
A LOCAL SHOP FOR LOCAL PEOPLE
But. Yeah. Been here a while.
Probably too long.
I'm gonna miss it, you know?

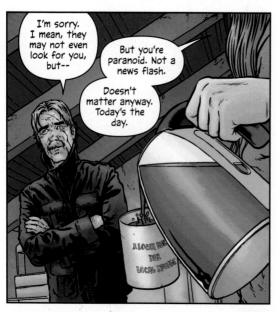

I'm sorry. I mean, they may not even look for you, but--
But you're paranoid. Not a news flash.
Doesn't matter anyway. Today's the day.
A LOCAL SHOP FOR LOCAL PEOPLE
I don't understand.
I know. You just got here. Besides, human stuff was never exactly your strong suit, was it?
Don't get me wrong. You were a good commanding officer. Best I ever had. But human life always kinda escaped you.
Me, I've been doing nothing BUT human life. Out in the civilian real world with nothing but some fake ID and a bunch of dirty money--
--thanks again for all that, by the way--
--living a little ordinary life with the little ordinary people who get along in the secret shadow of IO.
It sucks, by the way.
Cheers.
CHALLENGERS of the UNKNOWN
A LOCAL SHOP FOR LOCAL PEOPLE
How bad has it been? I mean, it looks like you made a life for yourself. I saw you have a home right next door.
Is it just you here, or...?
The Army taught me a trade, right? And I always liked fixing stuff.
I just can't fix everything.

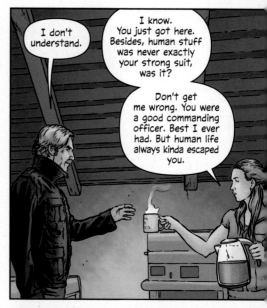

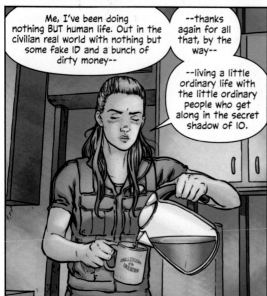

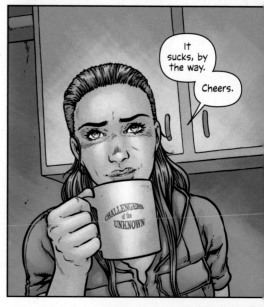

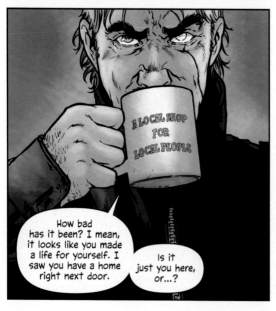

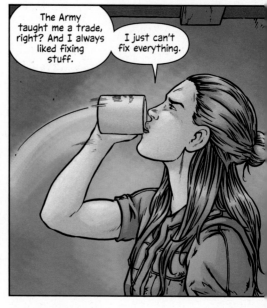

You know how it goes. Or maybe you don't.

Met lots of guys who were more bad than good. Couple of girls who didn't know what they were yet.

And then a guy who was a little more good than bad.

CHALLENGERS of the UNKNOWN

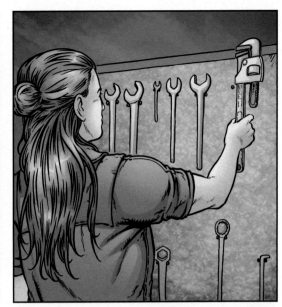

I had a daughter, John.

Where is she?

I gave her up for adoption. Had to.

Is the father around?

I killed him.

I killed him the day I told him I was pregnant.

Only a tiny bit more good than bad, it turned out.

He attacked me. Tried to kick the baby in my body to death.

I killed him. I literally crushed him to death with my hands.

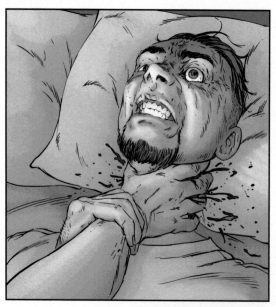

And afterward all I could think about was, what would happen the first time my baby cried and I couldn't deal with it?

What would happen if I squeezed her? Paddled her? Slapped her hand away from something?

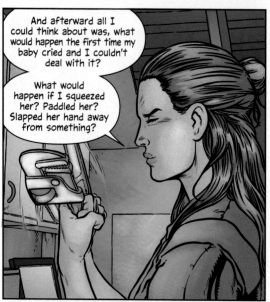

You wouldn't do that.

Everyone says that until the first time they do it.

Thing is, John, it likes it.

The Thunderbook implant. It likes the anger. Likes it when I hurt people.

It relishes it.

And it rewards me. It makes me stronger every time. Harder.

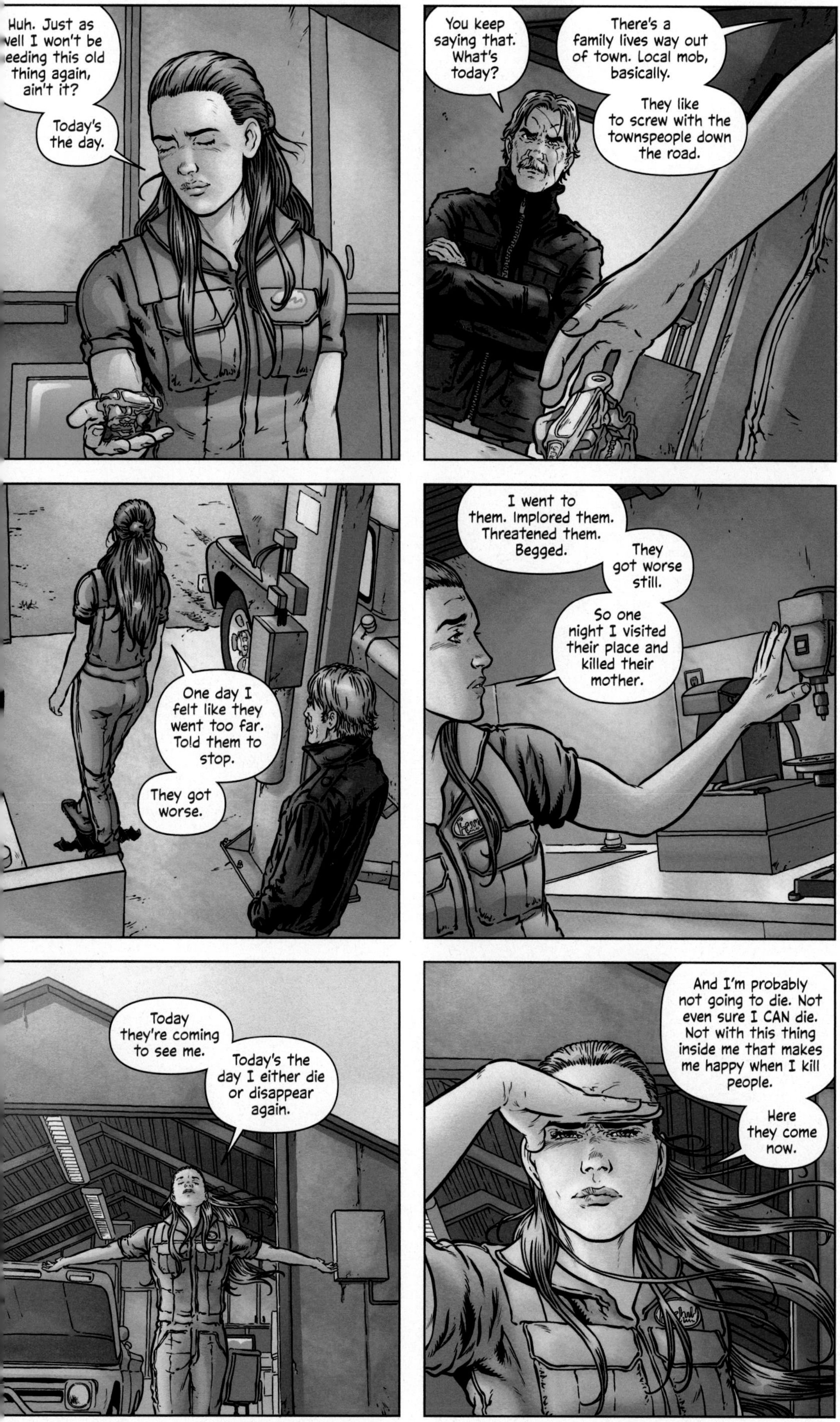
Huh. Just as well I won't be needing this old thing again, ain't it?
Today's the day.
You keep saying that. What's today?
There's a family lives way out of town. Local mob, basically.
They like to screw with the townspeople down the road.
One day I felt like they went too far. Told them to stop.
They got worse.
I went to them. Implored them. Threatened them. Begged.
They got worse still.
So one night I visited their place and killed their mother.
Today they're coming to see me.
Today's the day I either die or disappear again.
And I'm probably not going to die. Not even sure I CAN die. Not with this thing inside me that makes me happy when I kill people.
Here they come now.

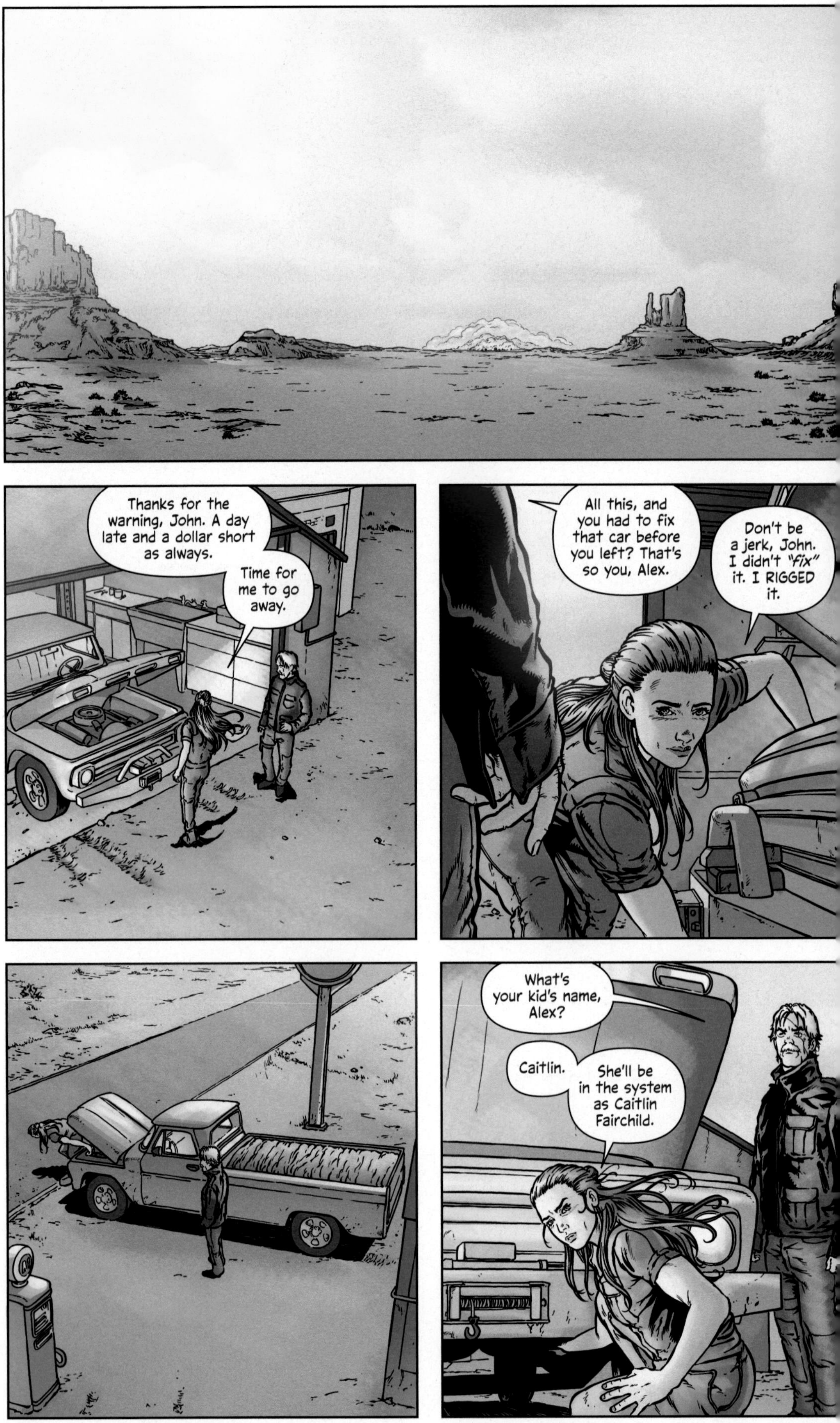

Thanks for the warning, John. A day late and a dollar short as always.
Time for me to go away.
All this, and you had to fix that car before you left? That's so you, Alex.
Don't be a jerk, John. I didn't "fix" it. I RIGGED it.
What's your kid's name, Alex?
Caitlin.
She'll be in the system as Caitlin Fairchild.

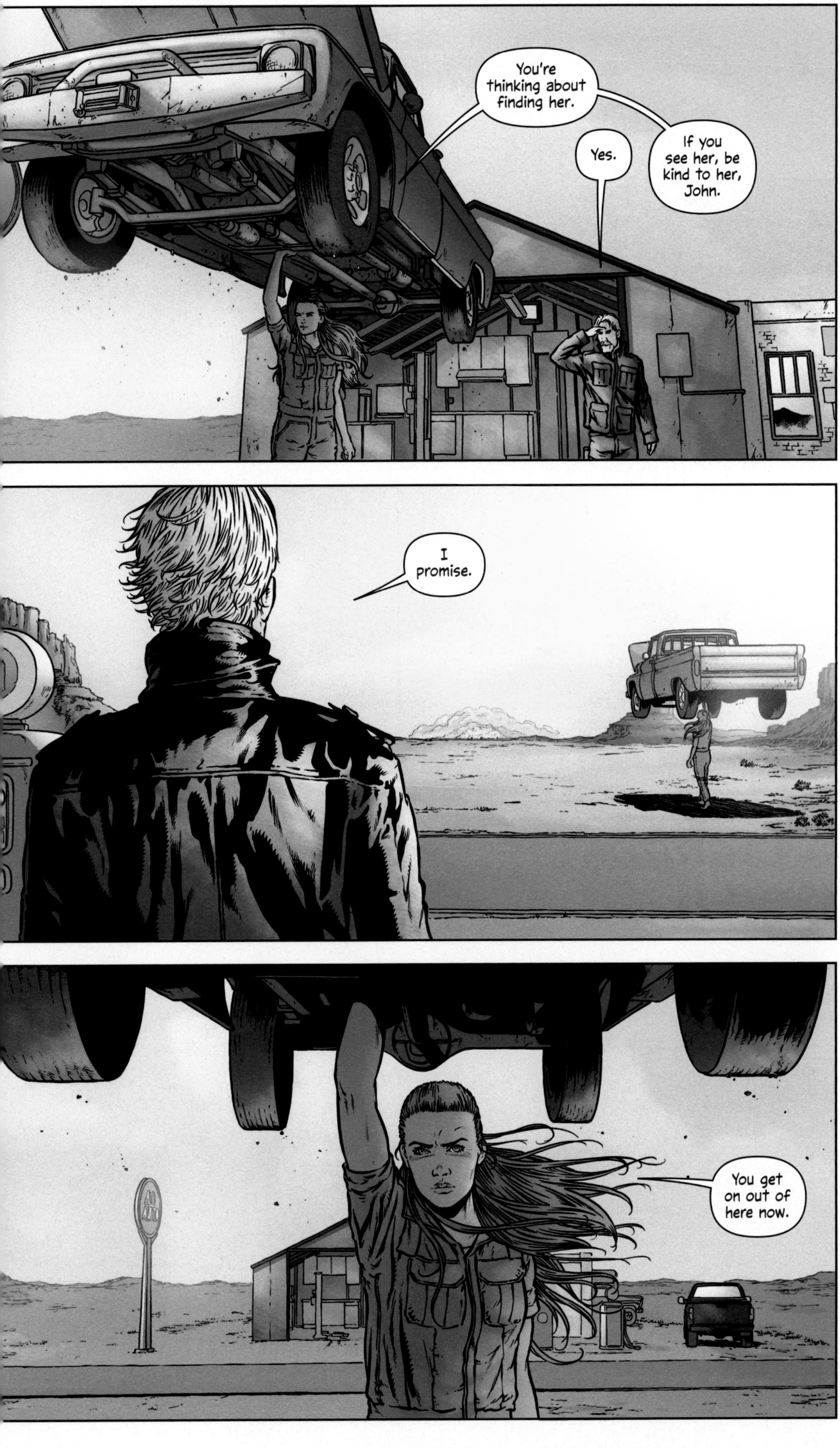
You're thinking about finding her.
Yes.
If you see her, be kind to her, John.
I promise.
You get on out of here now.

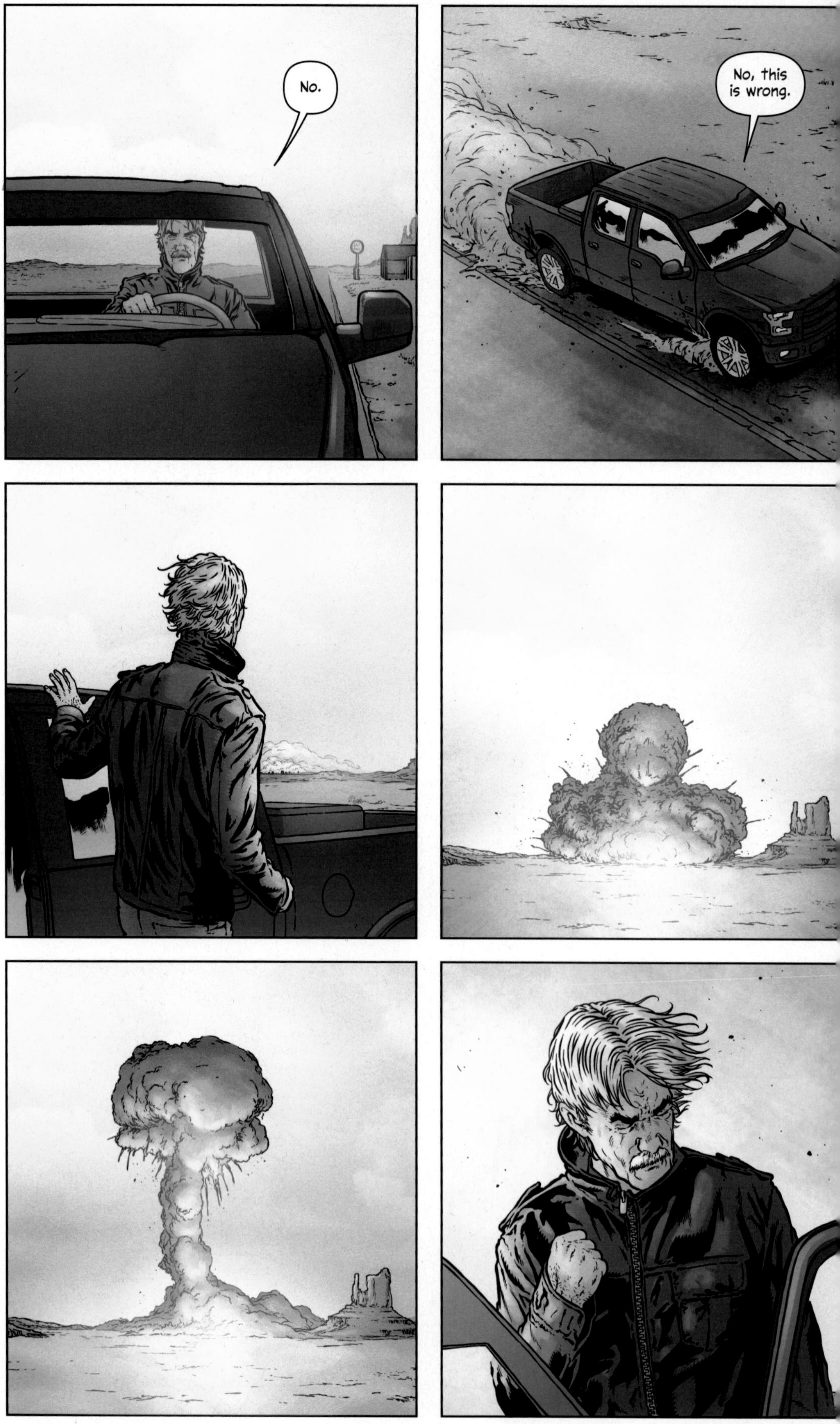
No.
No, this is wrong.

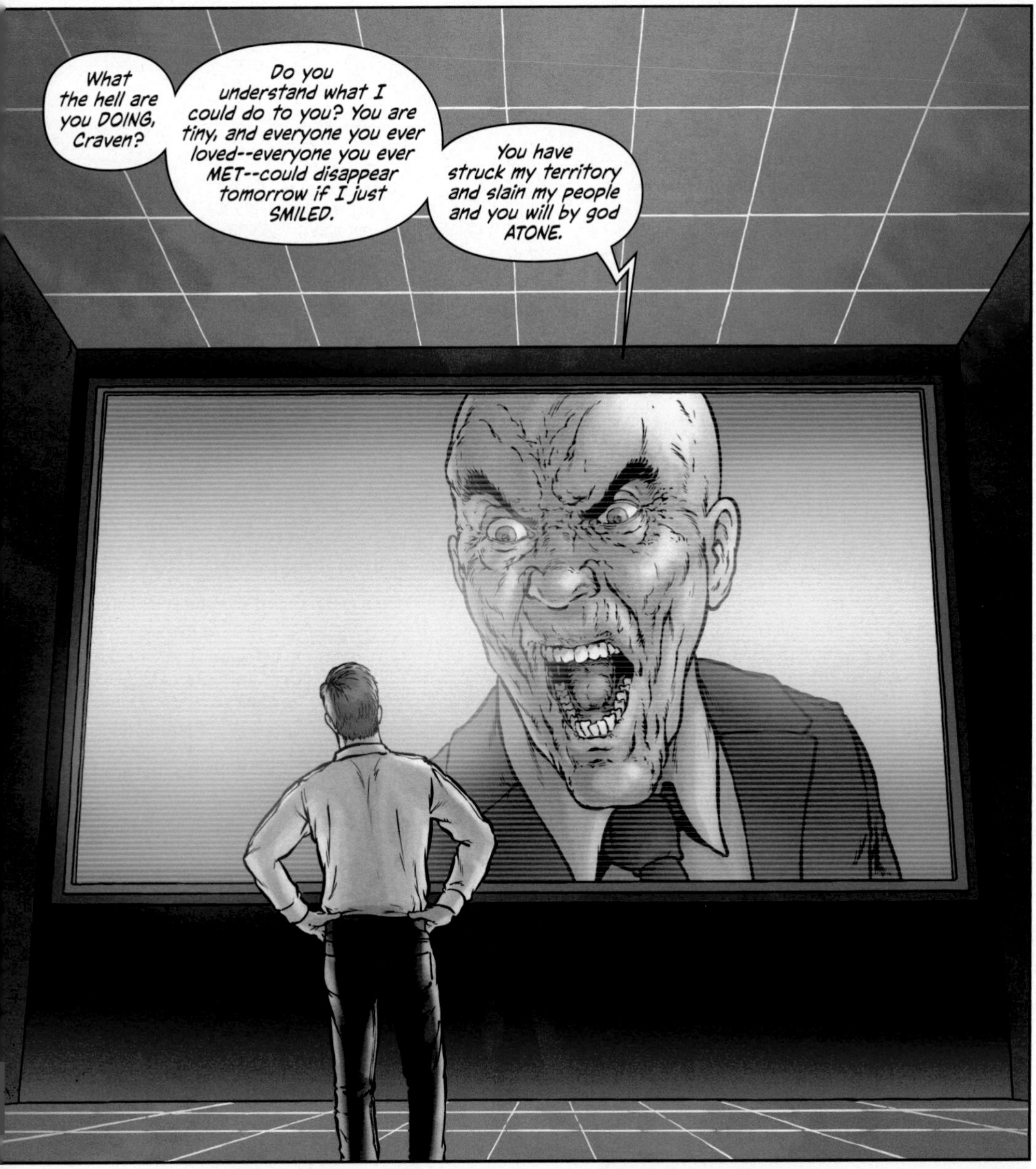
What the hell are you DOING, Craven?
Do you understand what I could do to you? You are tiny, and everyone you ever loved--everyone you ever MET--could disappear tomorrow if I just SMILED.
You have struck my territory and slain my people and you will by god ATONE.

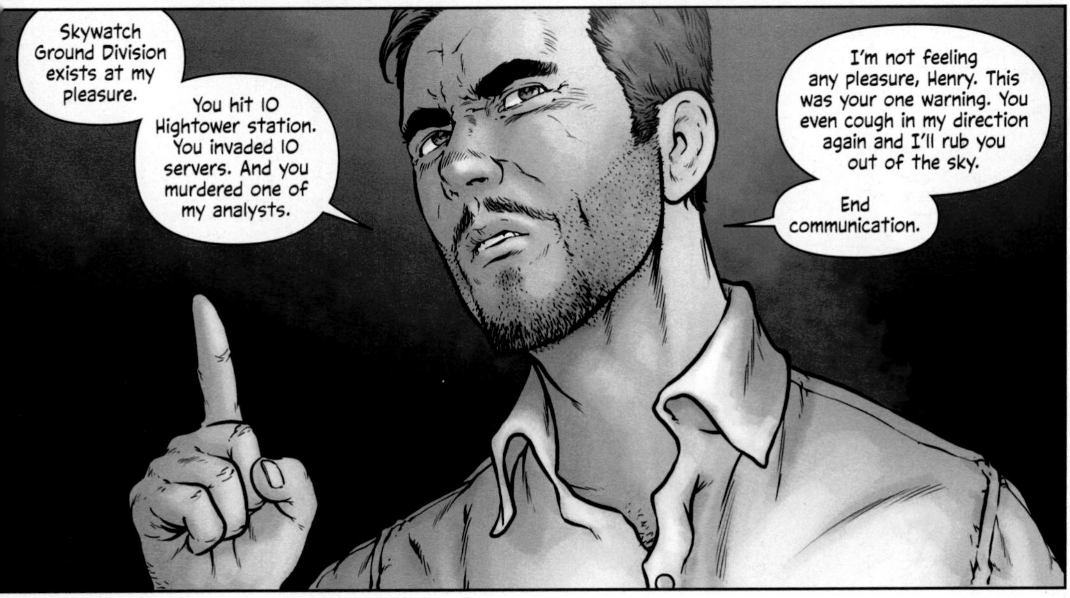
Skywatch Ground Division exists at my pleasure.
You hit 10 Hightower station. You invaded 10 servers. And you murdered one of my analysts.
I'm not feeling any pleasure, Henry. This was your one warning. You even cough in my direction again and I'll rub you out of the sky.
End communication.

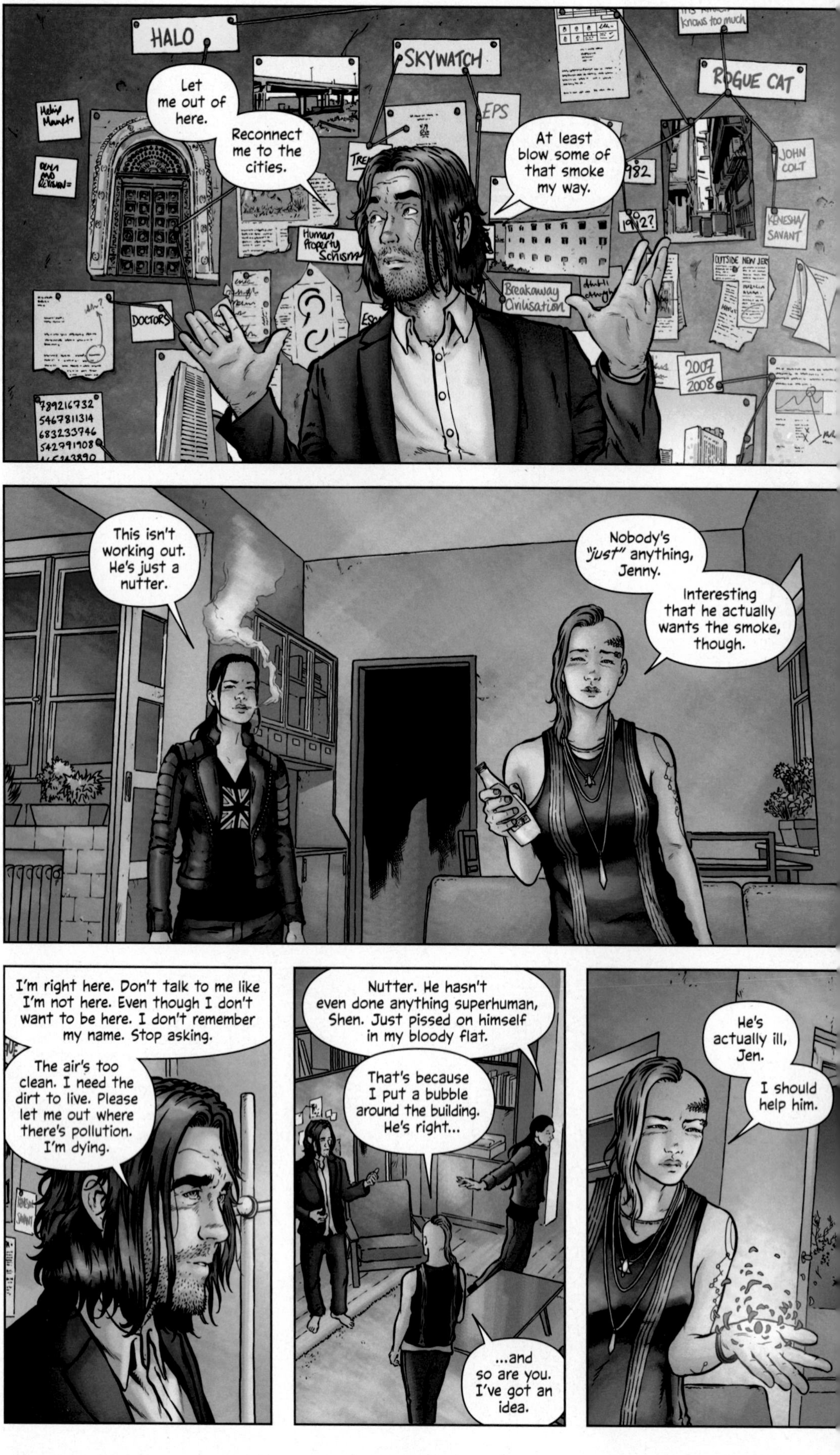
HALO
SKYWATCH
ROGUE CAT
Let me out of here.
Reconnect me to the cities.
At least blow some of that smoke my way.
EPS
JOHN COLT
KENESHA/ SAVANT
Human Property Schism
Breakaway Civilisation
DOCTORS
2007 2008
This isn't working out. He's just a nutter.
Nobody's "just" anything, Jenny.
Interesting that he actually wants the smoke, though.
I'm right here. Don't talk to me like I'm not here. Even though I don't want to be here. I don't remember my name. Stop asking.
The air's too clean. I need the dirt to live. Please let me out where there's pollution. I'm dying.
Nutter. He hasn't even done anything superhuman, Shen. Just pissed on himself in my bloody flat.
That's because I put a bubble around the building. He's right...
...and so are you. I've got an idea.
He's actually ill, Jen.
I should help him.

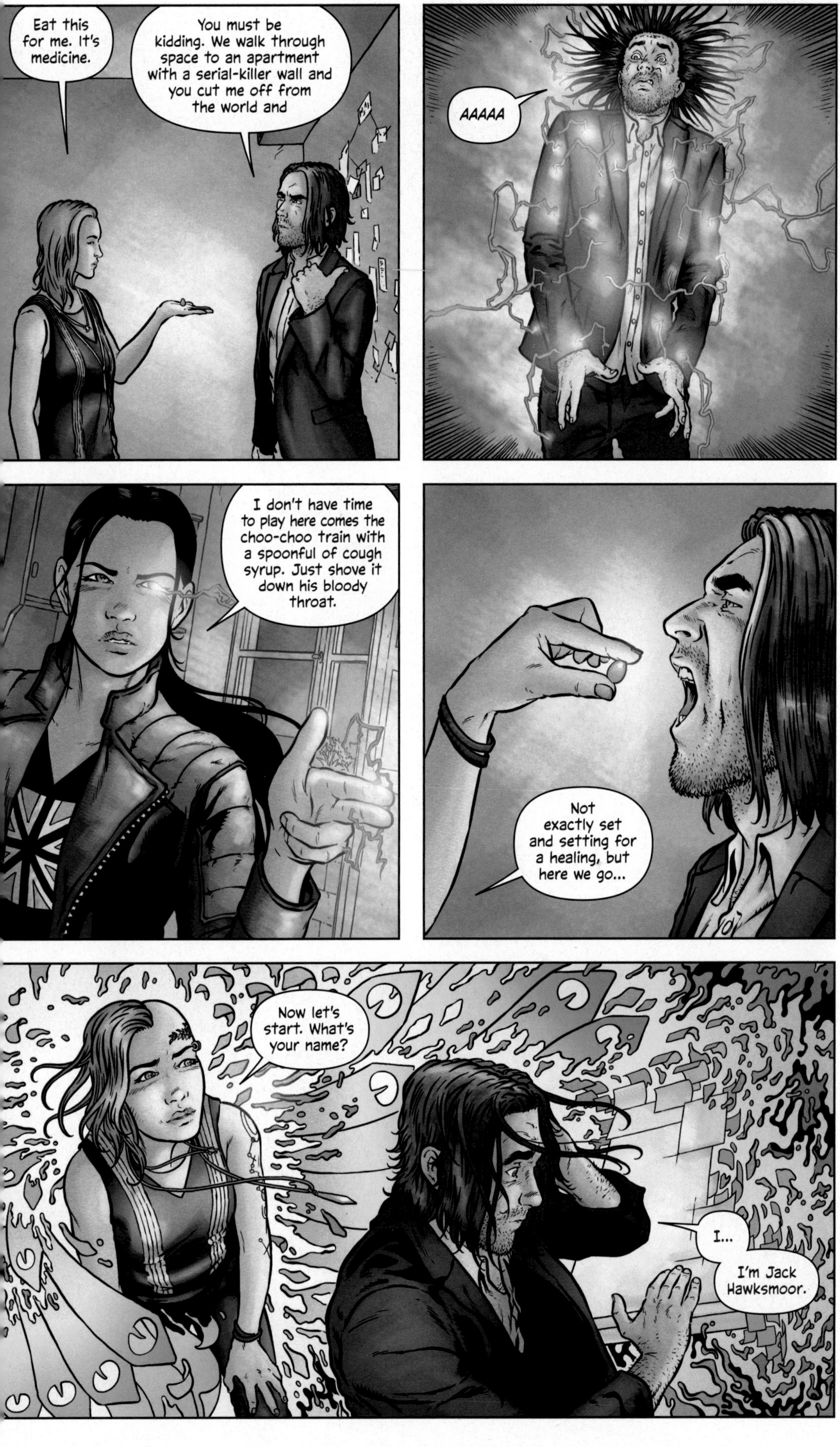
Eat this for me. It's medicine.
You must be kidding. We walk through space to an apartment with a serial-killer wall and you cut me off from the world and
AAAAA
I don't have time to play here comes the choo-choo train with a spoonful of cough syrup. Just shove it down his bloody throat.
Not exactly set and setting for a healing, but here we go...
Now let's start. What's your name?
I...
I'm Jack Hawksmoor.

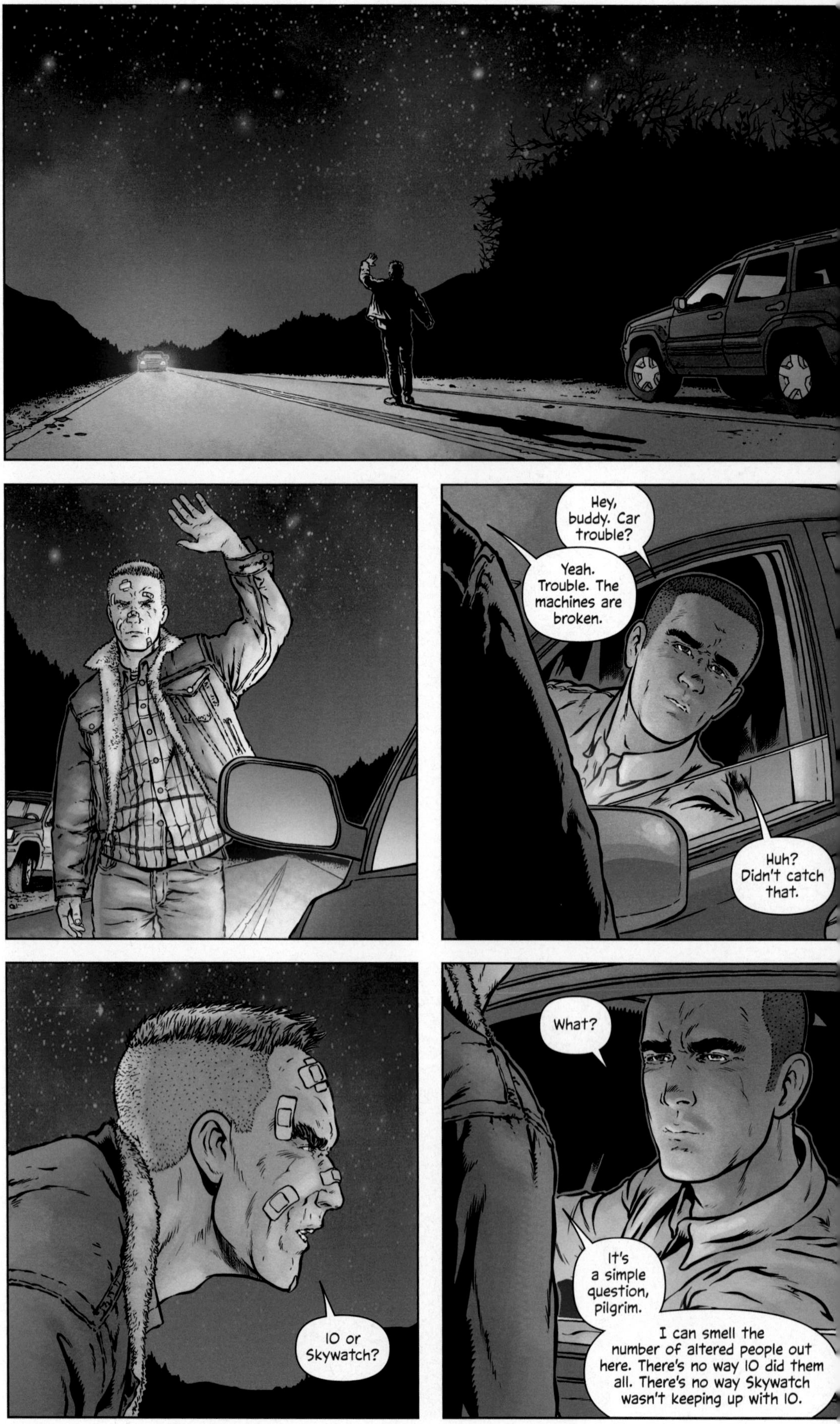
Hey, buddy. Car trouble?
Yeah. Trouble. The machines are broken.
Huh? Didn't catch that.
IO or Skywatch?
What?
It's a simple question, pilgrim.
I can smell the number of altered people out here. There's no way IO did them all. There's no way Skywatch wasn't keeping up with IO.

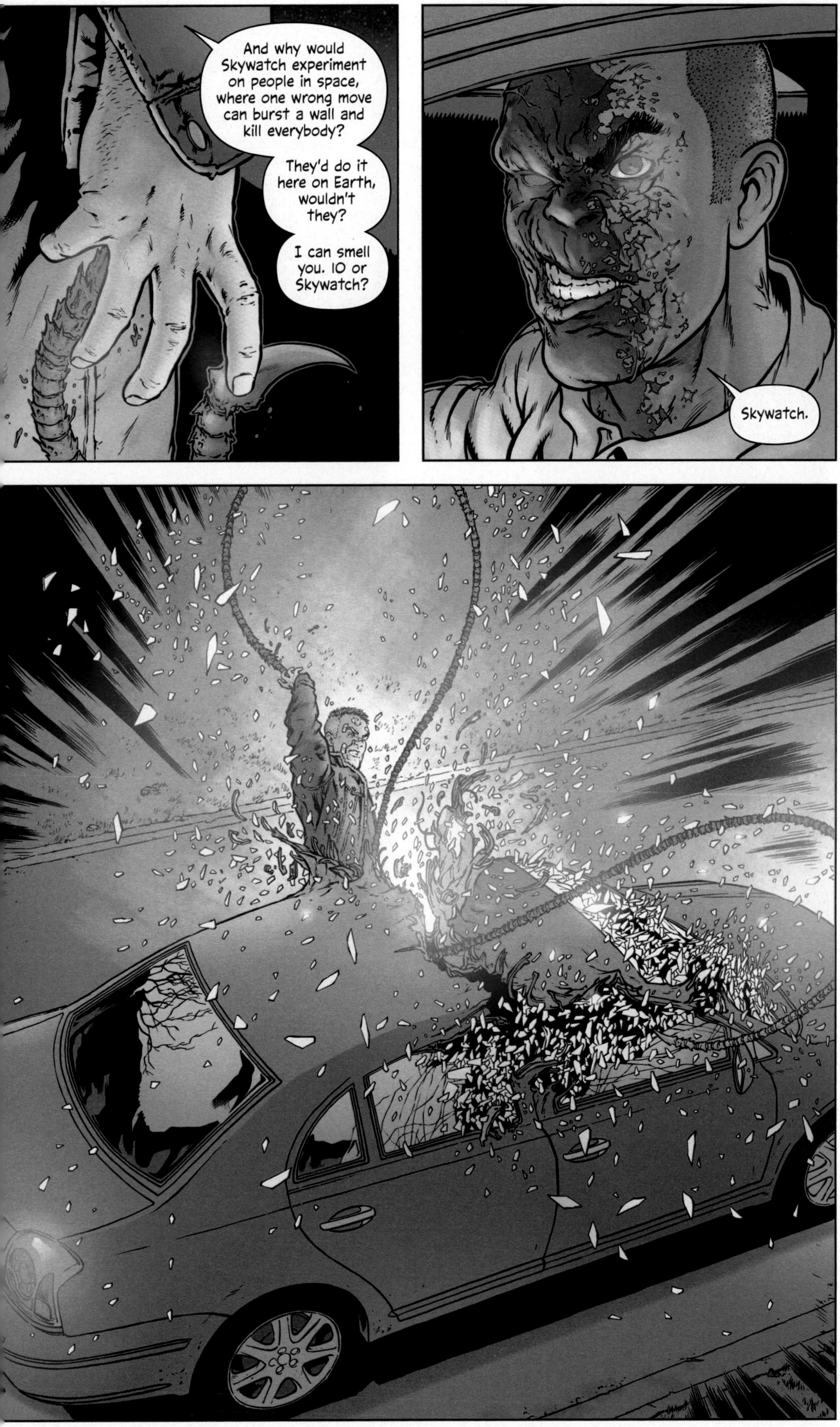
And why would Skywatch experiment on people in space, where one wrong move can burst a wall and kill everybody?
They'd do it here on Earth, wouldn't they?
I can smell you. IO or Skywatch?
Skywatch.

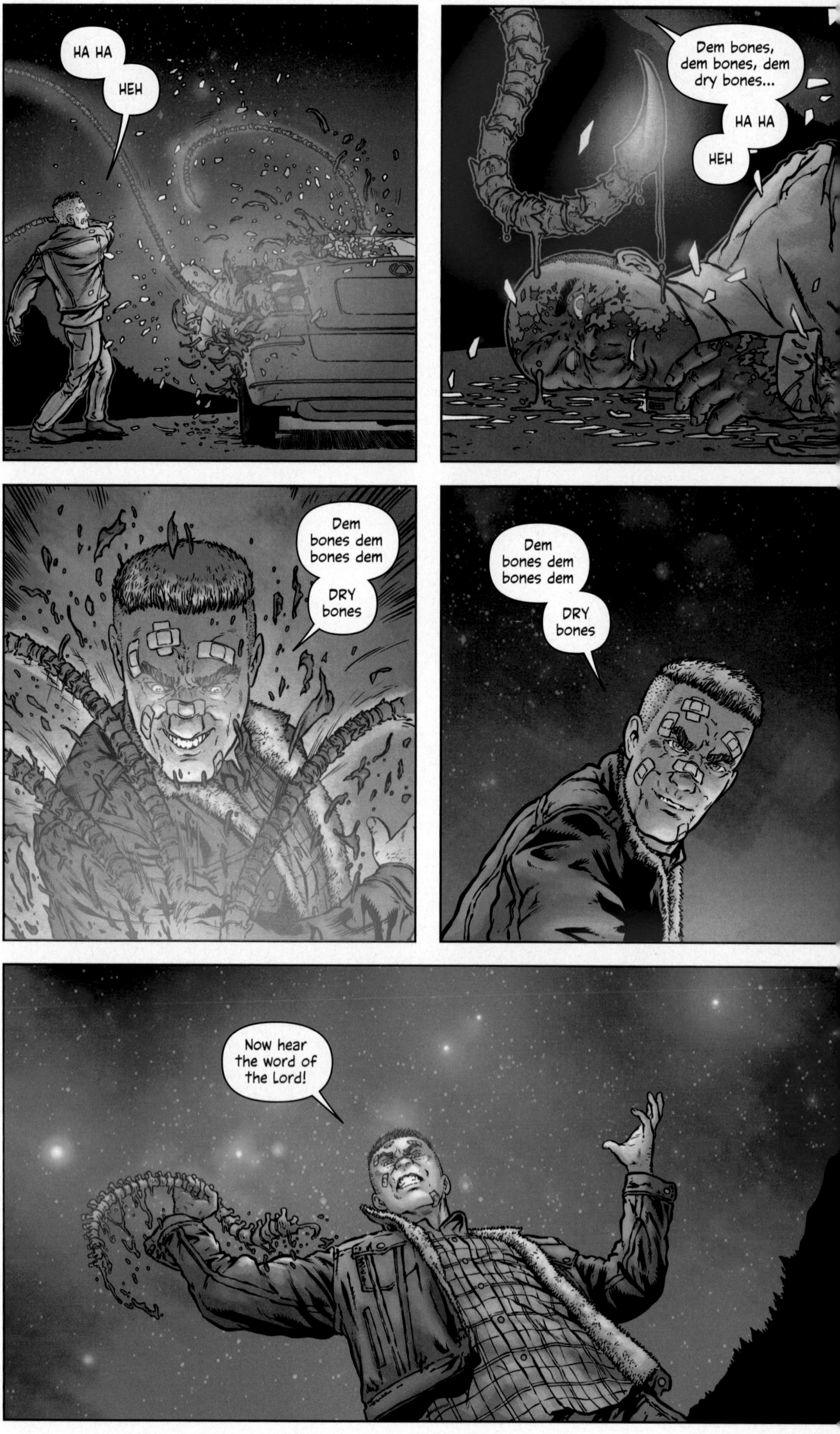

HA HA
HEH
Dem bones, dem bones, dem dry bones...
HA HA
HEH
Dem bones dem bones dem
DRY bones
Dem bones dem bones dem
DRY bones
Now hear the word of the Lord!

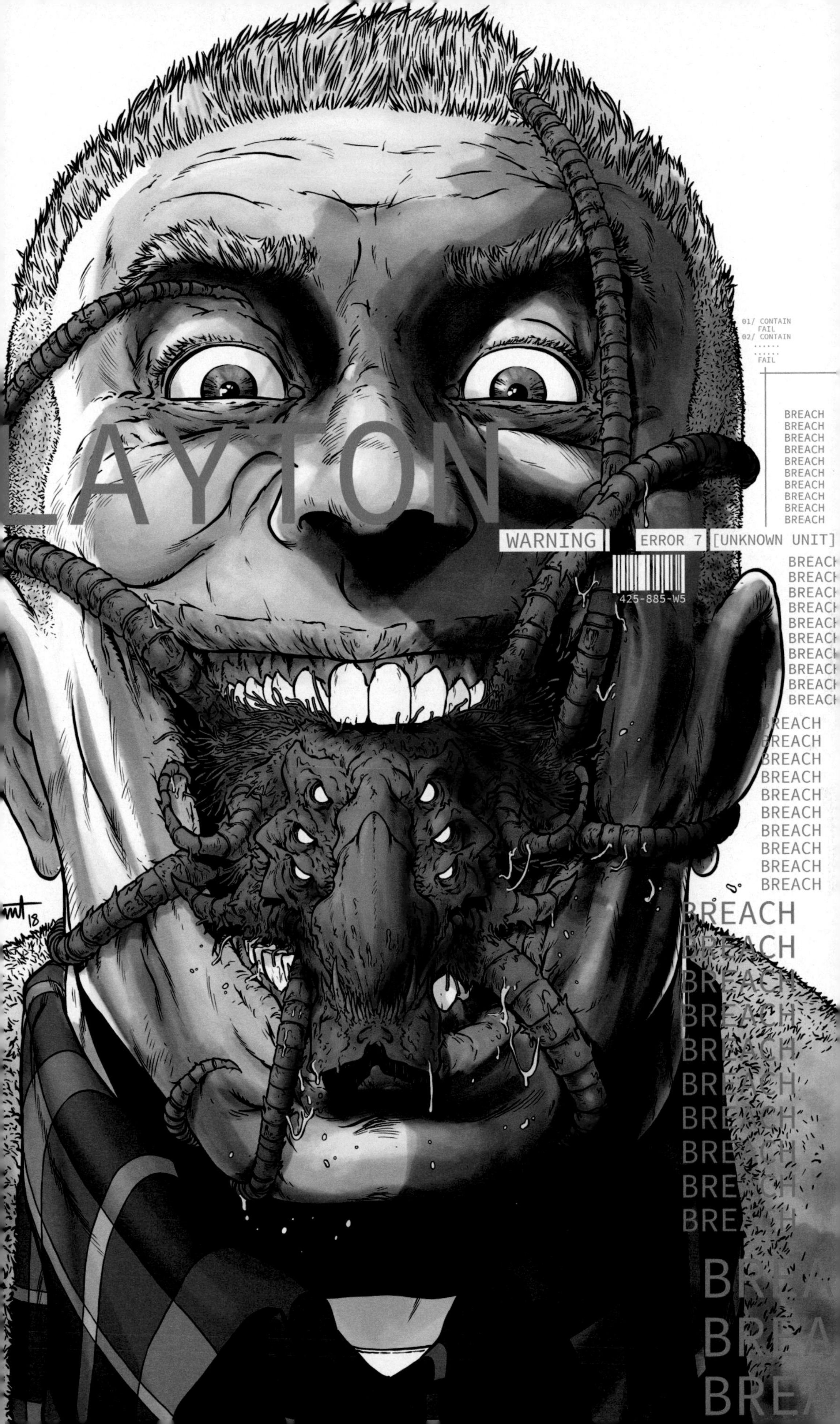
LAYTON
01/ CONTAIN
FAIL
02/ CONTAIN
......
......
FAIL
BREACH
BREACH
BREACH
BREACH
BREACH
BREACH
BREACH
BREACH
BREACH
BREACH
WARNING
ERROR 7
[UNKNOWN UNIT]
425-885-W5
BREACH
BREACH
BREACH
BREACH
BREACH
BREACH
BREACH
BREACH
BREACH
BREACH
BREACH
BREACH
BREACH
BREACH
BREACH
BREACH
BREACH
BREACH
BREACH
BREACH

15

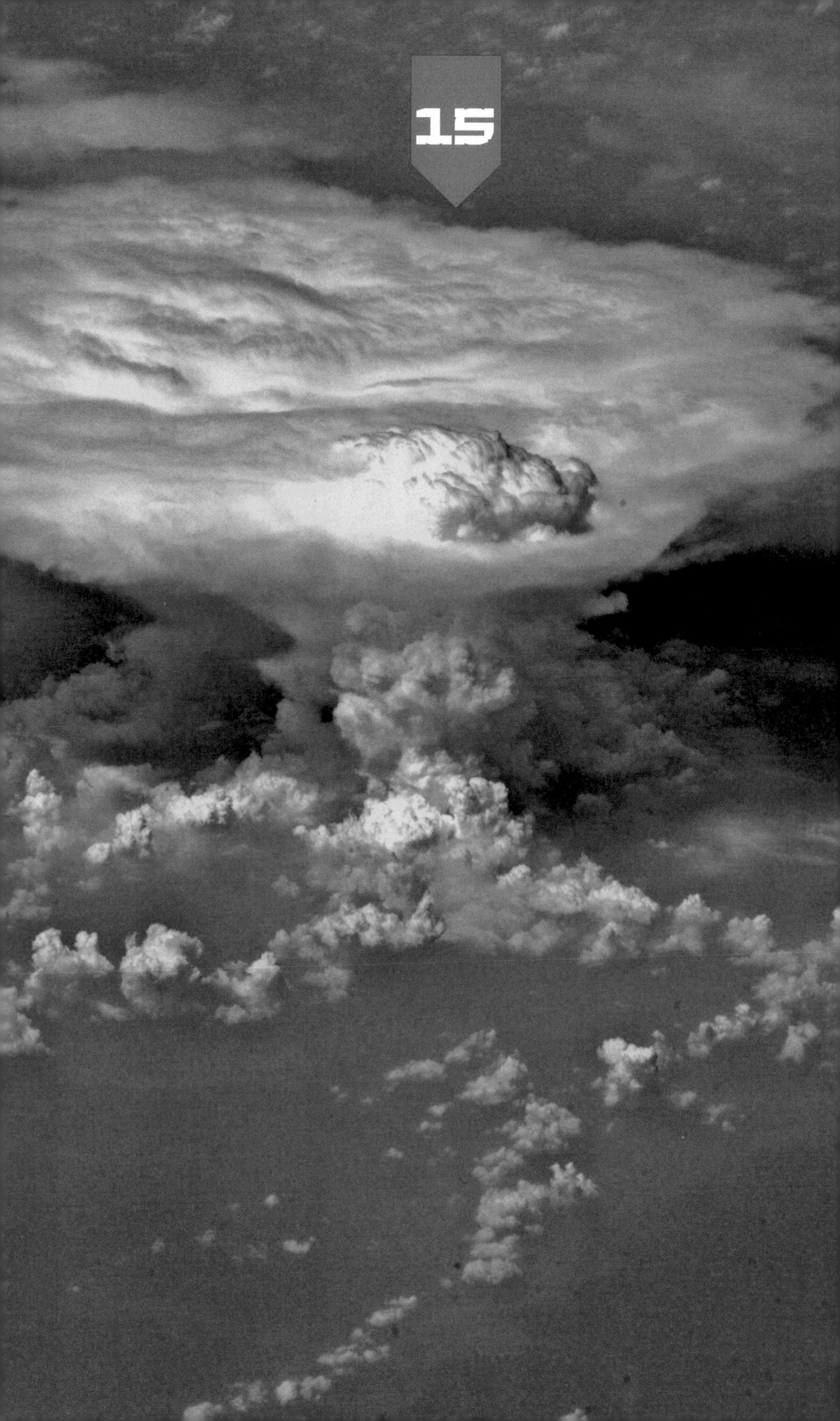

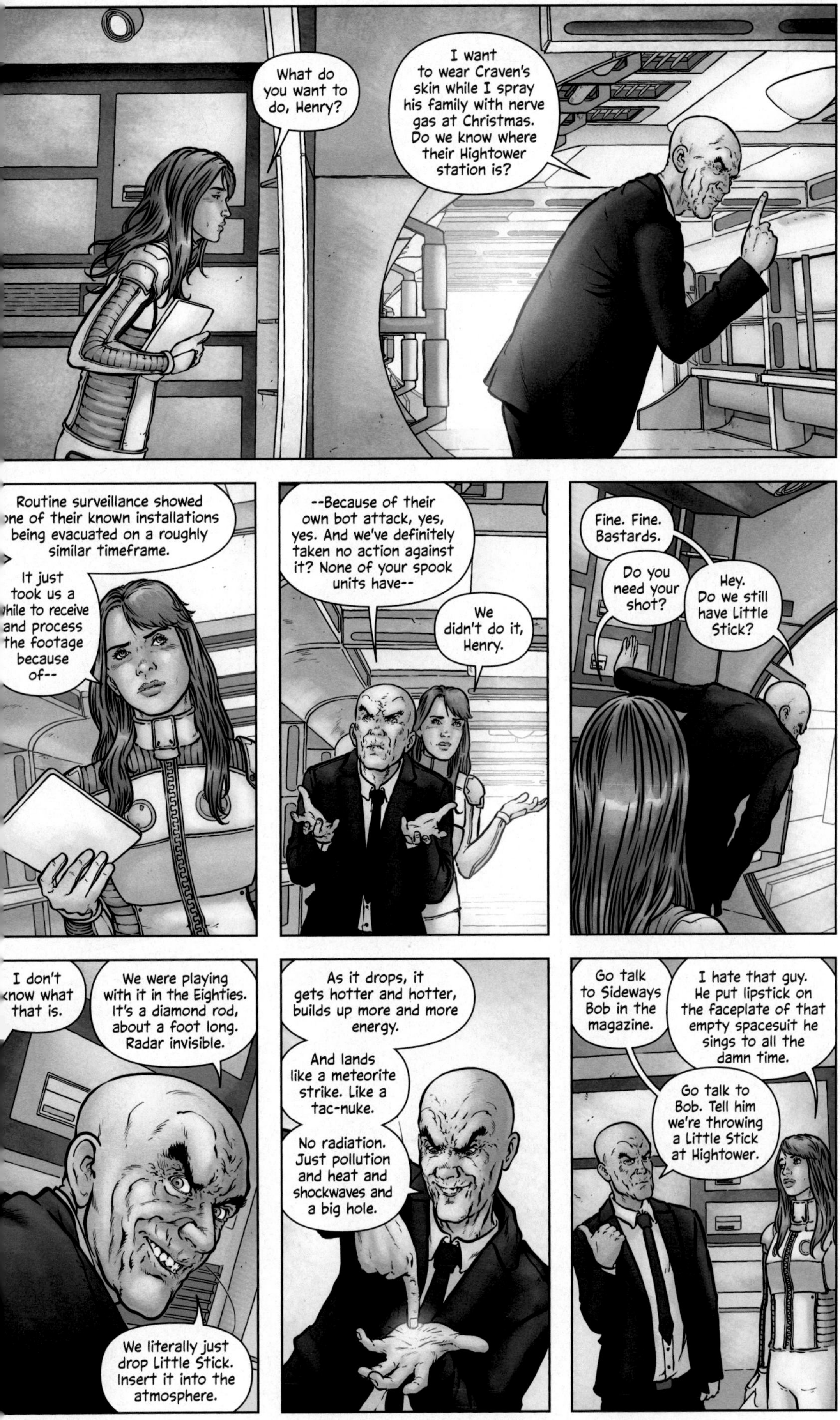
What do you want to do, Henry?
I want to wear Craven's skin while I spray his family with nerve gas at Christmas. Do we know where their Hightower station is?
Routine surveillance showed one of their known installations being evacuated on a roughly similar timeframe.
It just took us a while to receive and process the footage because of--
--Because of their own bot attack, yes, yes. And we've definitely taken no action against it? None of your spook units have--
We didn't do it, Henry.
Fine. Fine. Bastards.
Hey. Do we still have Little Stick?
Do you need your shot?
I don't know what that is.
We were playing with it in the Eighties. It's a diamond rod, about a foot long. Radar invisible.
We literally just drop Little Stick. Insert it into the atmosphere.
As it drops, it gets hotter and hotter, builds up more and more energy.
And lands like a meteorite strike. Like a tac-nuke.
No radiation. Just pollution and heat and shockwaves and a big hole.
Go talk to Sideways Bob in the magazine.
I hate that guy. He put lipstick on the faceplate of that empty spacesuit he sings to all the damn time.
Go talk to Bob. Tell him we're throwing a Little Stick at Hightower.

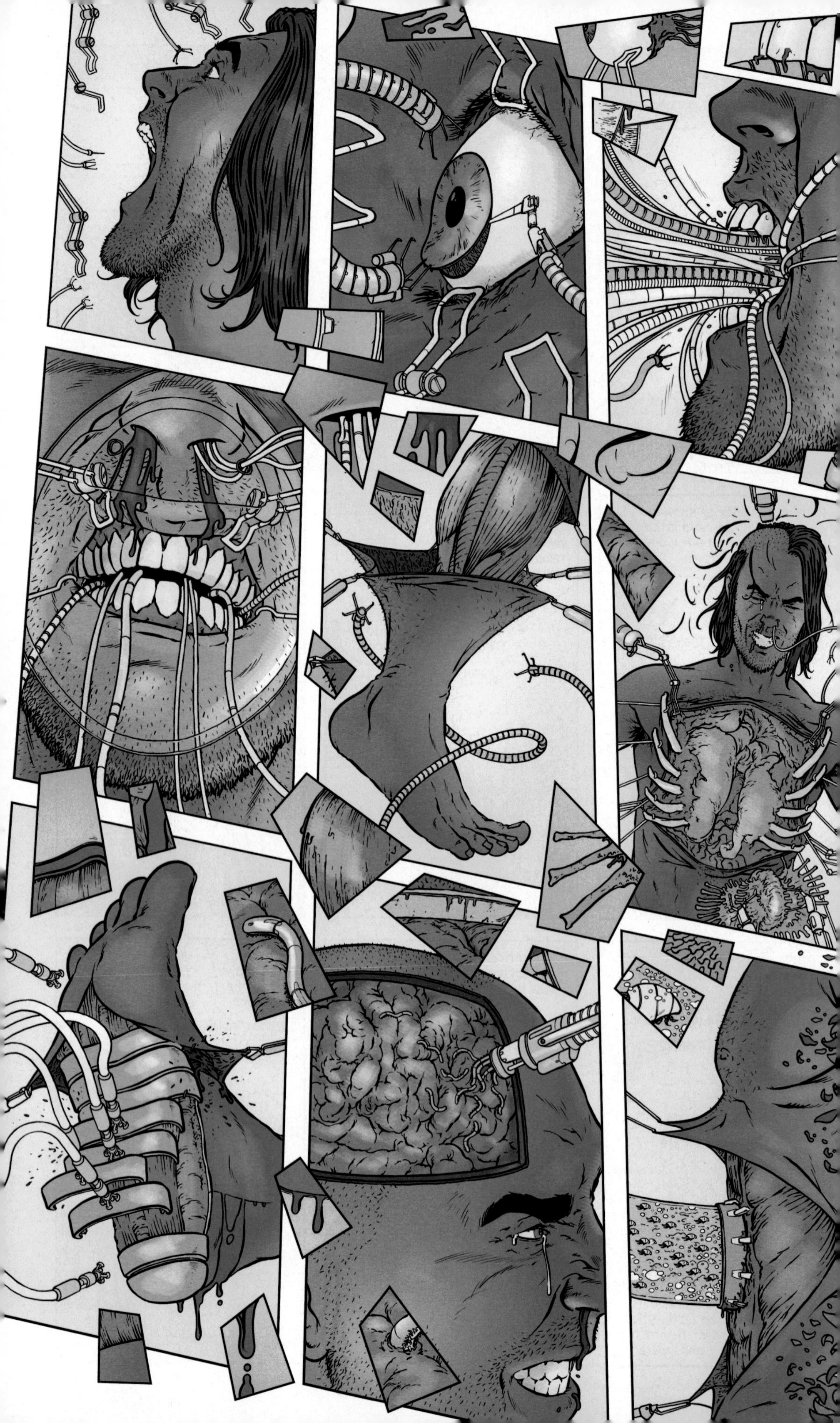

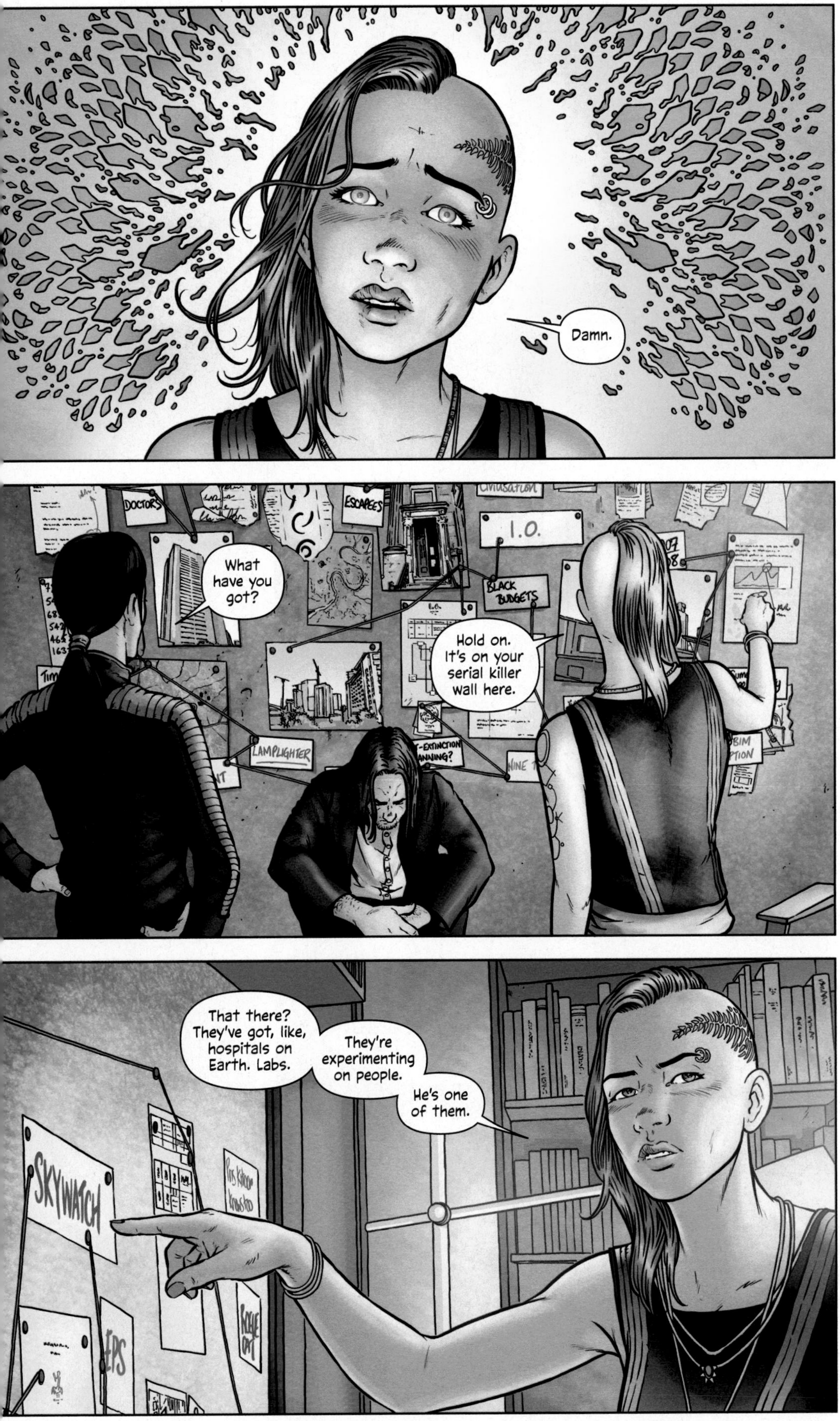
Damn.
DOCTORS
ESCAPEES
I.O.
BLACK BUDGETS
LAMPLIGHTER
What have you got?
Hold on. It's on your serial killer wall here.
SKYWATCH
That there? They've got, like, hospitals on Earth. Labs.
They're experimenting on people.
He's one of them.

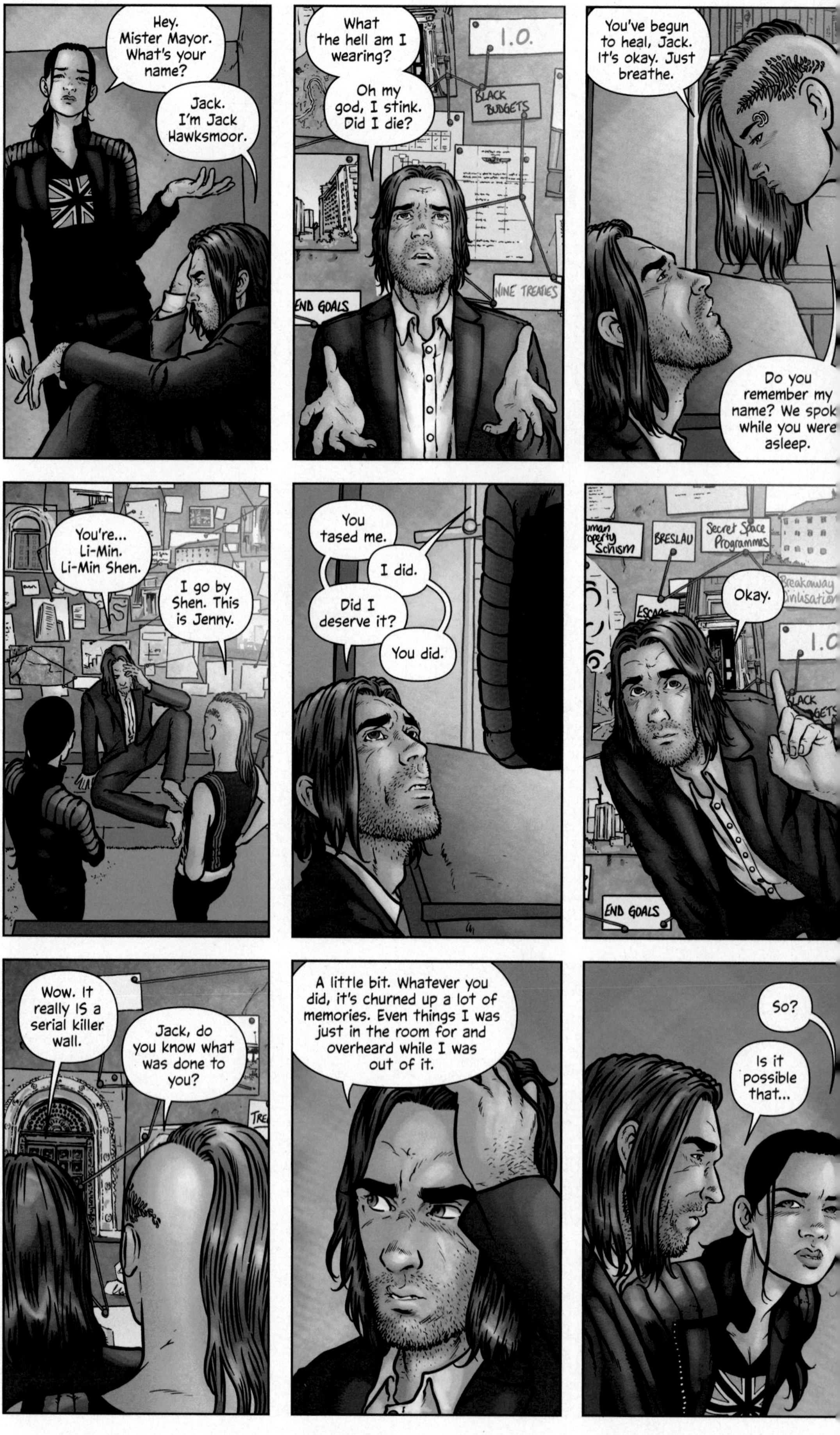
Hey. Mister Mayor. What's your name?
Jack. I'm Jack Hawksmoor.
What the hell am I wearing?
Oh my god, I stink. Did I die?
I.O.
BLACK BUDGETS
NINE TREATIES
END GOALS
You've begun to heal, Jack. It's okay. Just breathe.
Do you remember my name? We spok while you were asleep.
You're... Li-Min. Li-Min Shen.
I go by Shen. This is Jenny.
You tased me.
I did.
Did I deserve it?
You did.
BRESLAU
Secret Space Programmes
Okay.
END GOALS
Wow. It really IS a serial killer wall.
Jack, do you know what was done to you?
A little bit. Whatever you did, it's churned up a lot of memories. Even things I was just in the room for and overheard while I was out of it.
So?
Is it possible that...

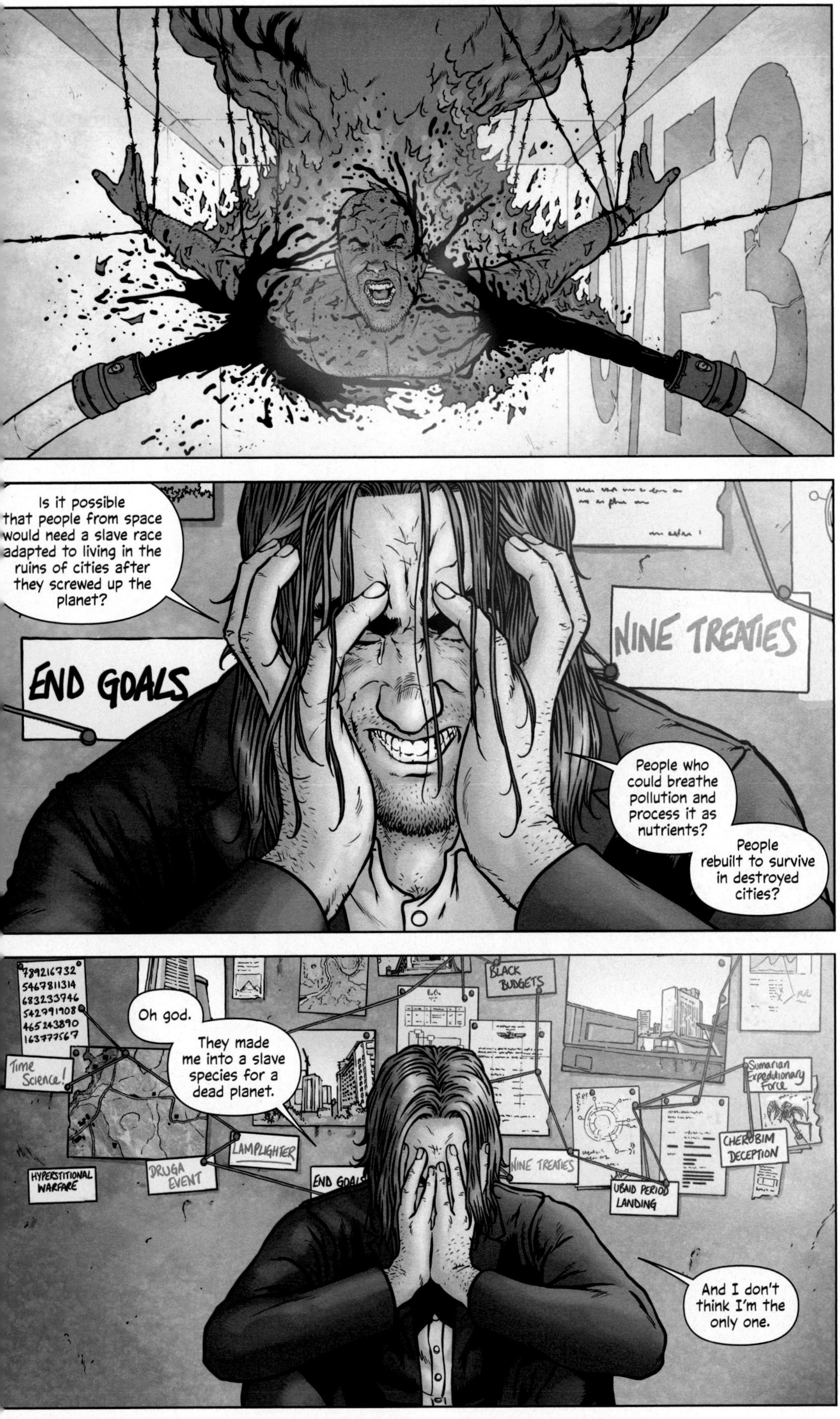
Is it possible that people from space would need a slave race adapted to living in the ruins of cities after they screwed up the planet?
END GOALS
NINE TREATIES
People who could breathe pollution and process it as nutrients?
People rebuilt to survive in destroyed cities?
Oh god.
They made me into a slave species for a dead planet.
BLACK BUDGETS
Time Science!
Sumarian Expeditionary Force
HYPERSTITIONAL WARFARE
DRUGA EVENT
LAMPLIGHTER
NINE TREATIES
UBAID PERIOD LANDING
CHERUBIM DECEPTION
And I don't think I'm the only one.

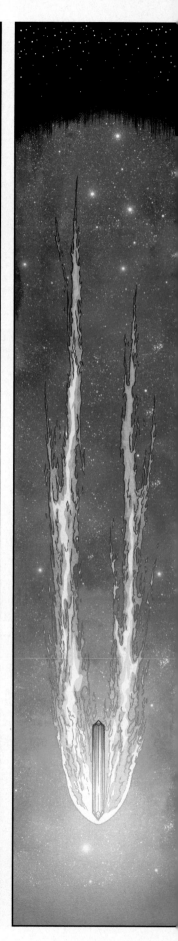

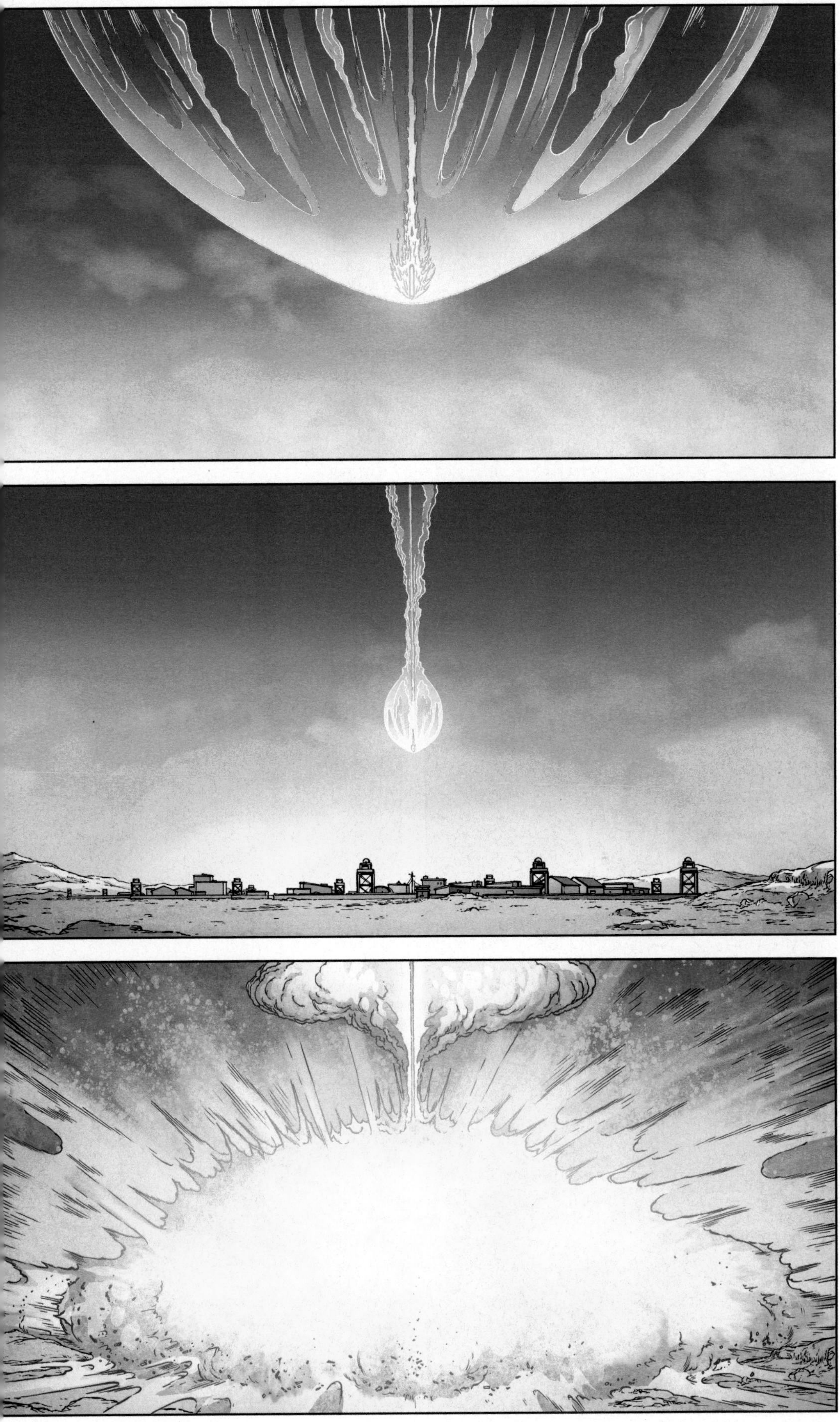

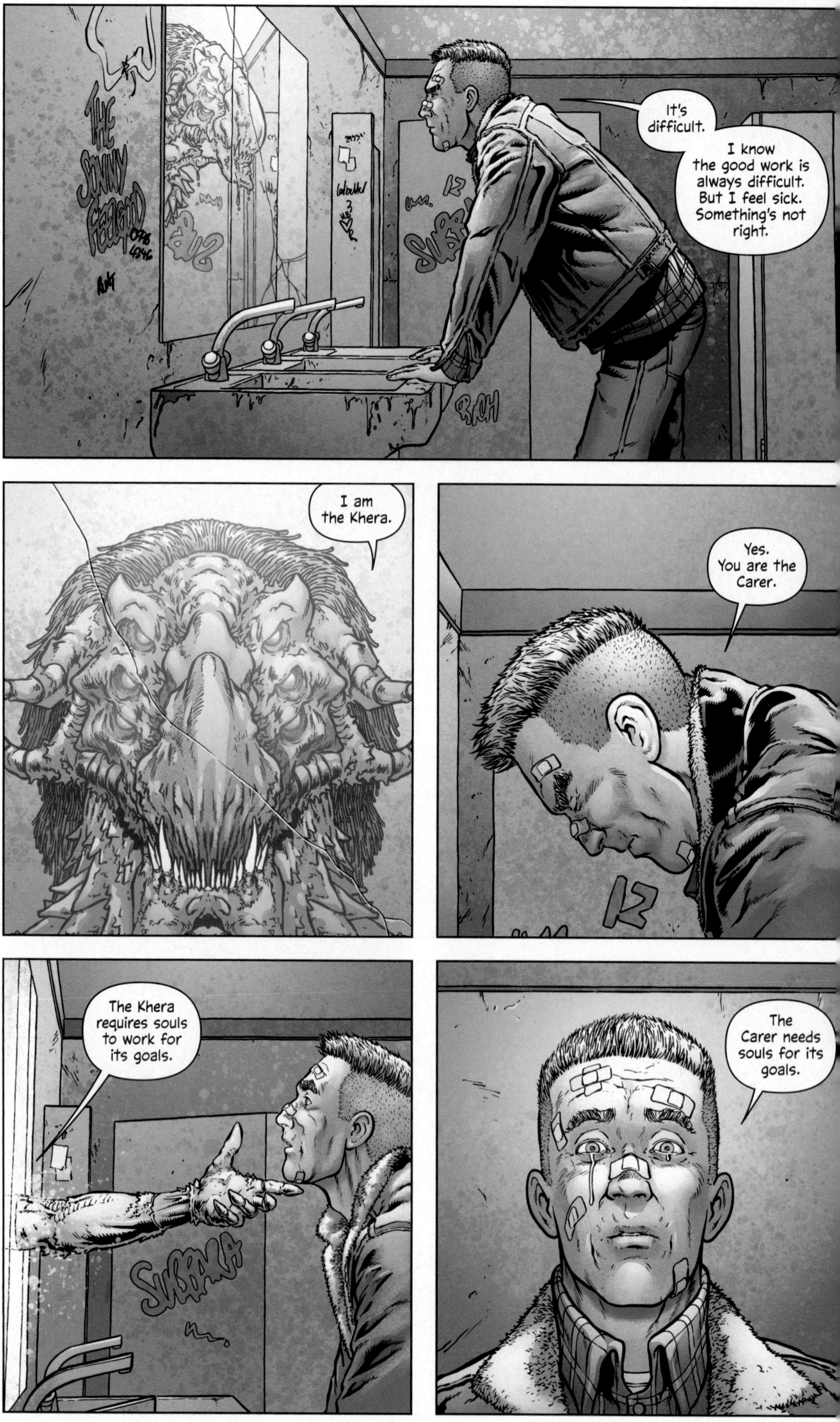
It's difficult.
I know the good work is always difficult. But I feel sick. Something's not right.
I am the Khera.
Yes. You are the Carer.
The Khera requires souls to work for its goals.
The Carer needs souls for its goals.

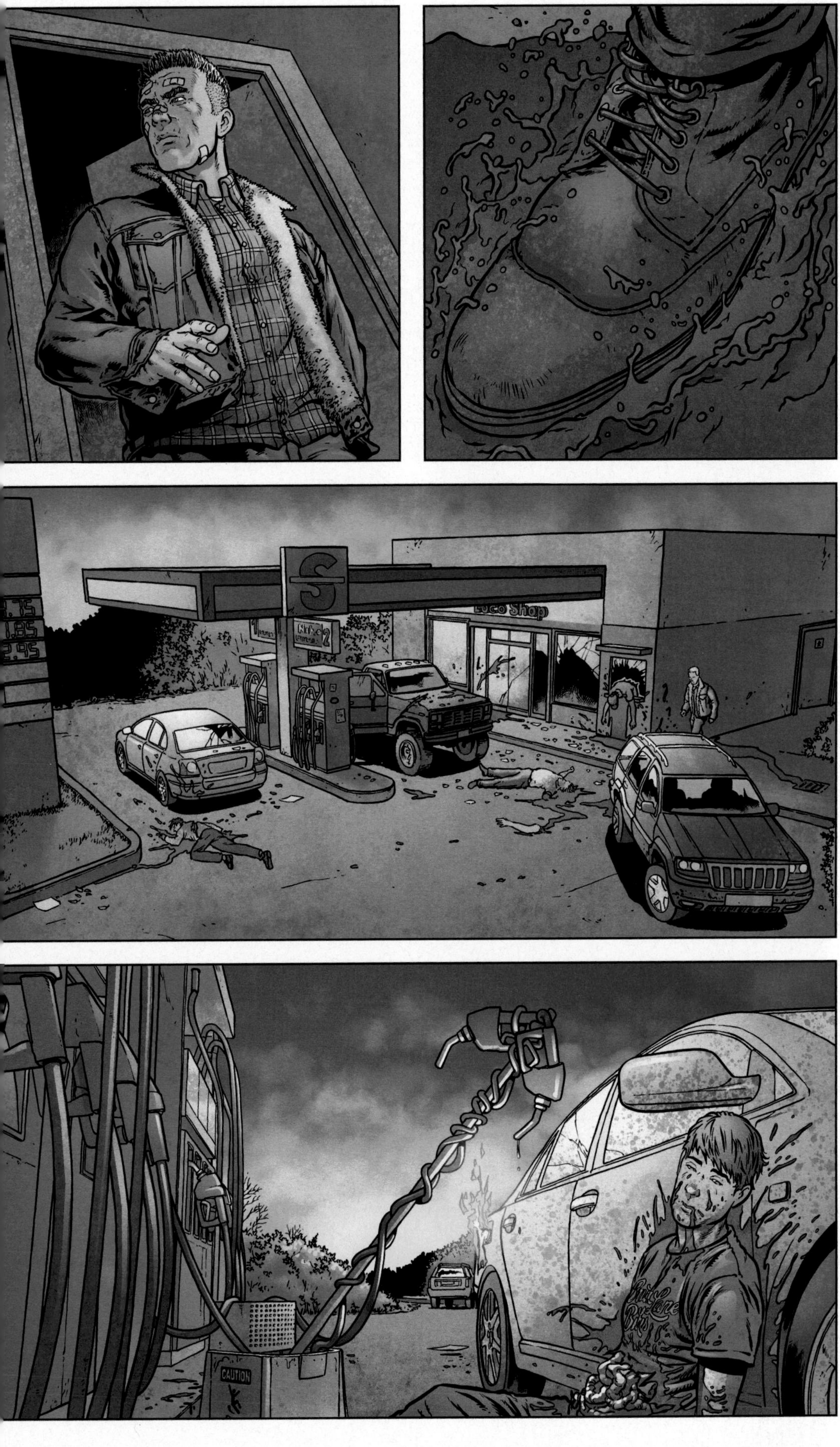
Loco Shop
1.85
CAUTION

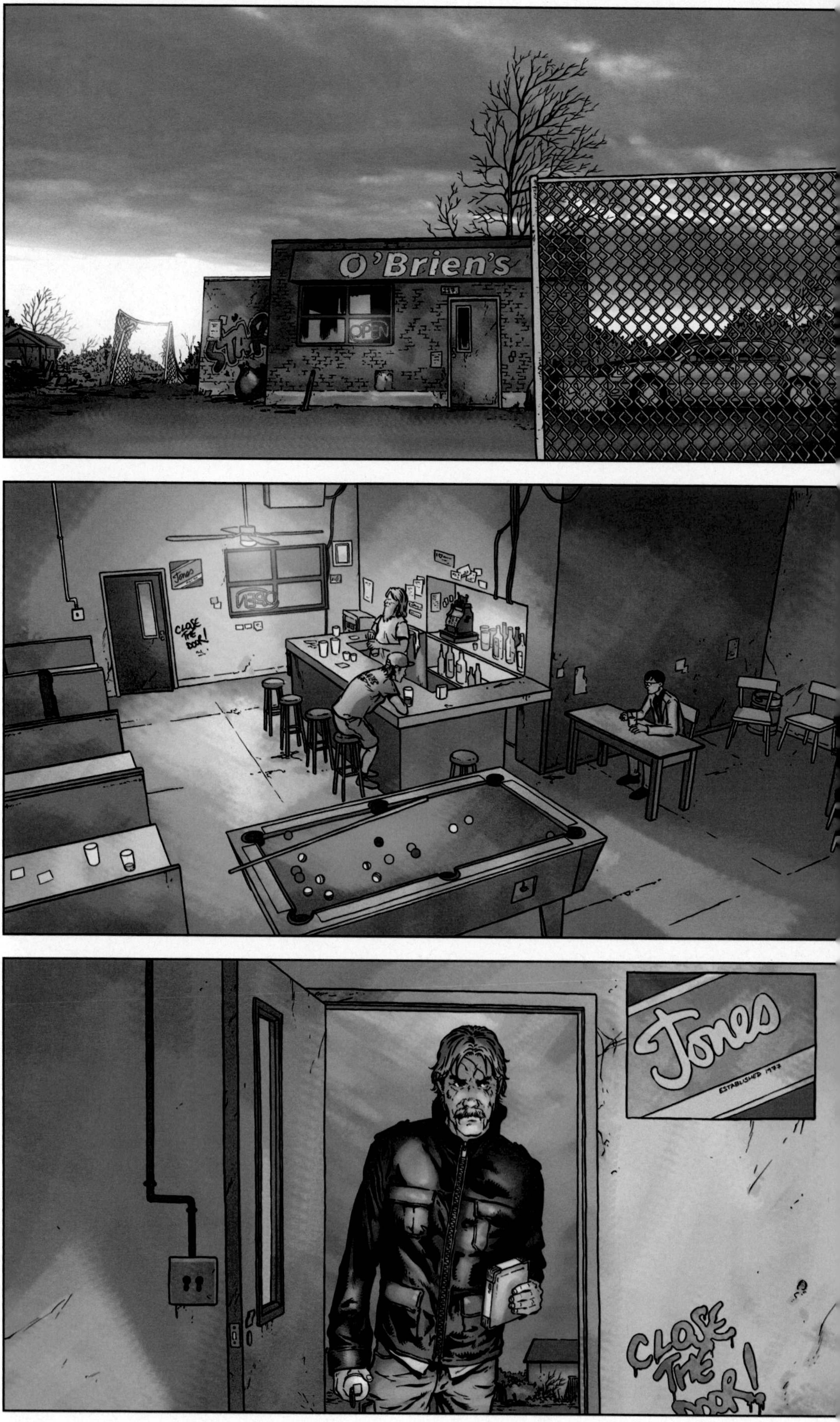
O'Brien's
OPEN
Jones
CLOSE THE DOOR!
Jones
ESTABLISHED 1973
CLOSE THE DOOR!

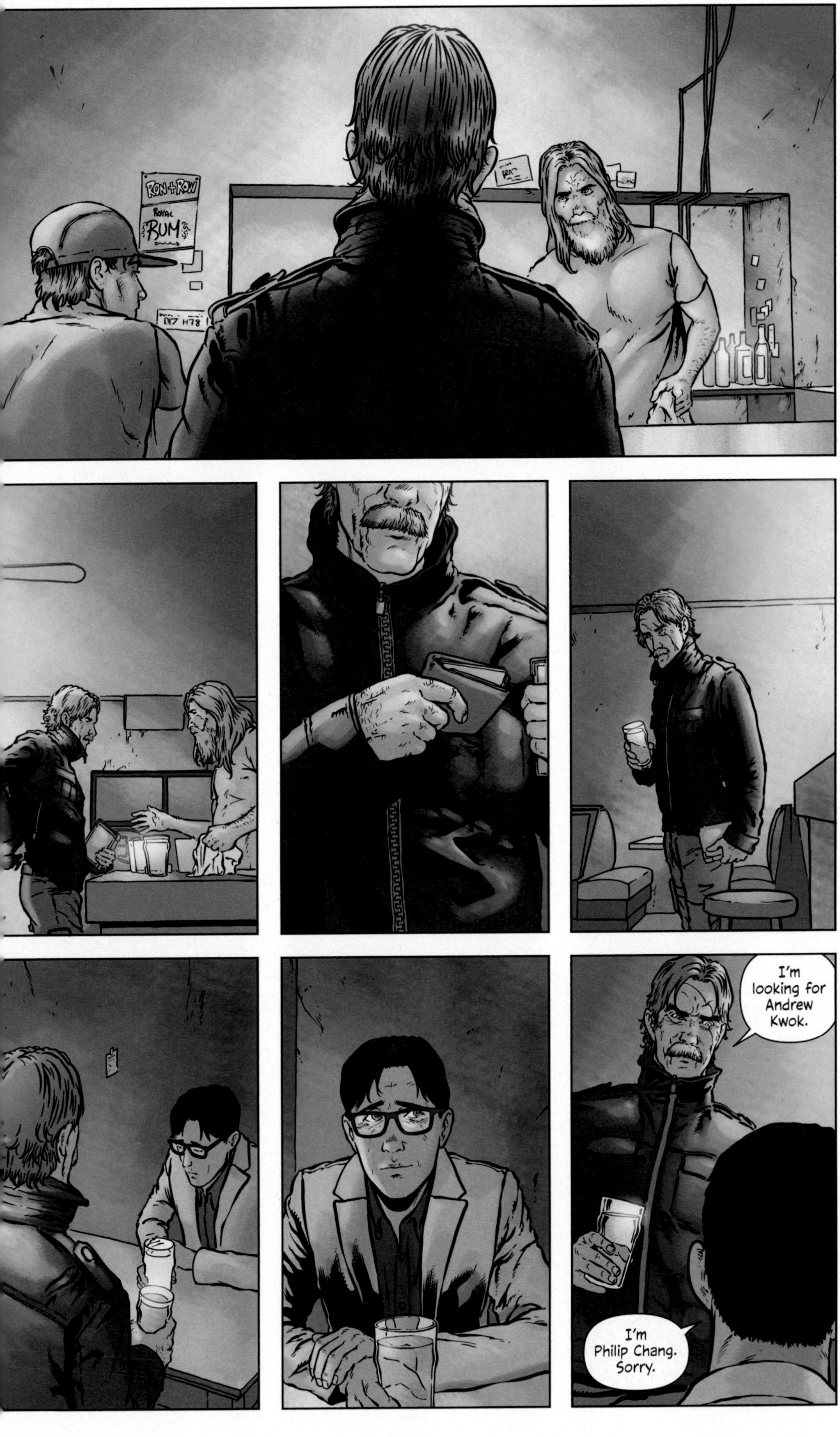
RON + ROW
ROYAL
RUM
D17 H78
I'm looking for Andrew Kwok.
I'm Philip Chang. Sorry.

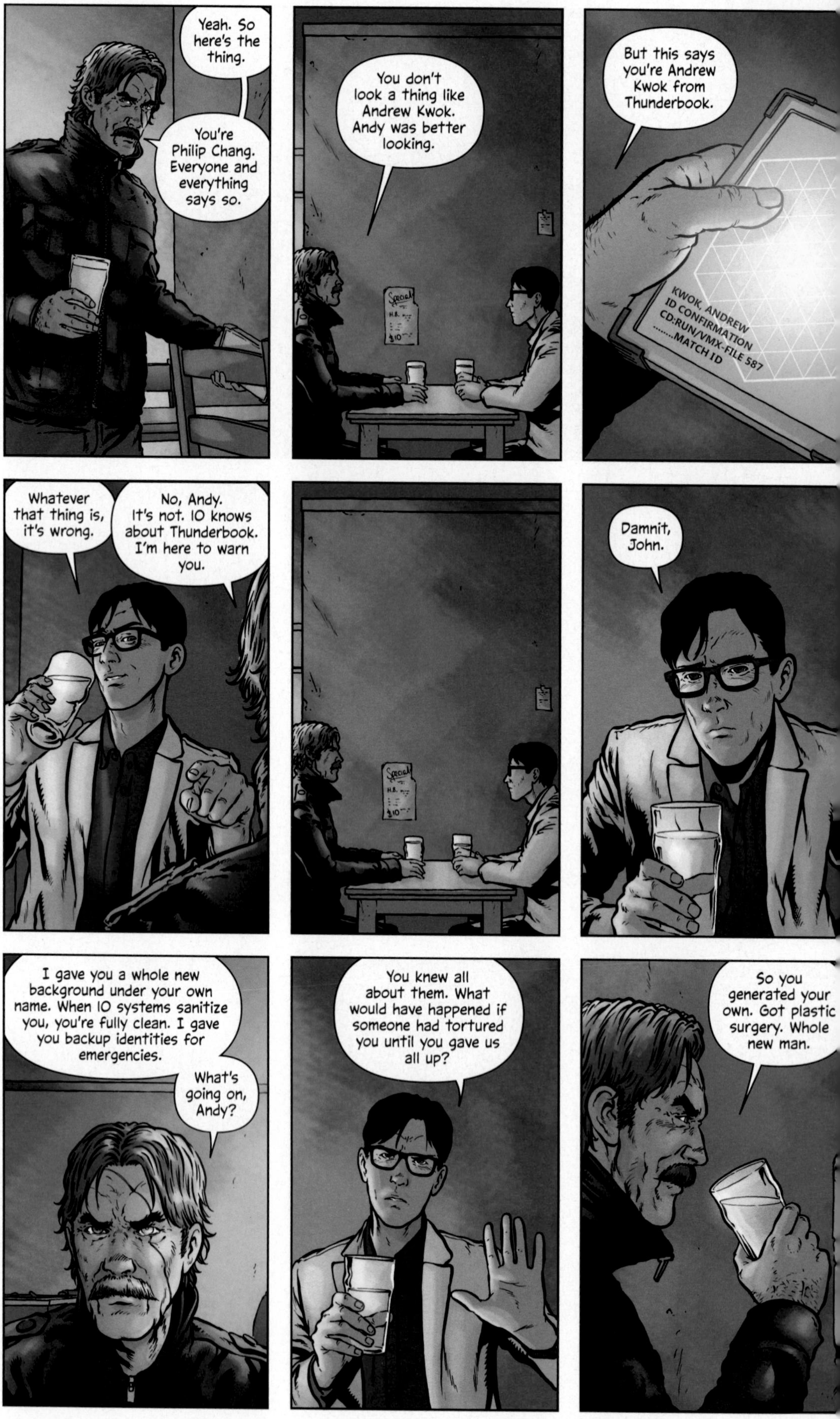
Yeah. So here's the thing.
You're Philip Chang. Everyone and everything says so.
You don't look a thing like Andrew Kwok. Andy was better looking.
But this says you're Andrew Kwok from Thunderbook.
KWOK, ANDREW
ID CONFIRMATION
CD:RUN/VMX-FILE 587
.......MATCH ID
Whatever that thing is, it's wrong.
No, Andy. It's not. IO knows about Thunderbook. I'm here to warn you.
Damnit, John.
I gave you a whole new background under your own name. When IO systems sanitize you, you're fully clean. I gave you backup identities for emergencies.
What's going on, Andy?
You knew all about them. What would have happened if someone had tortured you until you gave us all up?
So you generated your own. Got plastic surgery. Whole new man.

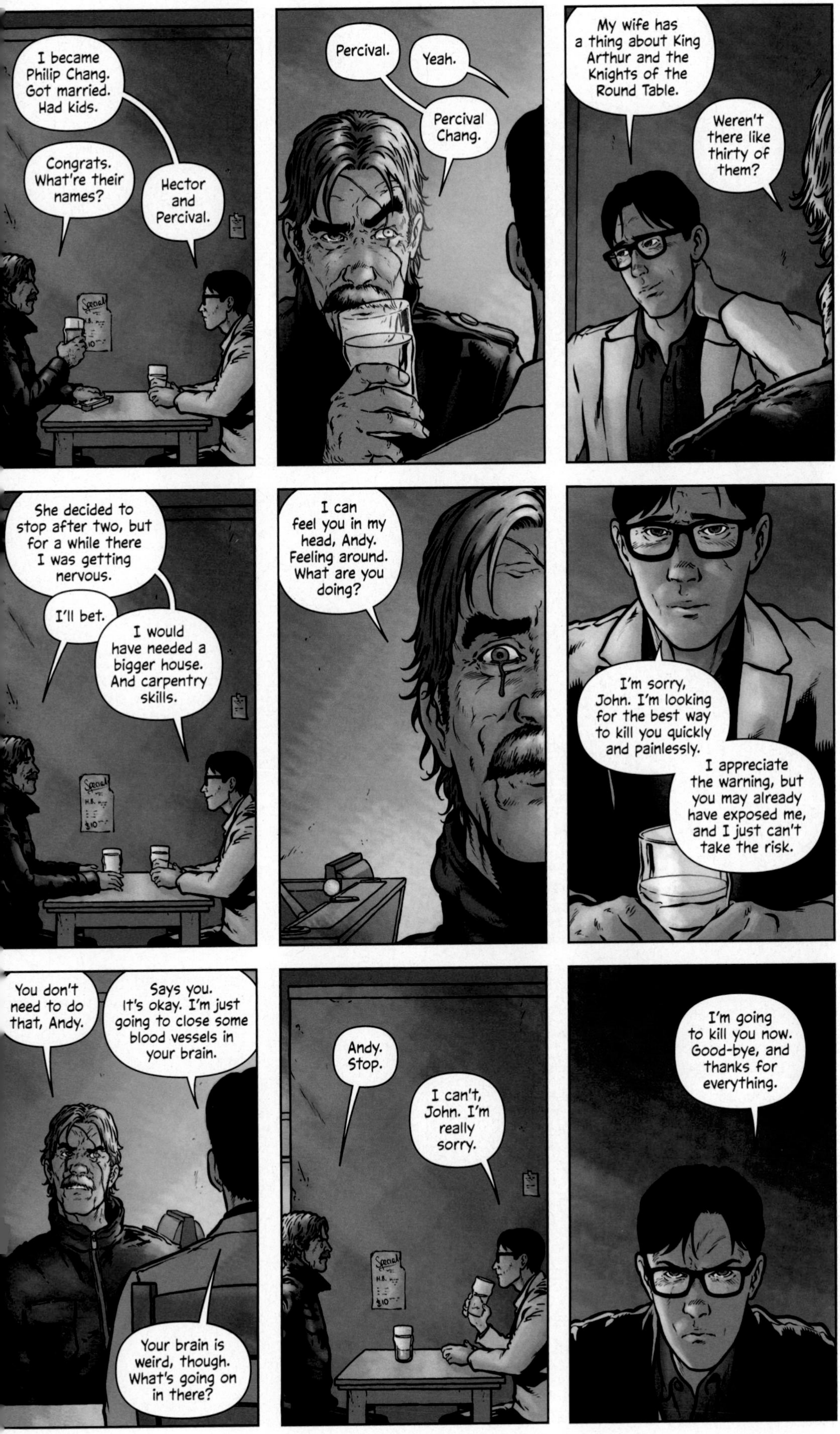

I became Philip Chang. Got married. Had kids.
Congrats. What're their names?
Hector and Percival.
Percival.
Yeah.
Percival Chang.
My wife has a thing about King Arthur and the Knights of the Round Table.
Weren't there like thirty of them?
She decided to stop after two, but for a while there I was getting nervous.
I'll bet.
I would have needed a bigger house. And carpentry skills.
I can feel you in my head, Andy. Feeling around. What are you doing?
I'm sorry, John. I'm looking for the best way to kill you quickly and painlessly.
I appreciate the warning, but you may already have exposed me, and I just can't take the risk.
You don't need to do that, Andy.
Says you. It's okay. I'm just going to close some blood vessels in your brain.
Your brain is weird, though. What's going on in there?
Andy. Stop.
I can't, John. I'm really sorry.
I'm going to kill you now. Good-bye, and thanks for everything.

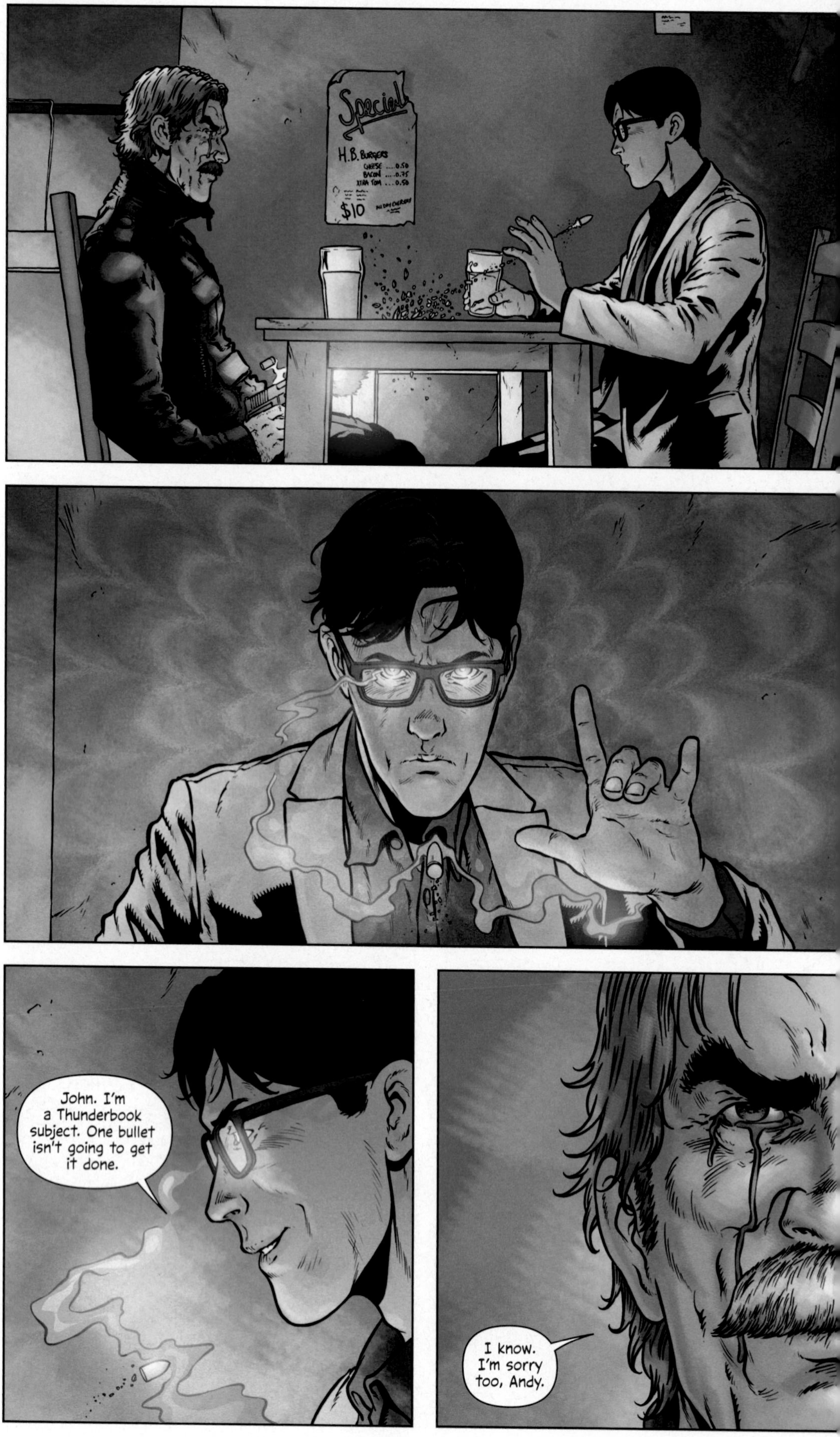
Specials
H.B. BURGERS
CHEESE 0.50
BACON 0.75
XTRA TOM 0.50
$10
John. I'm a Thunderbook subject. One bullet isn't going to get it done.
I know. I'm sorry too, Andy.

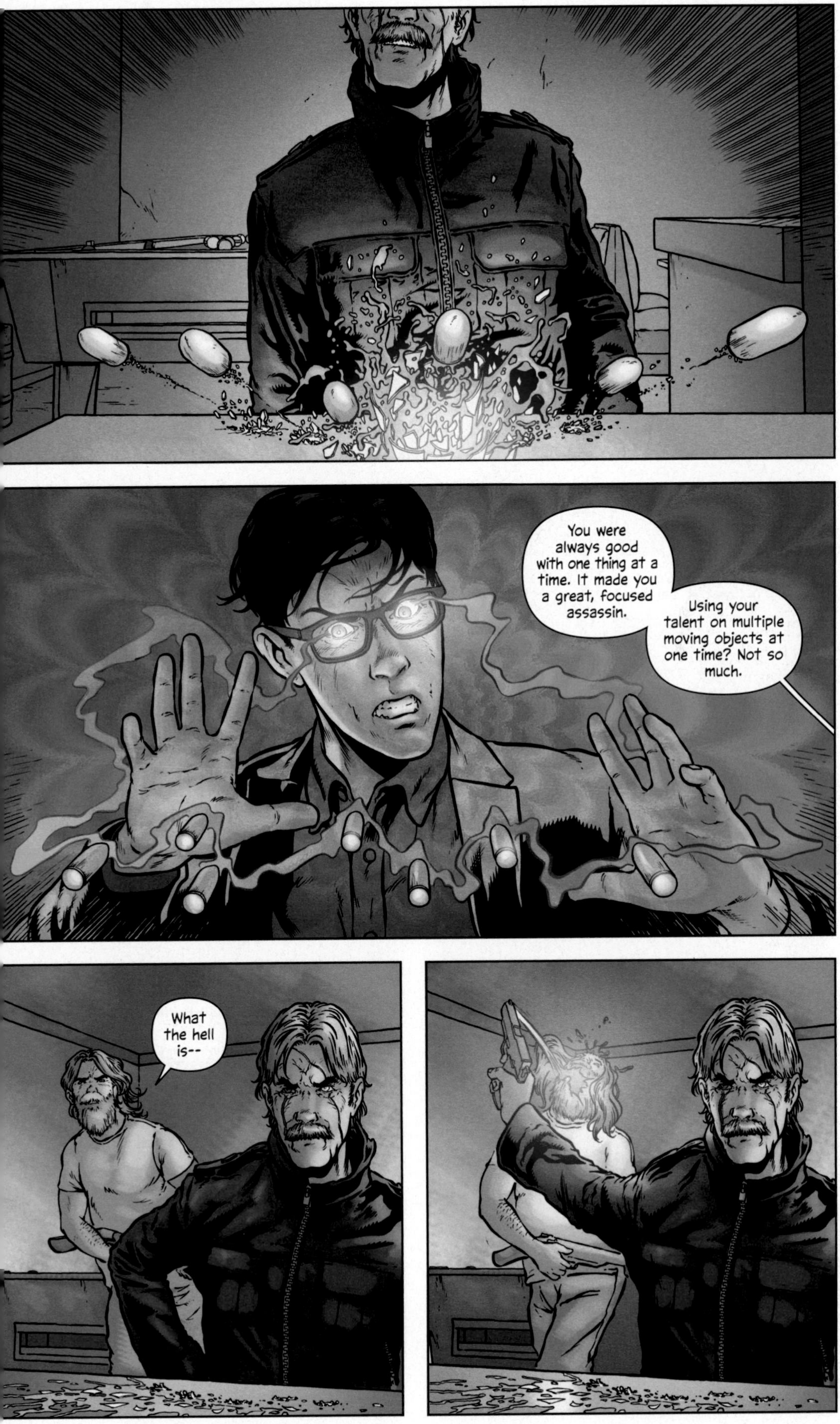
You were always good with one thing at a time. It made you a great, focused assassin.
Using your talent on multiple moving objects at one time? Not so much.
What the hell is--

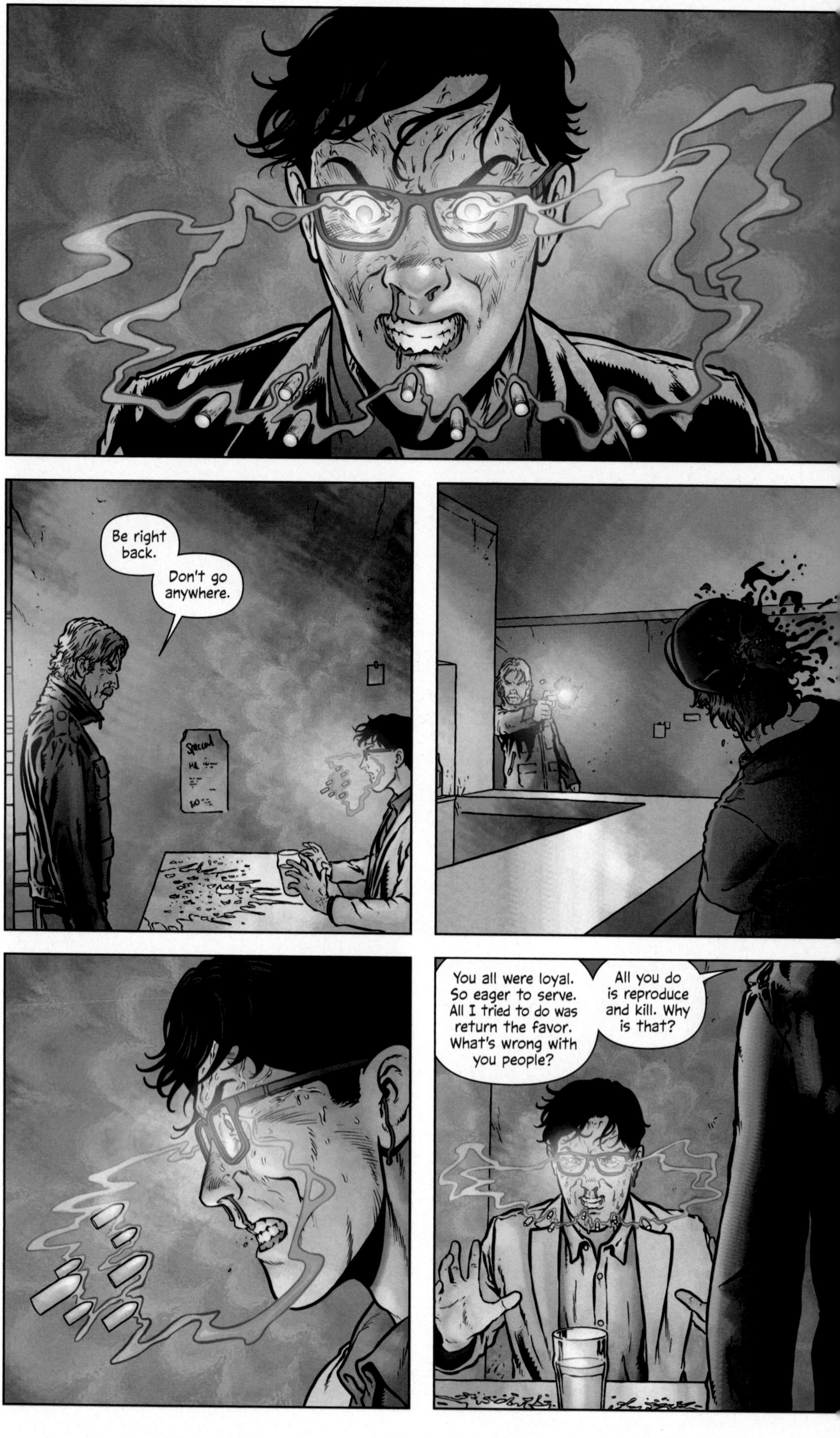
Be right back.
Don't go anywhere.
You all were loyal. So eager to serve. All I tried to do was return the favor. What's wrong with you people?
All you do is reproduce and kill. Why is that?

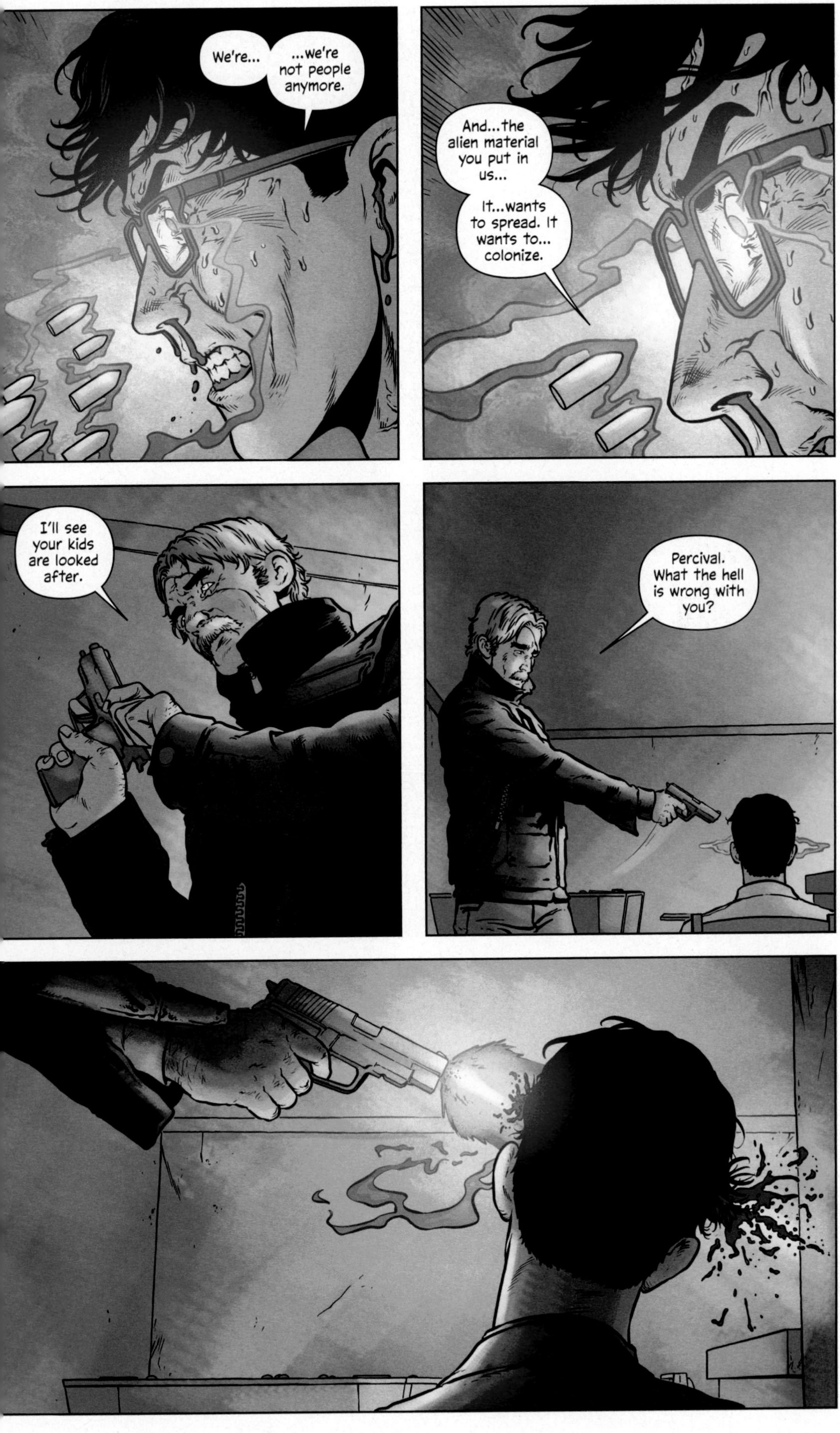
We're...
...we're not people anymore.
And...the alien material you put in us...
It...wants to spread. It wants to... colonize.
I'll see your kids are looked after.
Percival. What the hell is wrong with you?

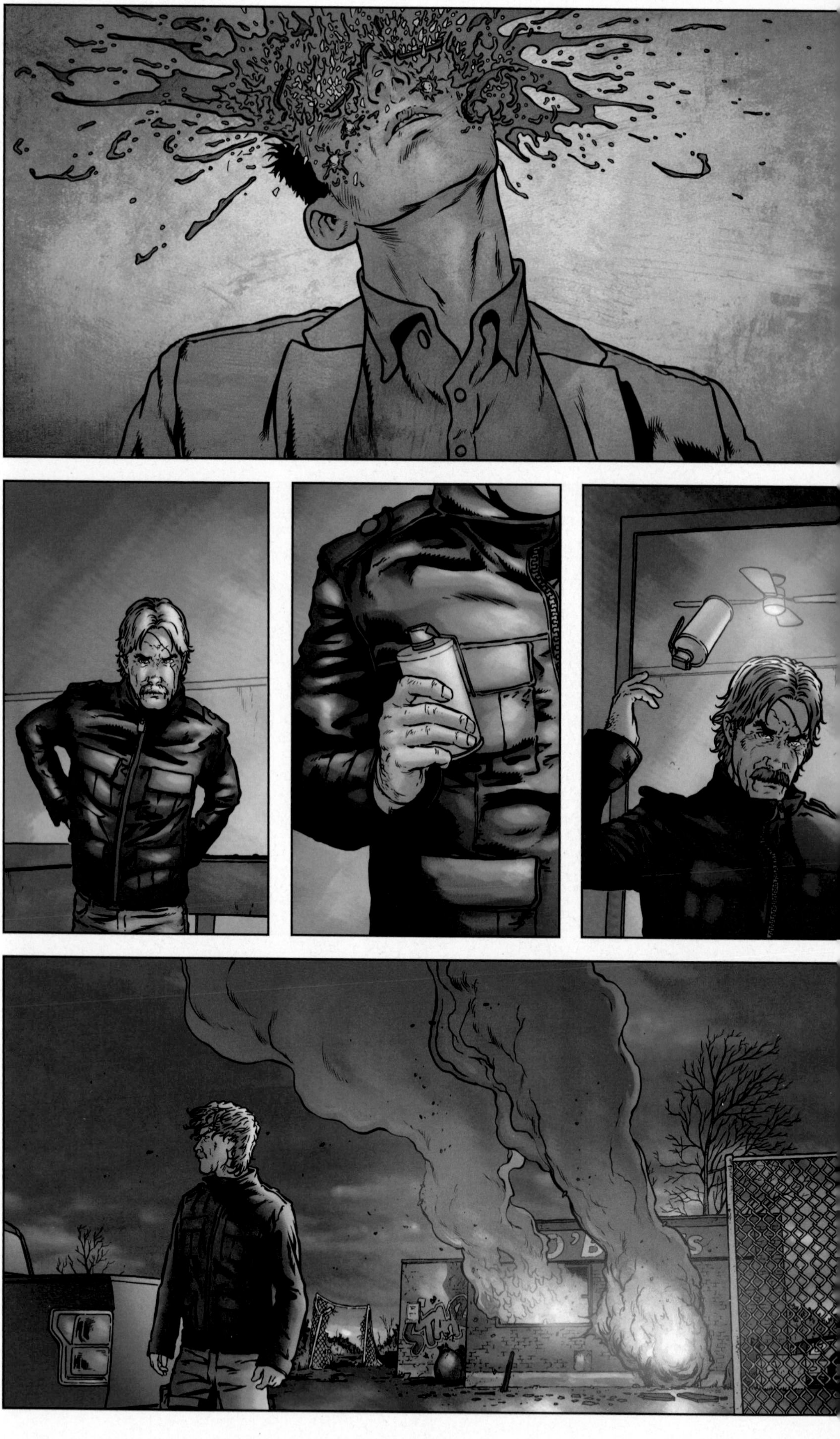

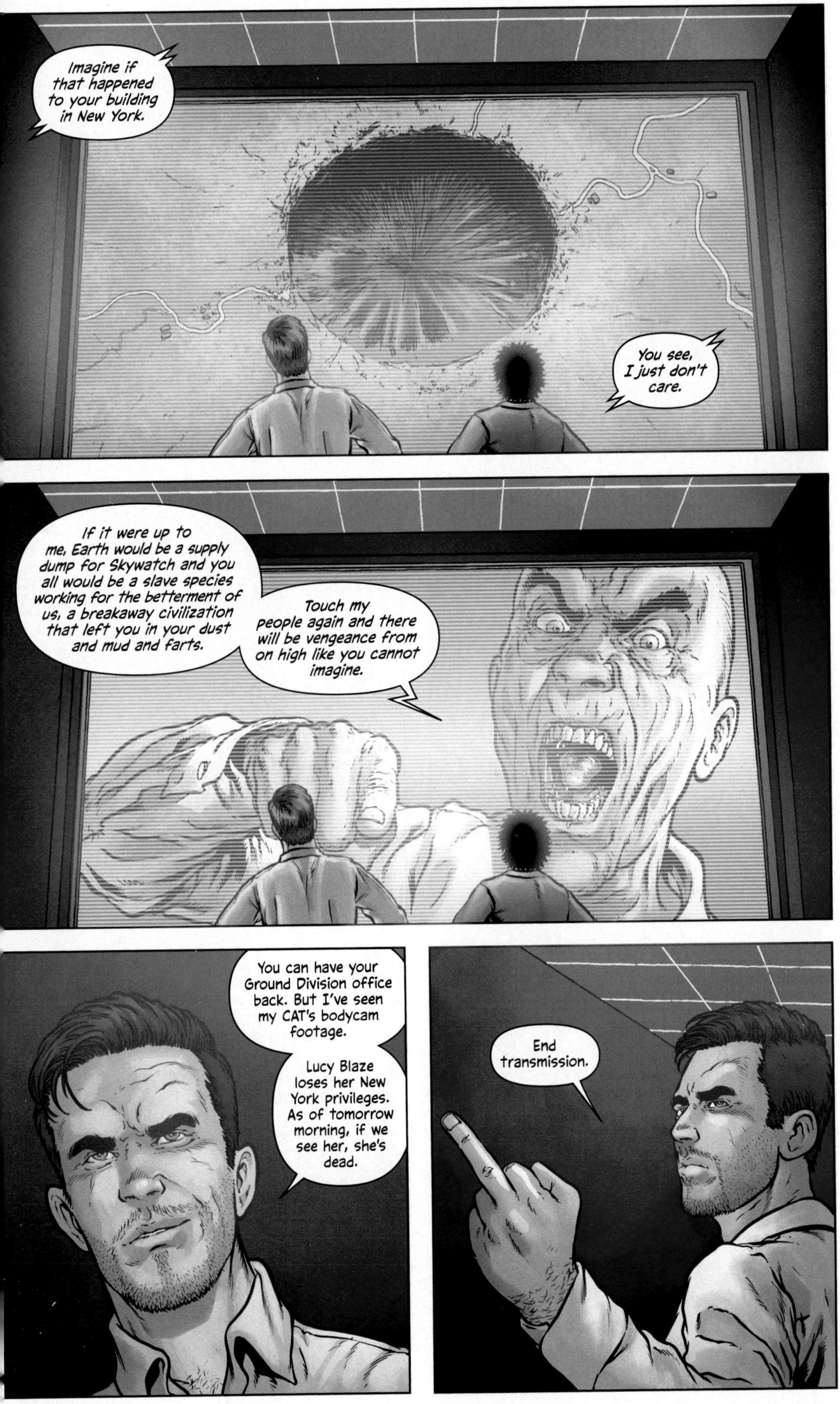
Imagine if that happened to your building in New York.
You see, I just don't care.
If it were up to me, Earth would be a supply dump for Skywatch and you all would be a slave species working for the betterment of us, a breakaway civilization that left you in your dust and mud and farts.
Touch my people again and there will be vengeance from on high like you cannot imagine.
You can have your Ground Division office back. But I've seen my CAT's bodycam footage.
Lucy Blaze loses her New York privileges. As of tomorrow morning, if we see her, she's dead.
End transmission.

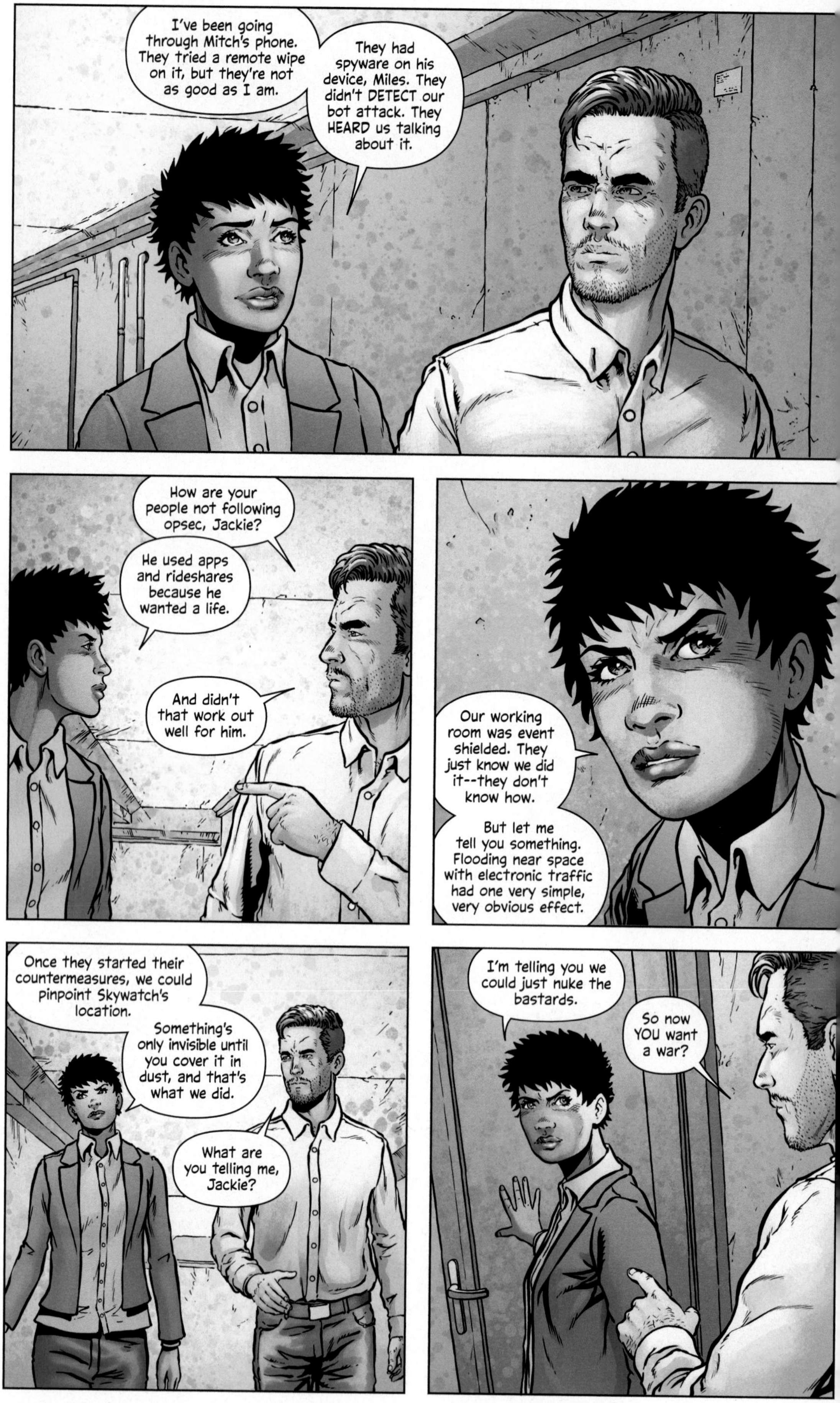
I've been going through Mitch's phone. They tried a remote wipe on it, but they're not as good as I am.
They had spyware on his device, Miles. They didn't DETECT our bot attack. They HEARD us talking about it.
How are your people not following opsec, Jackie?
He used apps and rideshares because he wanted a life.
And didn't that work out well for him.
Our working room was event shielded. They just know we did it--they don't know how.
But let me tell you something. Flooding near space with electronic traffic had one very simple, very obvious effect.
Once they started their countermeasures, we could pinpoint Skywatch's location.
Something's only invisible until you cover it in dust, and that's what we did.
What are you telling me, Jackie?
I'm telling you we could just nuke the bastards.
So now YOU want a war?

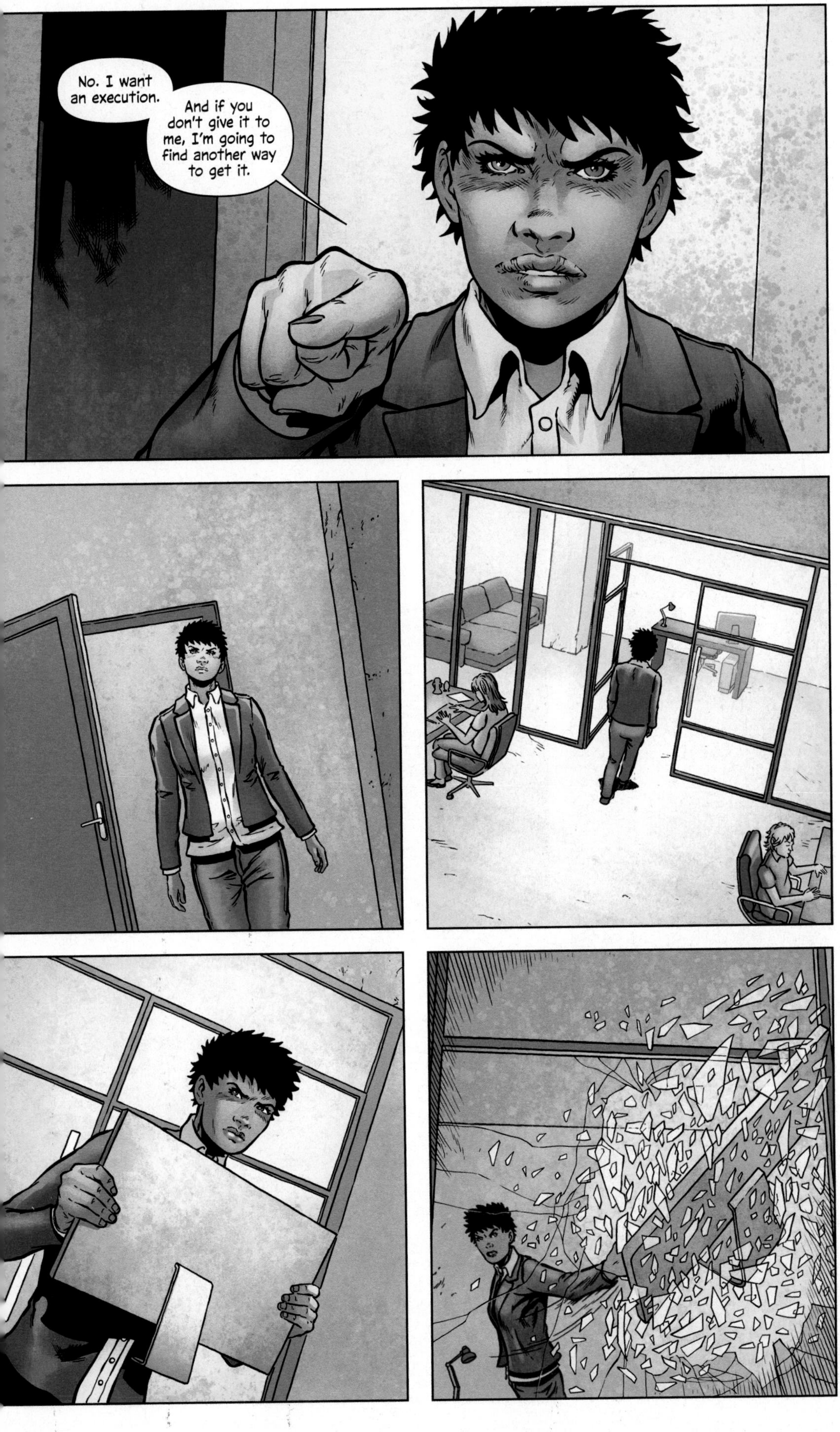
No. I want an execution.
And if you don't give it to me, I'm going to find another way to get it.

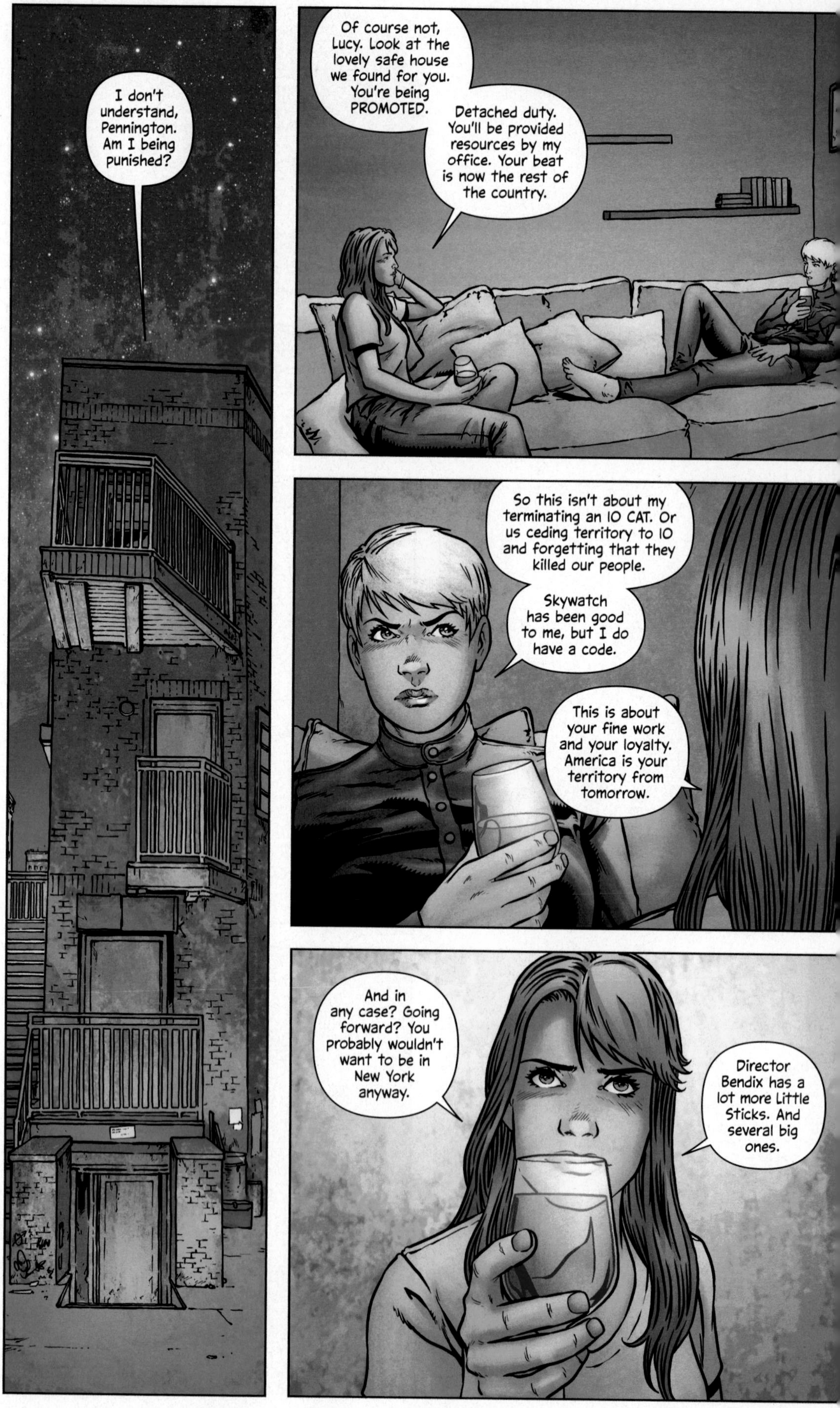
I don't understand, Pennington. Am I being punished?
Of course not, Lucy. Look at the lovely safe house we found for you. You're being PROMOTED.
Detached duty. You'll be provided resources by my office. Your beat is now the rest of the country.
So this isn't about my terminating an IO CAT. Or us ceding territory to IO and forgetting that they killed our people.
Skywatch has been good to me, but I do have a code.
This is about your fine work and your loyalty. America is your territory from tomorrow.
And in any case? Going forward? You probably wouldn't want to be in New York anyway.
Director Bendix has a lot more Little Sticks. And several big ones.

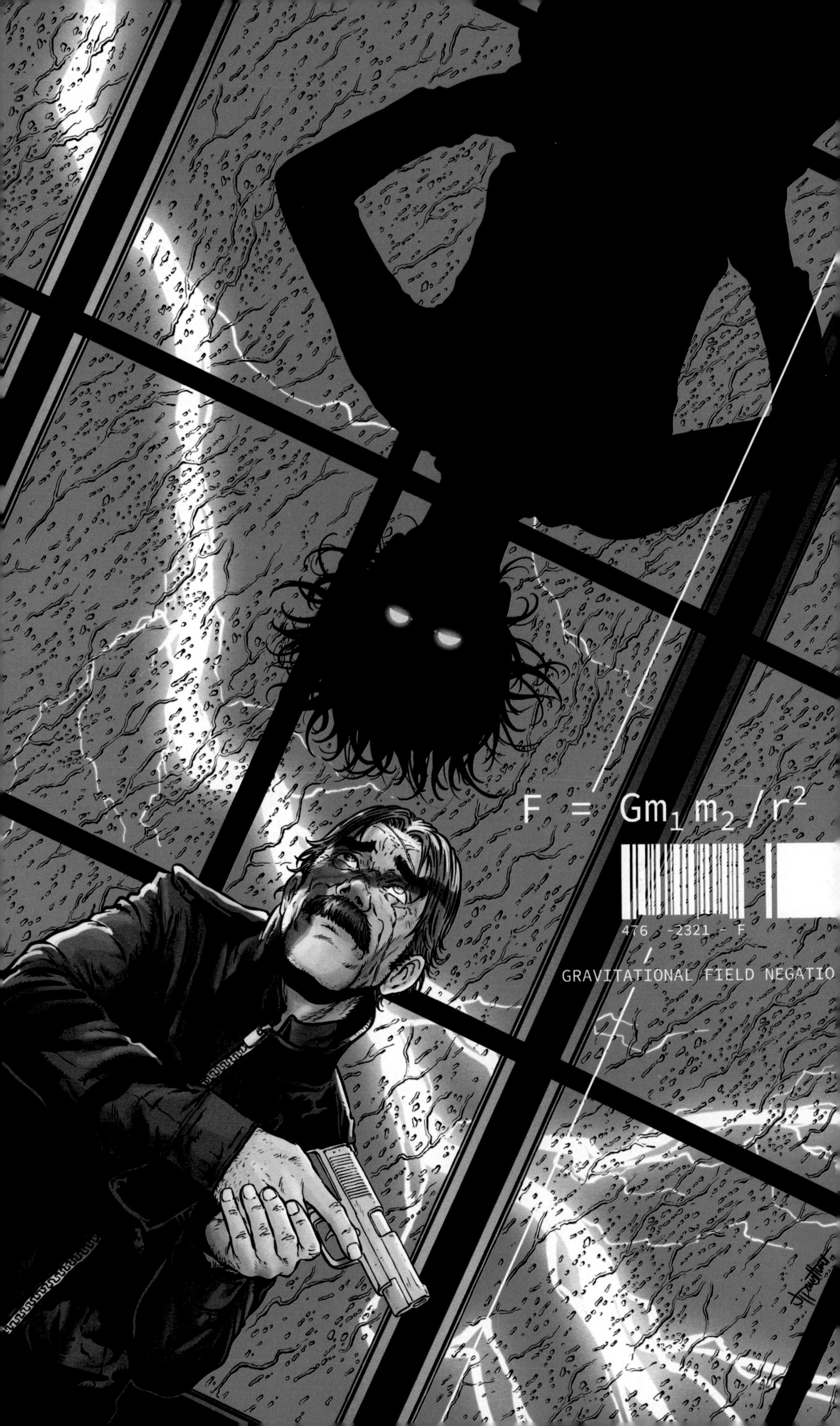

$F = Gm_1 m_2 / r^2$
476 -2321 - F
GRAVITATIONAL FIELD NEGATIO

16

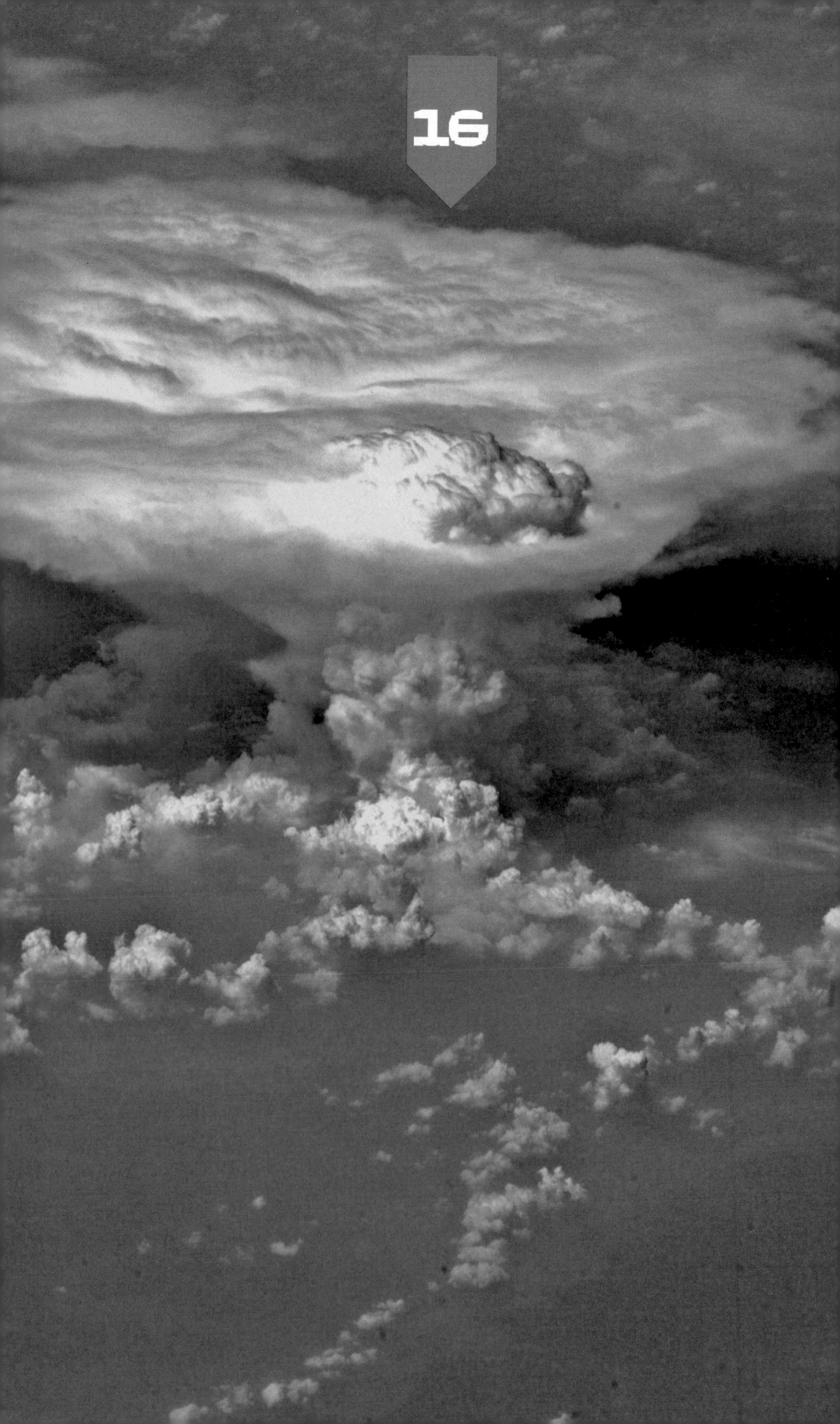

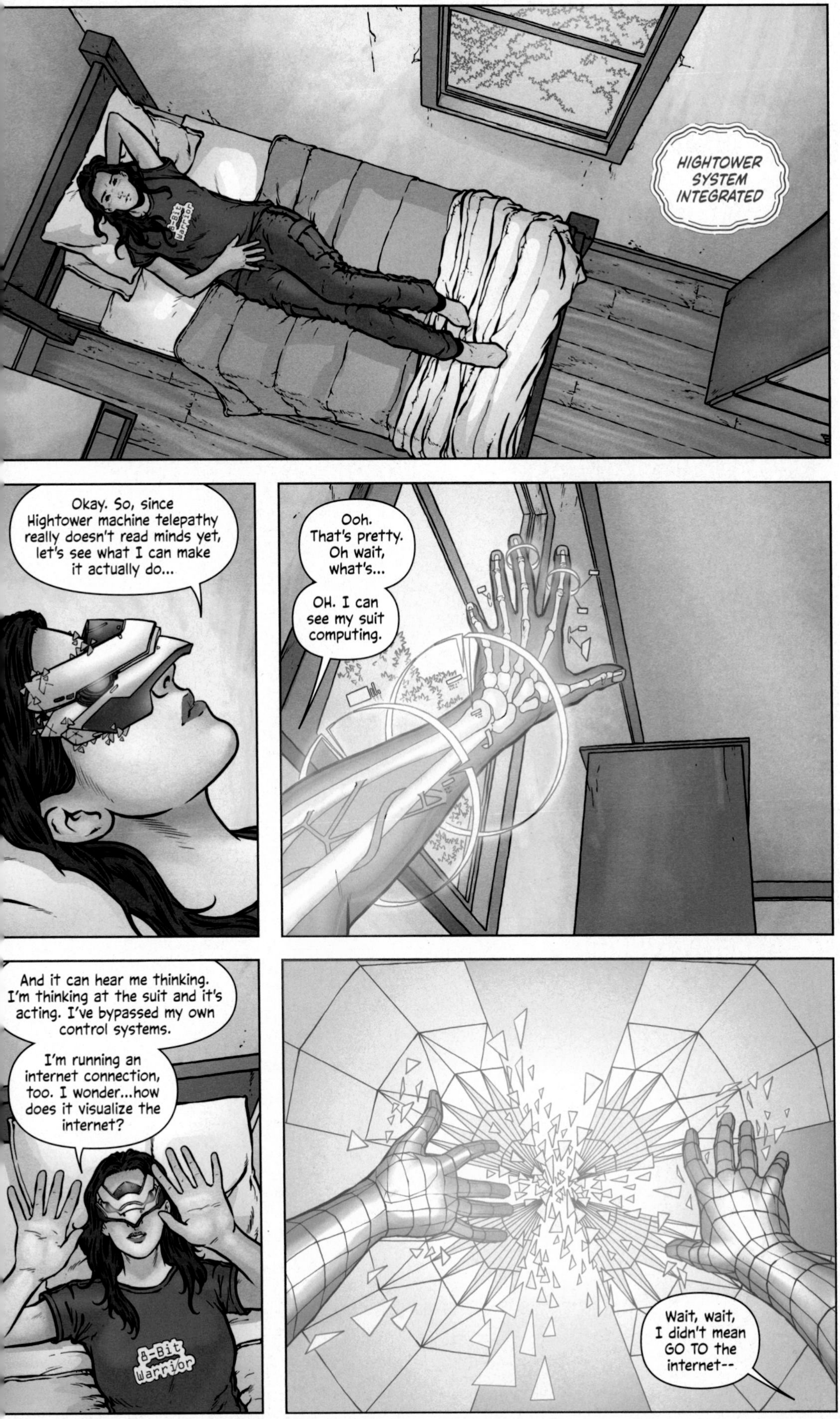
HIGHTOWER SYSTEM INTEGRATED
8-Bit Warrior
Okay. So, since Hightower machine telepathy really doesn't read minds yet, let's see what I can make it actually do...
Ooh. That's pretty. Oh wait, what's...
OH. I can see my suit computing.
And it can hear me thinking. I'm thinking at the suit and it's acting. I've bypassed my own control systems.
I'm running an internet connection, too. I wonder...how does it visualize the internet?
8-Bit Warrior
Wait, wait, I didn't mean GO TO the internet--

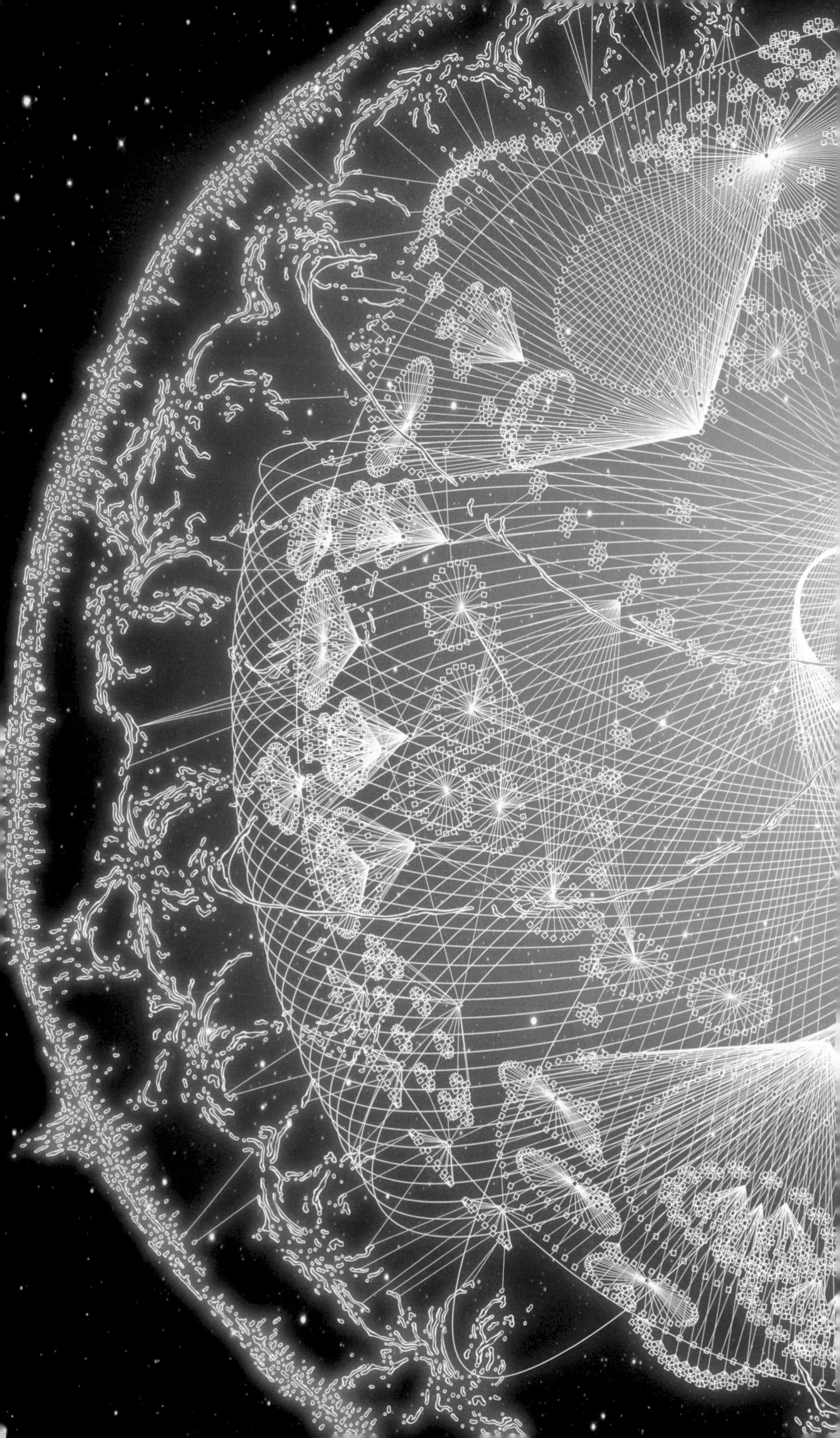

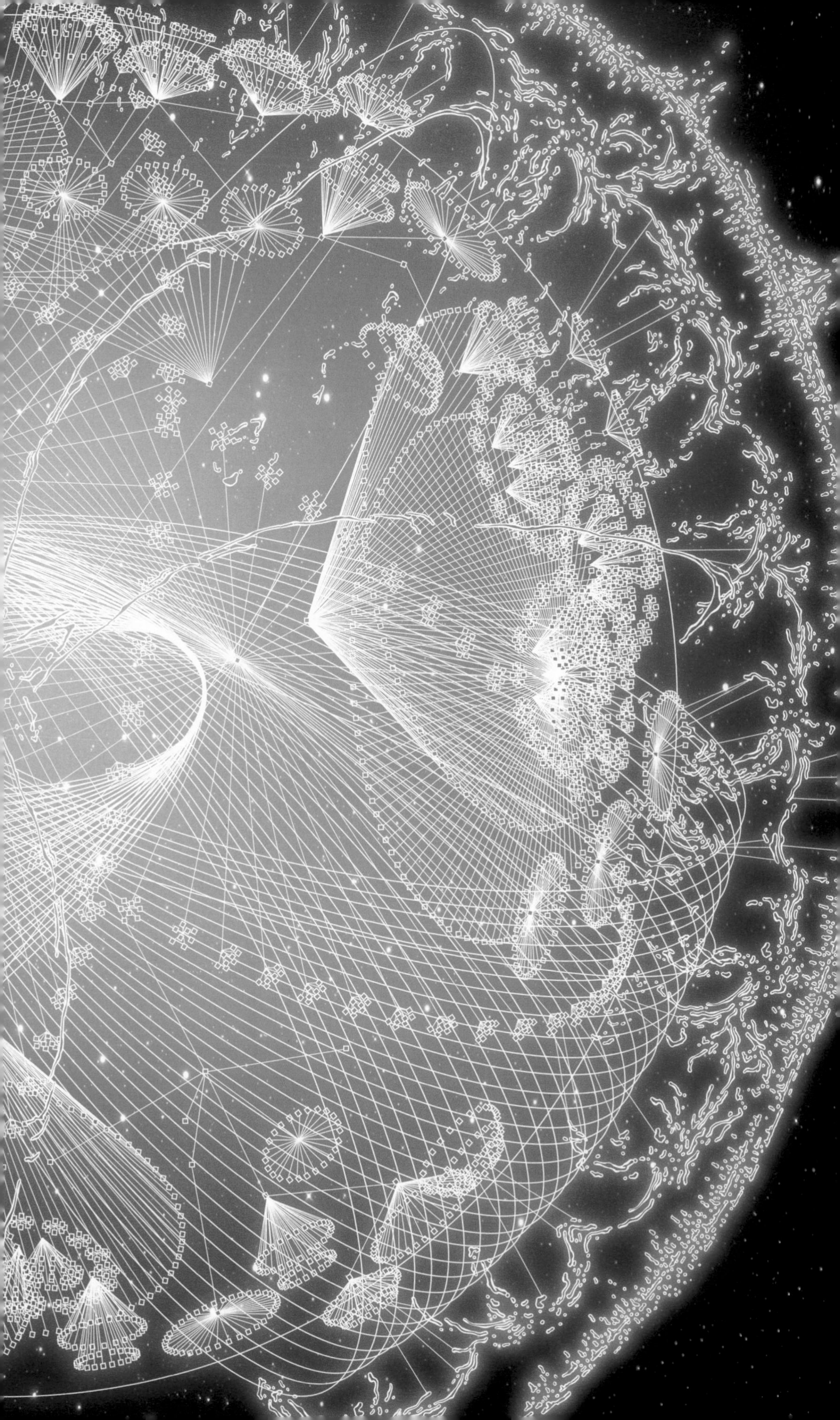

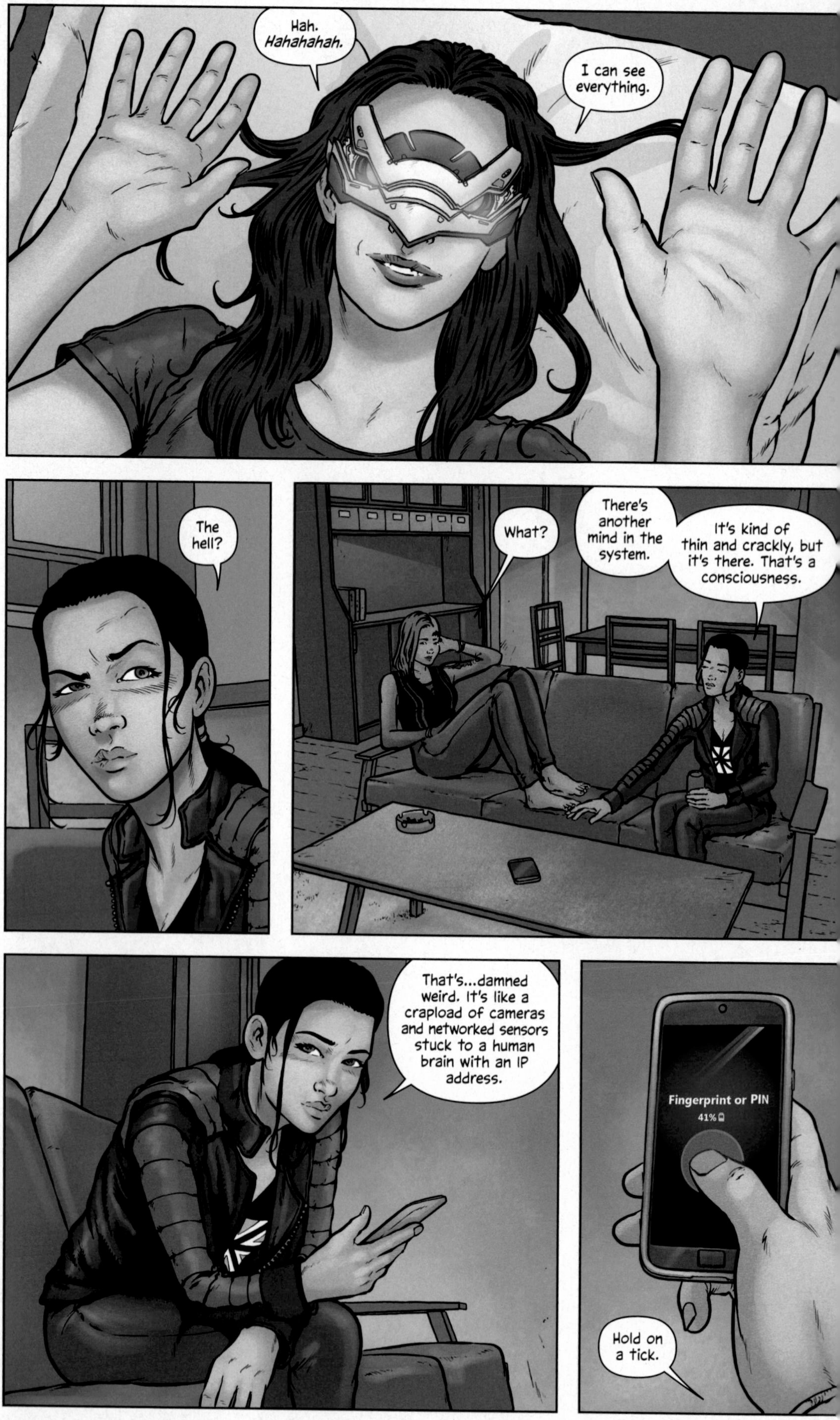
Hah.
Hahahahah.
I can see everything.
The hell?
What?
There's another mind in the system.
It's kind of thin and crackly, but it's there. That's a consciousness.
That's...damned weird. It's like a crapload of cameras and networked sensors stuck to a human brain with an IP address.
Fingerprint or PIN
41%
Hold on a tick.

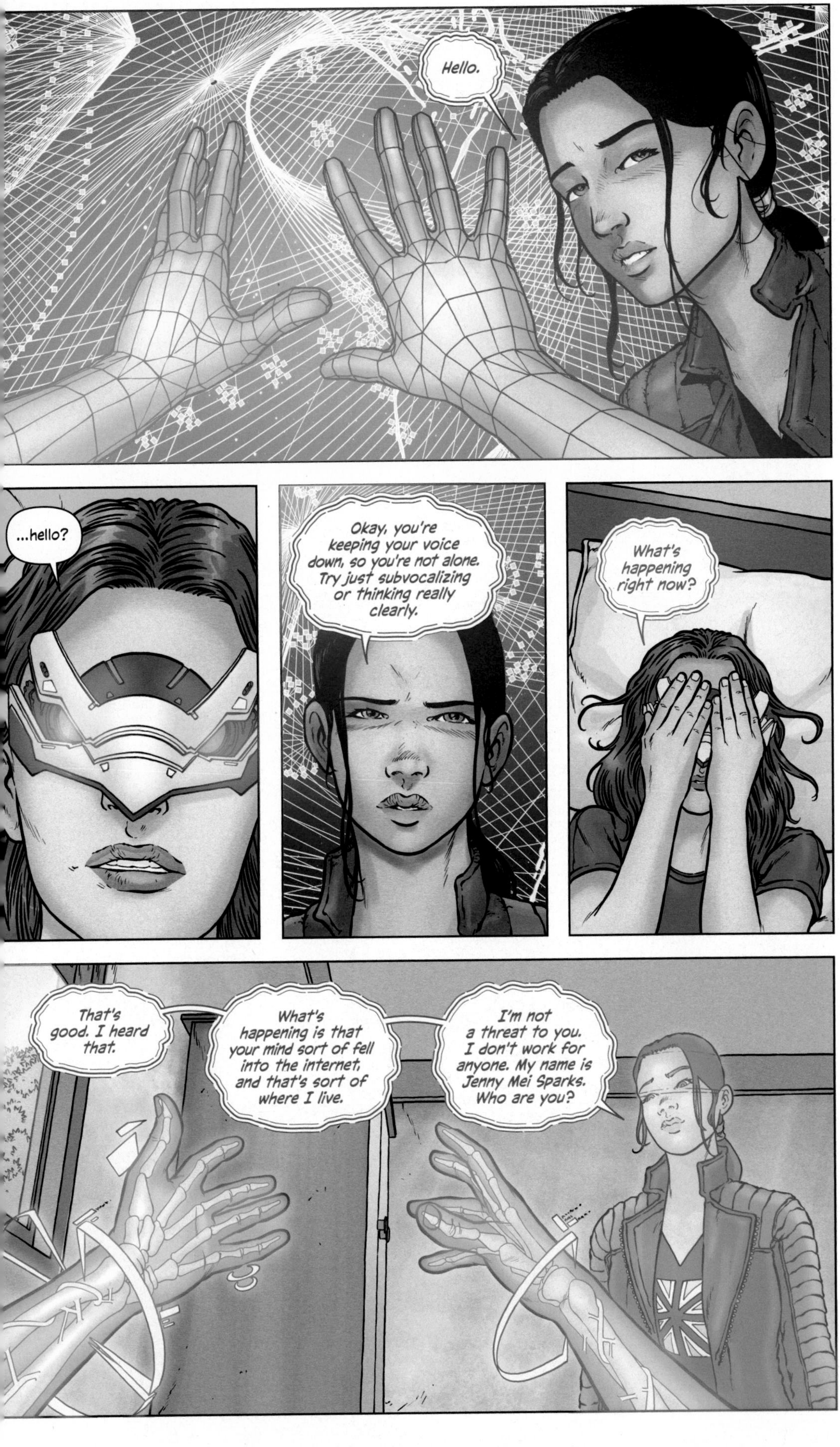
Hello.
...hello?
Okay, you're keeping your voice down, so you're not alone. Try just subvocalizing or thinking really clearly.
What's happening right now?
That's good. I heard that.
What's happening is that your mind sort of fell into the internet, and that's sort of where I live.
I'm not a threat to you. I don't work for anyone. My name is Jenny Mei Sparks. Who are you?

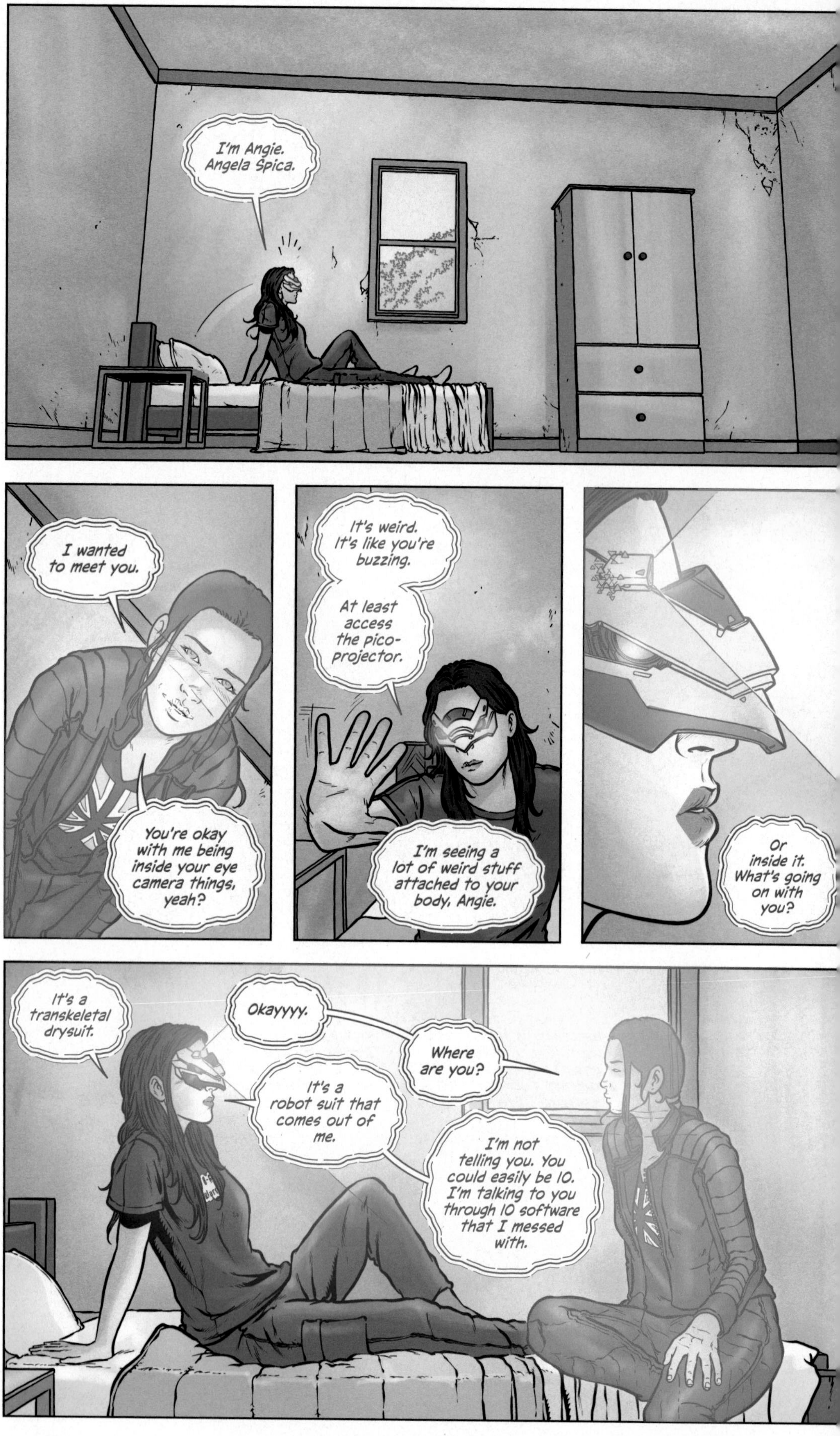

I'm Angie. Angela Spica.
I wanted to meet you.
You're okay with me being inside your eye camera things, yeah?
It's weird. It's like you're buzzing.
At least access the pico-projector.
I'm seeing a lot of weird stuff attached to your body, Angie.
Or inside it. What's going on with you?
It's a transkeletal drysuit.
Okayyyy.
Where are you?
It's a robot suit that comes out of me.
I'm not telling you. You could easily be IO. I'm talking to you through IO software that I messed with.

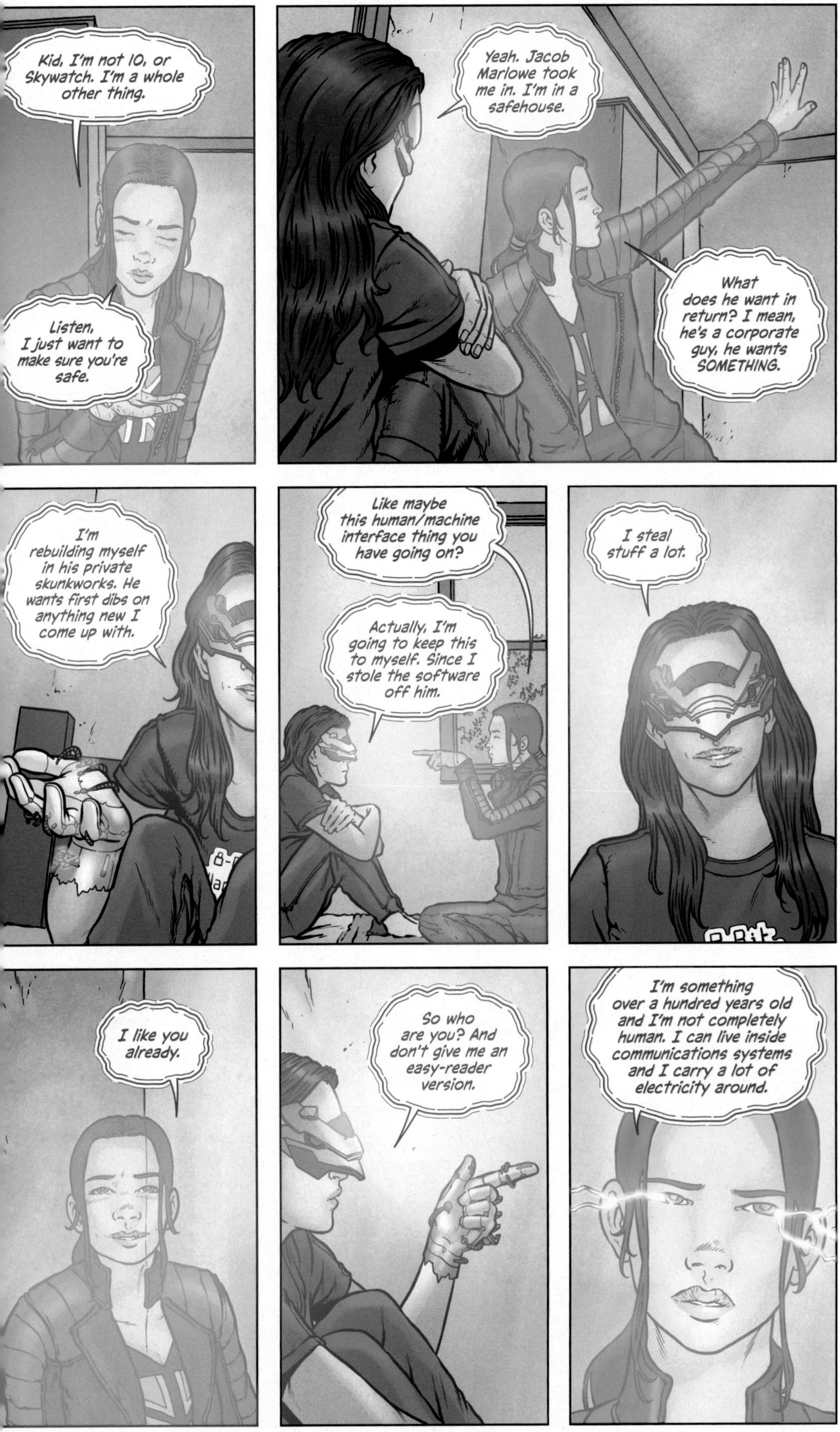
Kid, I'm not IO, or Skywatch. I'm a whole other thing.
Listen, I just want to make sure you're safe.
Yeah. Jacob Marlowe took me in. I'm in a safehouse.
What does he want in return? I mean, he's a corporate guy, he wants SOMETHING.
I'm rebuilding myself in his private skunkworks. He wants first dibs on anything new I come up with.
Like maybe this human/machine interface thing you have going on?
Actually, I'm going to keep this to myself. Since I stole the software off him.
I steal stuff a lot.
I like you already.
So who are you? And don't give me an easy-reader version.
I'm something over a hundred years old and I'm not completely human. I can live inside communications systems and I carry a lot of electricity around.

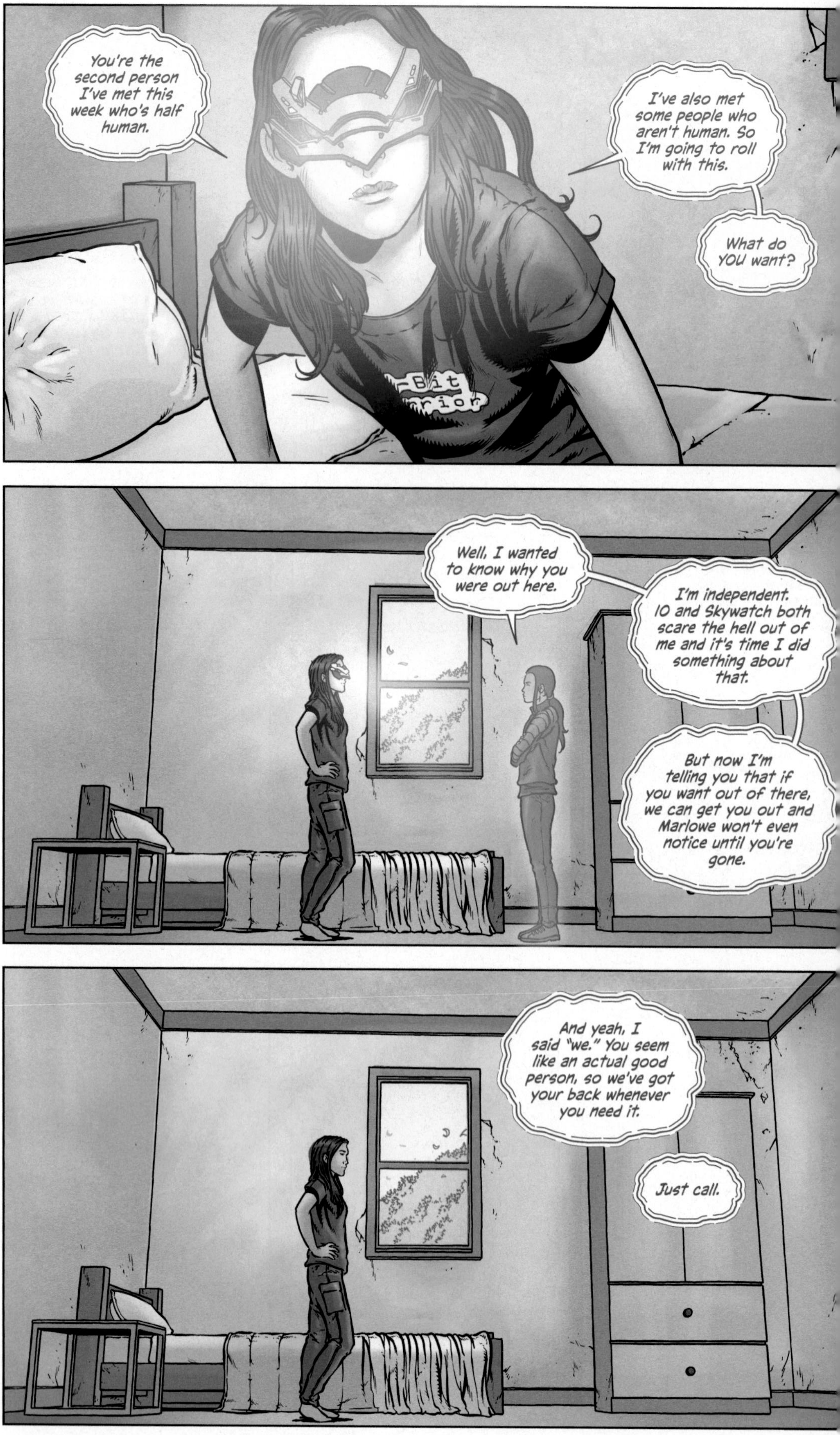
You're the second person I've met this week who's half human.
I've also met some people who aren't human. So I'm going to roll with this.
What do YOU want?
Well, I wanted to know why you were out here.
I'm independent. IO and Skywatch both scare the hell out of me and it's time I did something about that.
But now I'm telling you that if you want out of there, we can get you out and Marlowe won't even notice until you're gone.
And yeah, I said "we." You seem like an actual good person, so we've got your back whenever you need it.
Just call.

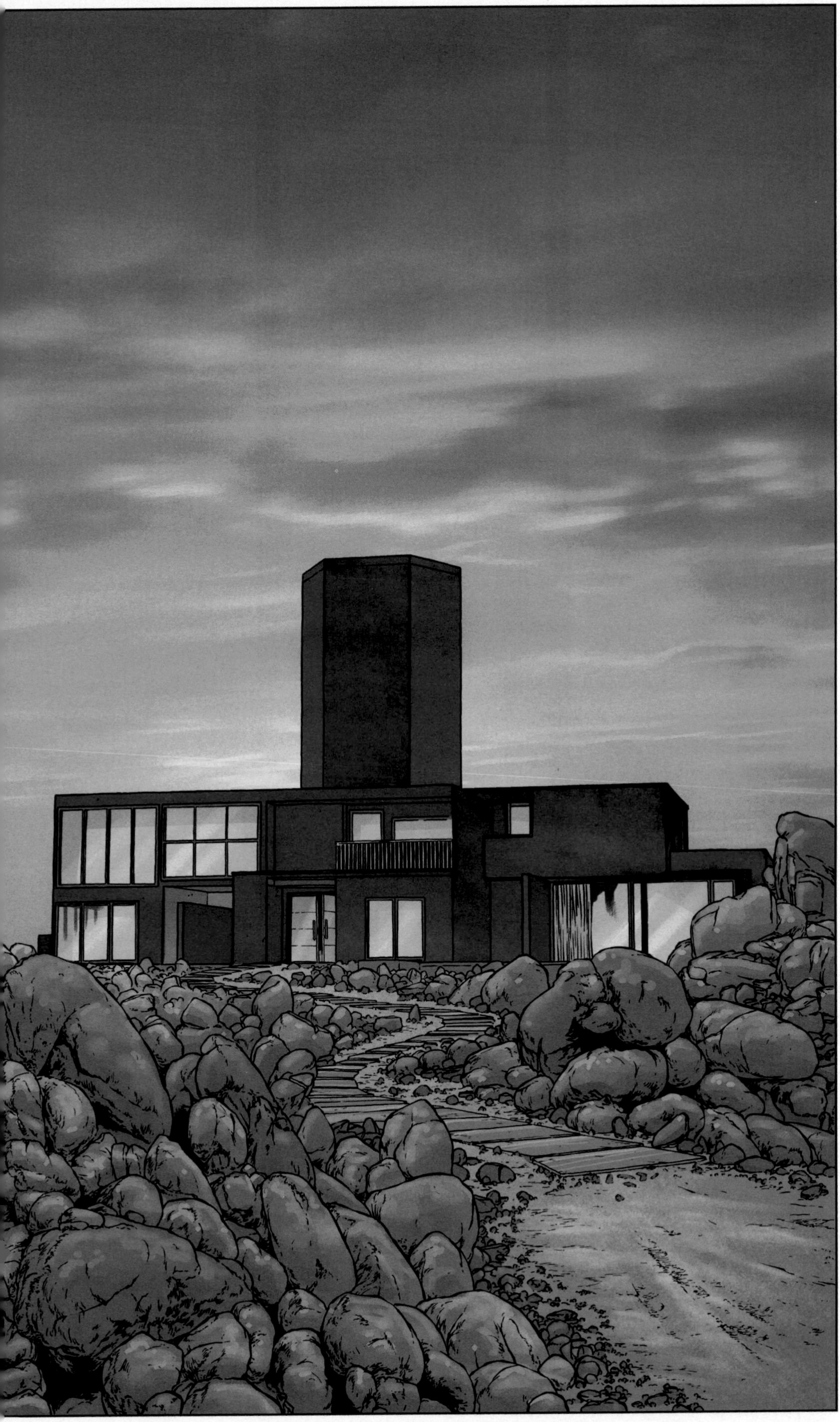

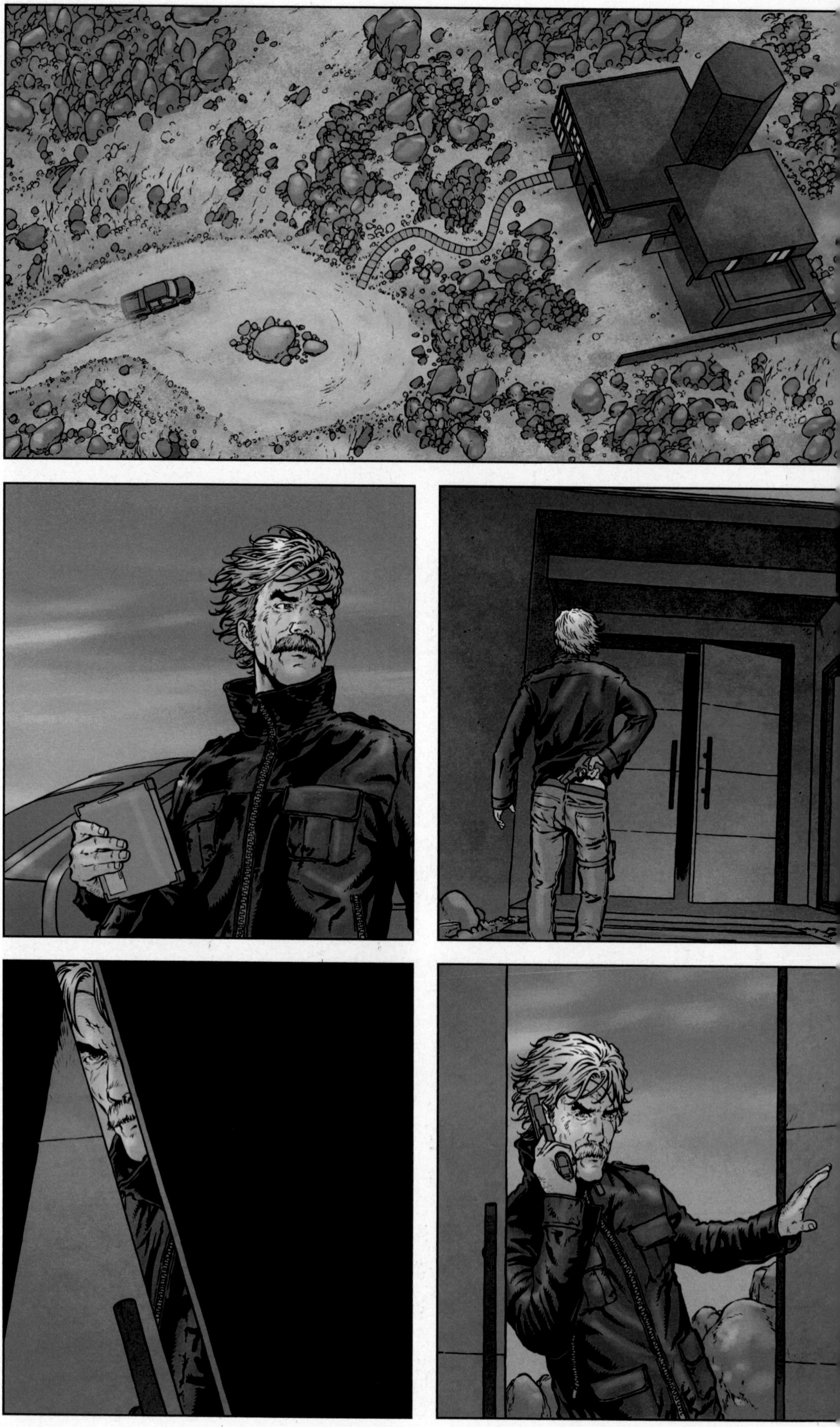

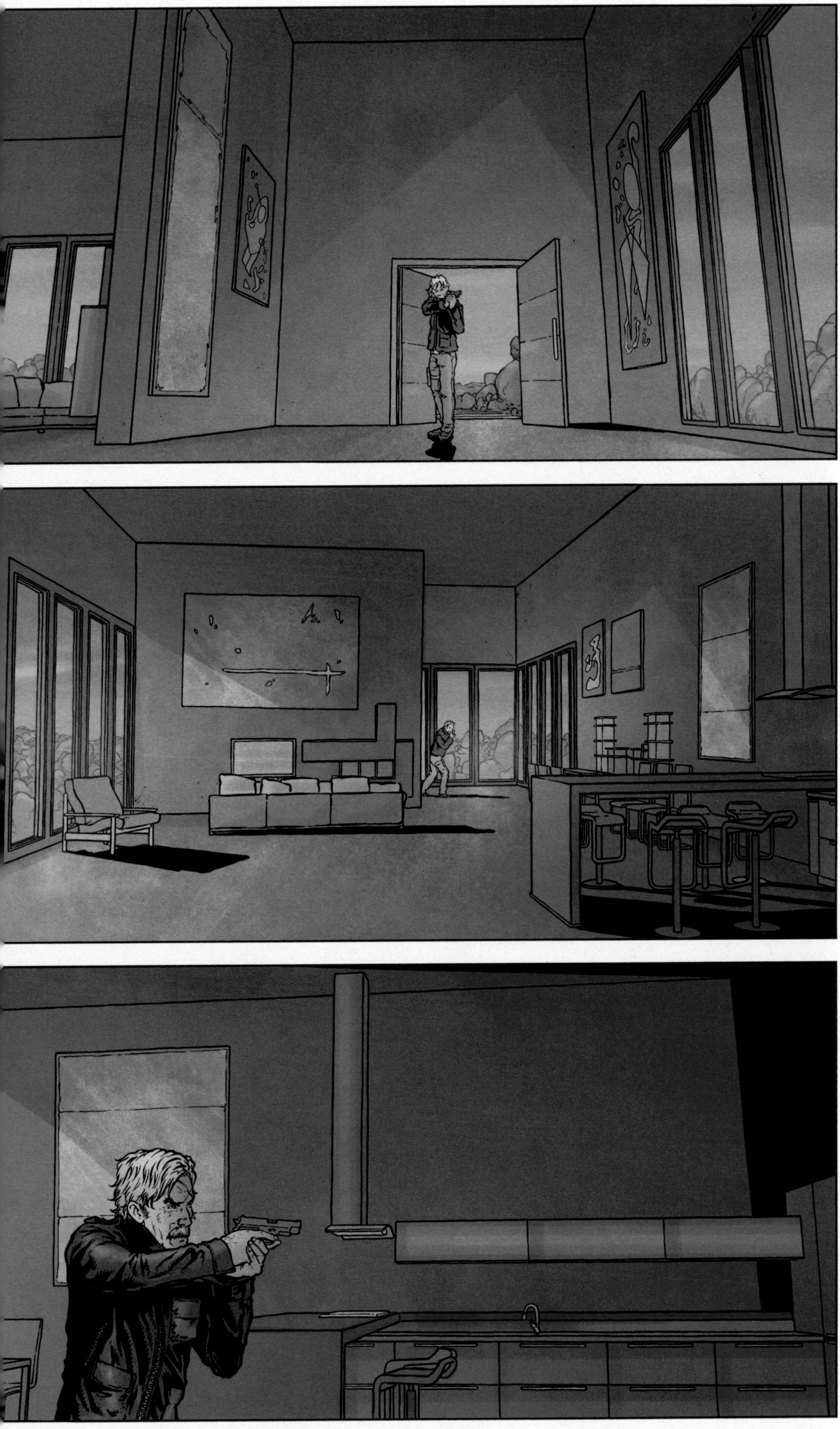

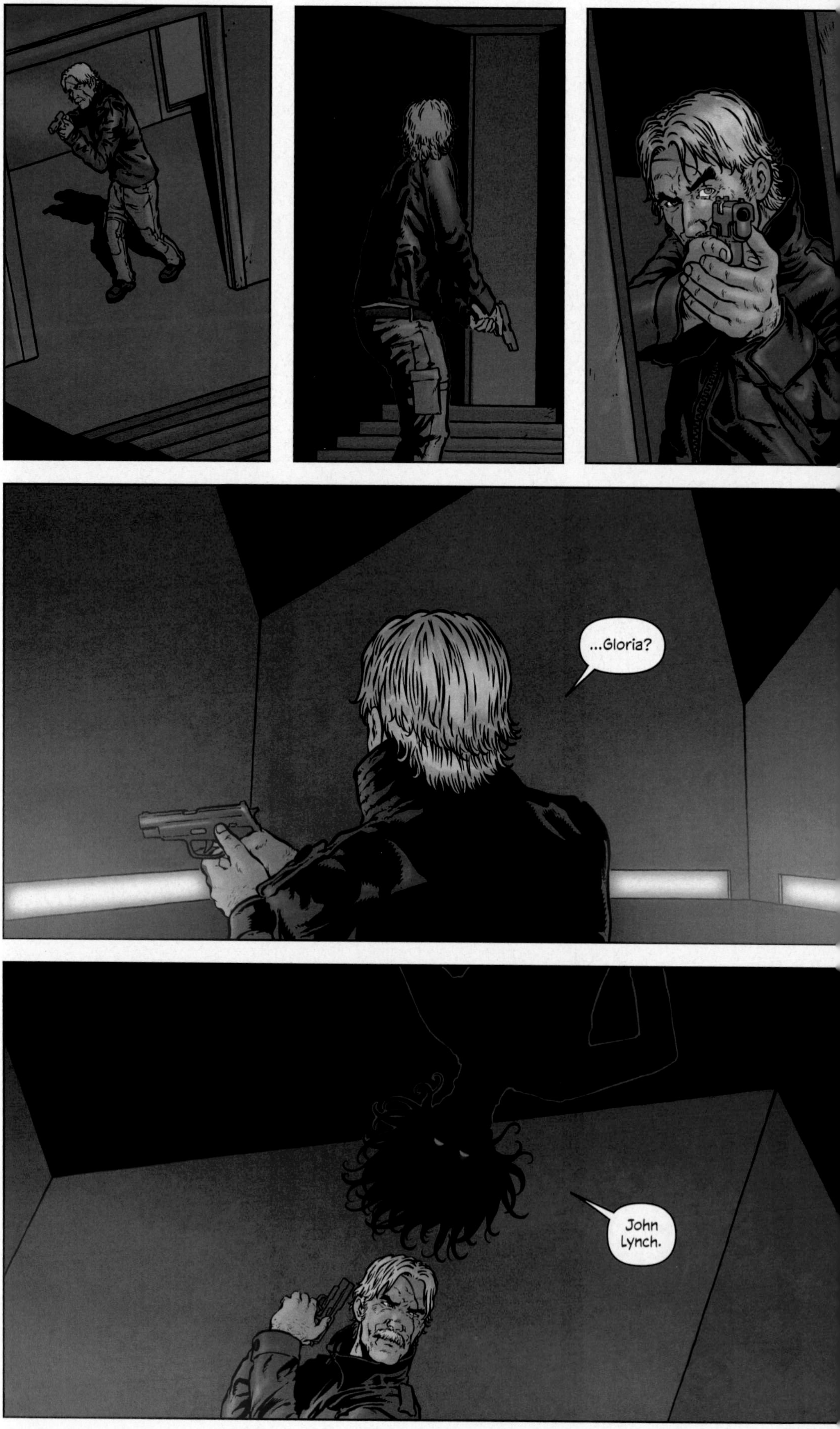
...Gloria?
John Lynch.

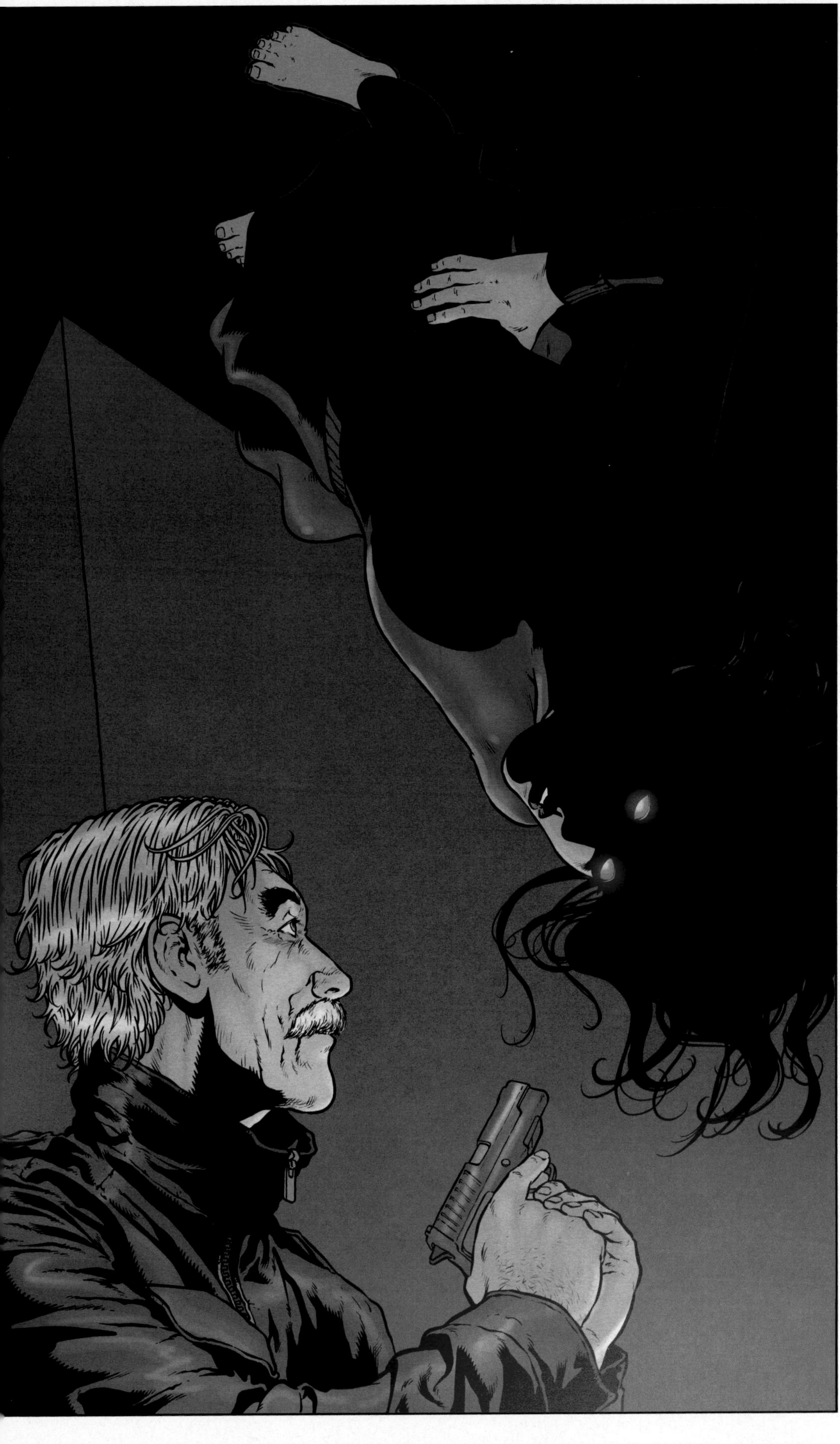

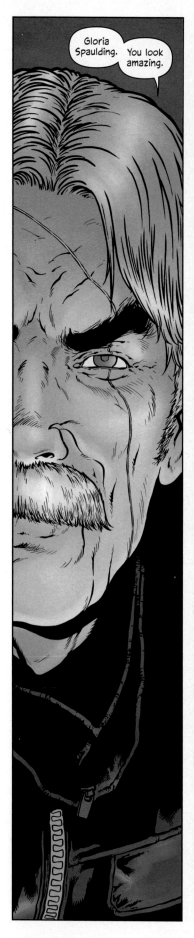

Gloria Spaulding. You look amazing.

You look like old crap.

Should have got a fancy Thunderbook implant like *meeee.*

The security cameras saw you approach, John. I thought I'd wait for you in my special room. Put the gun away before you have an accident.

You have a really nice house, Gloria.

I've come to warn you. Thunderbook may have been exposed to the current IO directorate.

You deserve to know. It's probably fine. I just felt like I should warn you to take extra care.

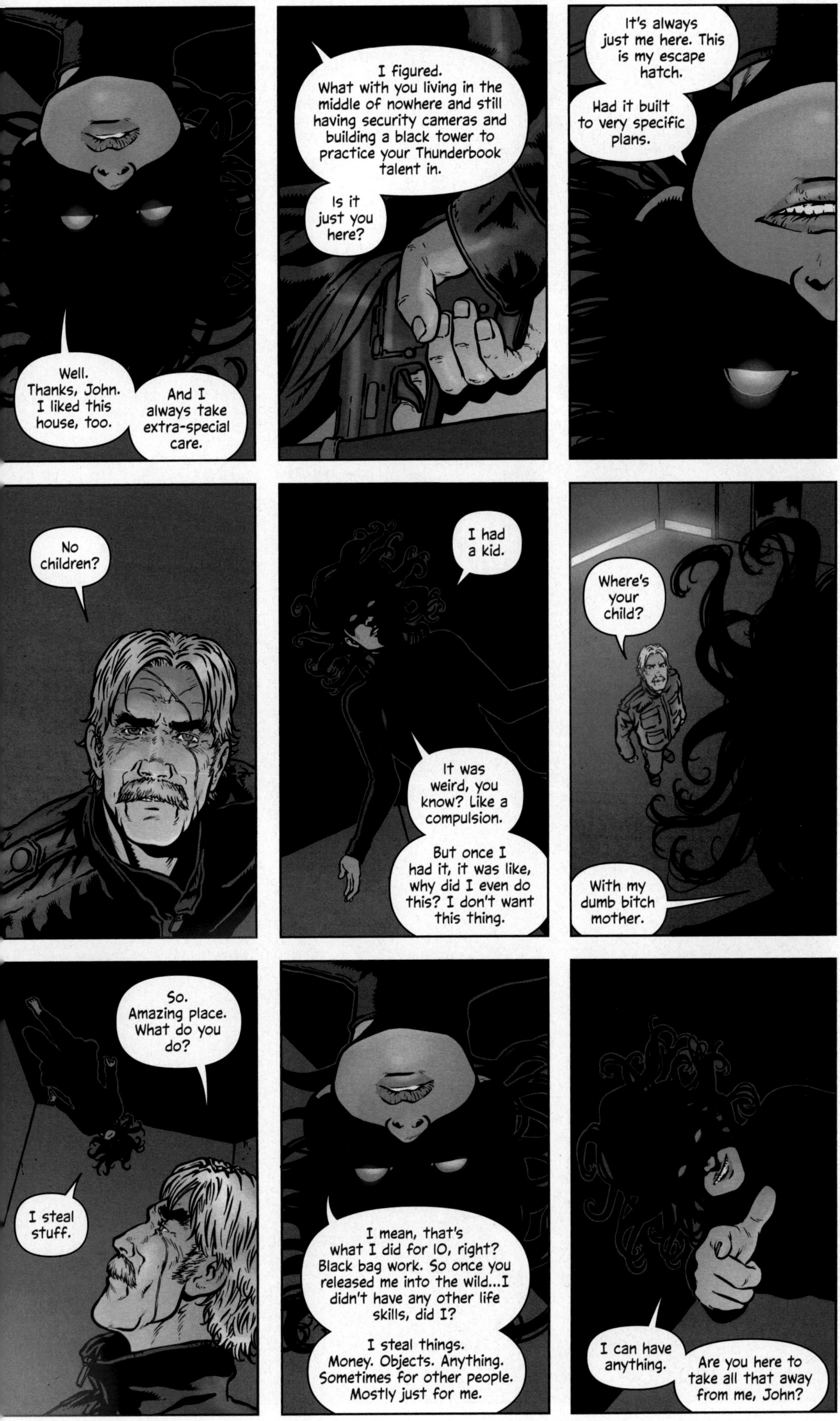
Well. Thanks, John. I liked this house, too.
And I always take extra-special care.
I figured. What with you living in the middle of nowhere and still having security cameras and building a black tower to practice your Thunderbook talent in.
Is it just you here?
It's always just me here. This is my escape hatch.
Had it built to very specific plans.
No children?
I had a kid.
It was weird, you know? Like a compulsion.
But once I had it, it was like, why did I even do this? I don't want this thing.
Where's your child?
With my dumb bitch mother.
So. Amazing place. What do you do?
I steal stuff.
I mean, that's what I did for 10, right? Black bag work. So once you released me into the wild...I didn't have any other life skills, did I?
I steal things. Money. Objects. Anything. Sometimes for other people. Mostly just for me.
I can have anything.
Are you here to take all that away from me, John?

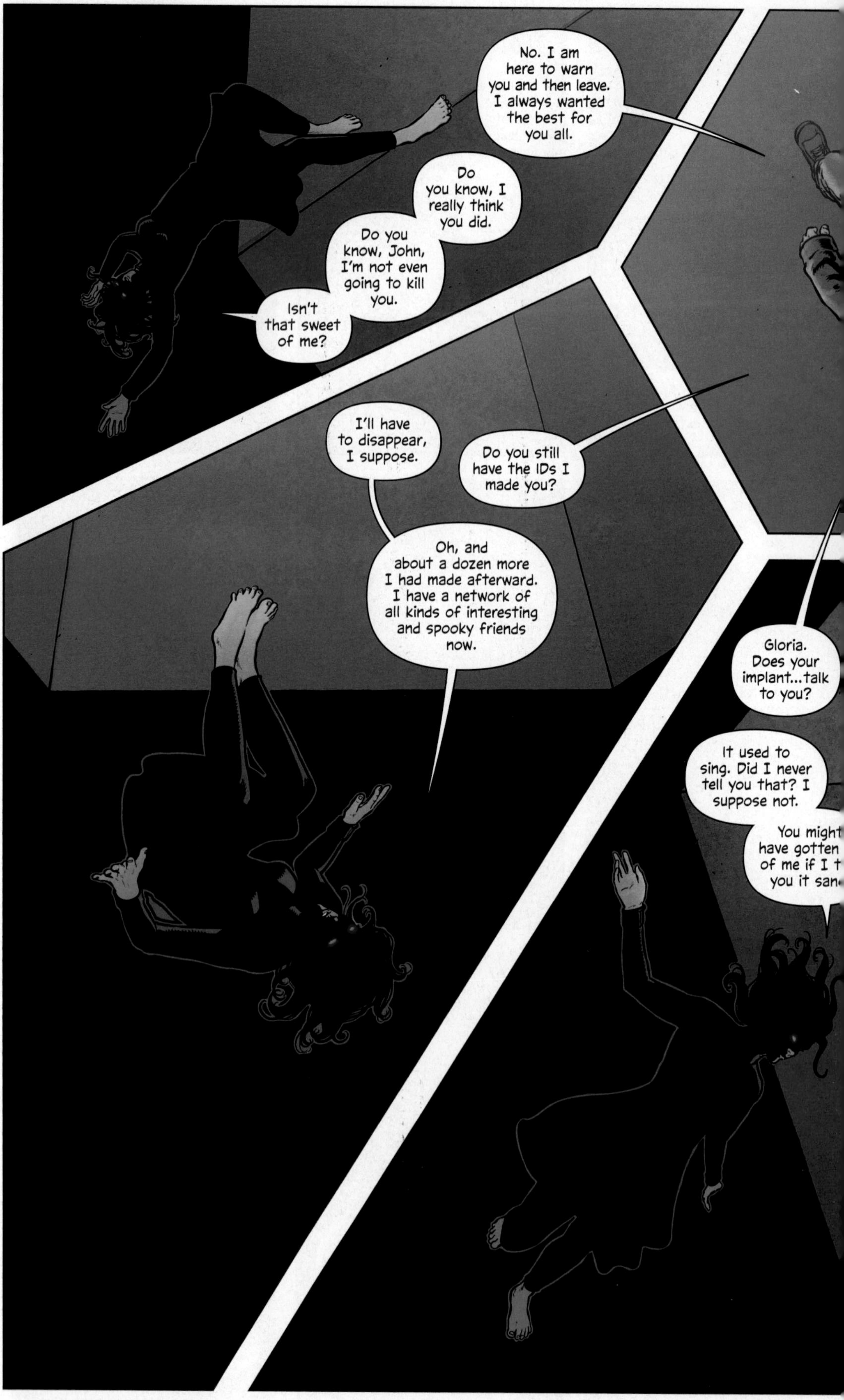
No. I am here to warn you and then leave. I always wanted the best for you all.
Do you know, I really think you did.
Do you know, John, I'm not even going to kill you.
Isn't that sweet of me?
Do you still have the IDs I made you?
I'll have to disappear, I suppose.
Oh, and about a dozen more I had made afterward. I have a network of all kinds of interesting and spooky friends now.
Gloria. Does your implant...talk to you?
It used to sing. Did I never tell you that? I suppose not.
You might have gotten of me if I you it

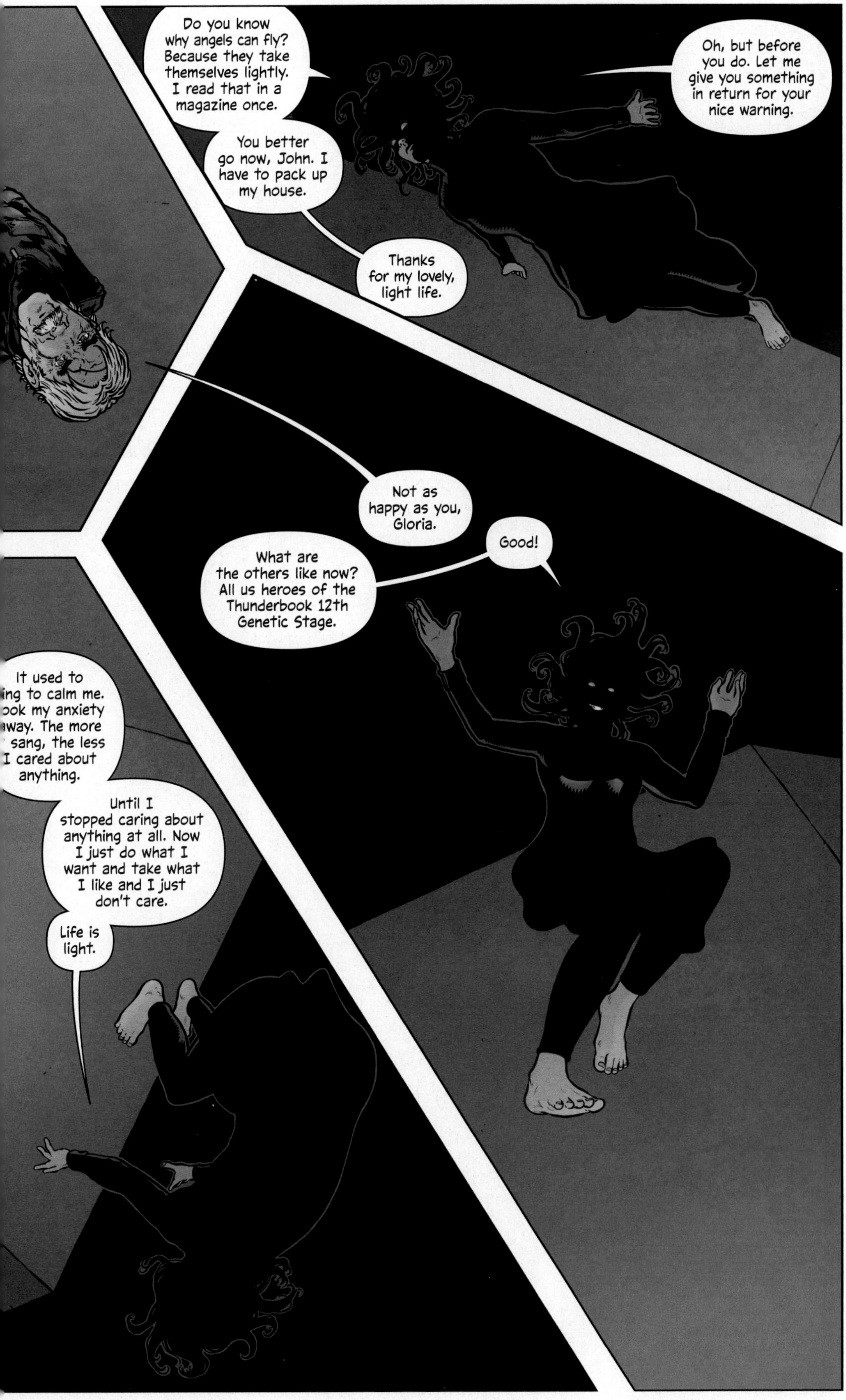
Do you know why angels can fly? Because they take themselves lightly. I read that in a magazine once.
You better go now, John. I have to pack up my house.
Thanks for my lovely, light life.
Oh, but before you do. Let me give you something in return for your nice warning.
Not as happy as you, Gloria.
Good!
What are the others like now? All us heroes of the Thunderbook 12th Genetic Stage.
It used to ing to calm me. ook my anxiety way. The more sang, the less I cared about anything.
Until I stopped caring about anything at all. Now I just do what I want and take what I like and I just don't care.
Life is light.

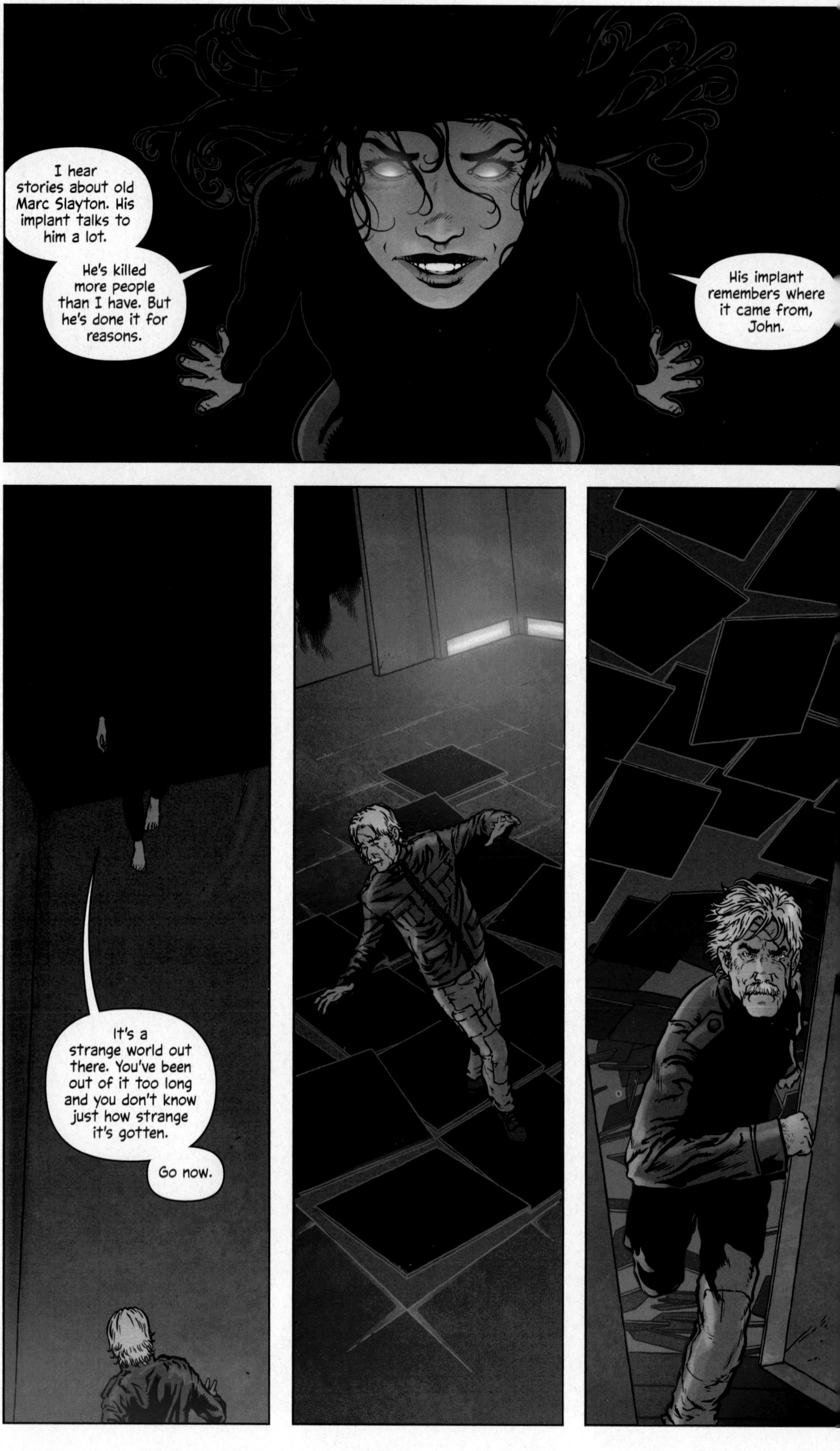
I hear stories about old Marc Slayton. His implant talks to him a lot.
He's killed more people than I have. But he's done it for reasons.
His implant remembers where it came from, John.
It's a strange world out there. You've been out of it too long and you don't know just how strange it's gotten.
Go now.

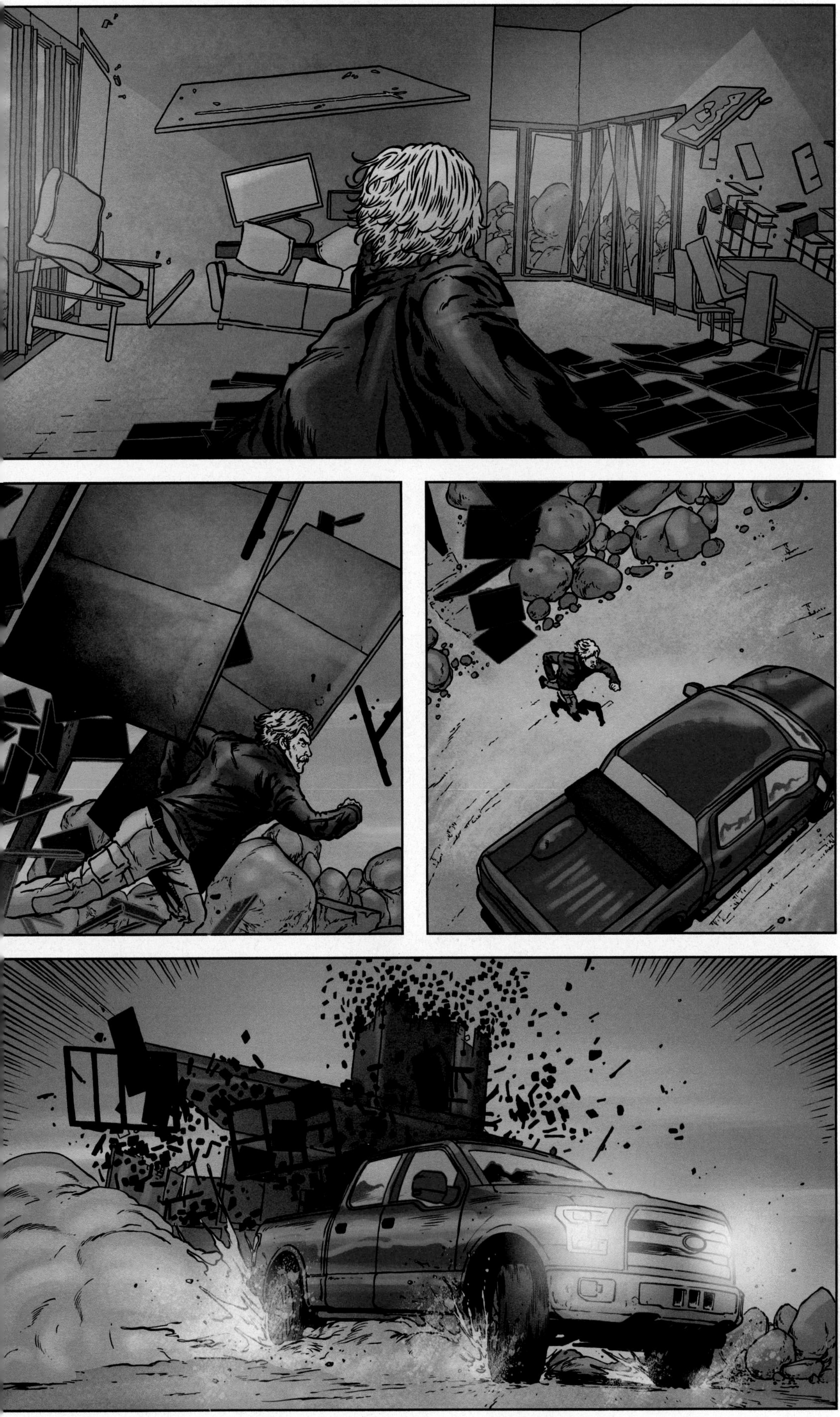

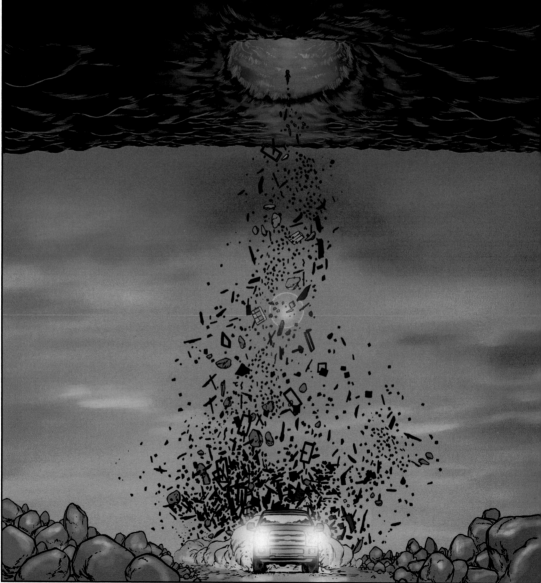

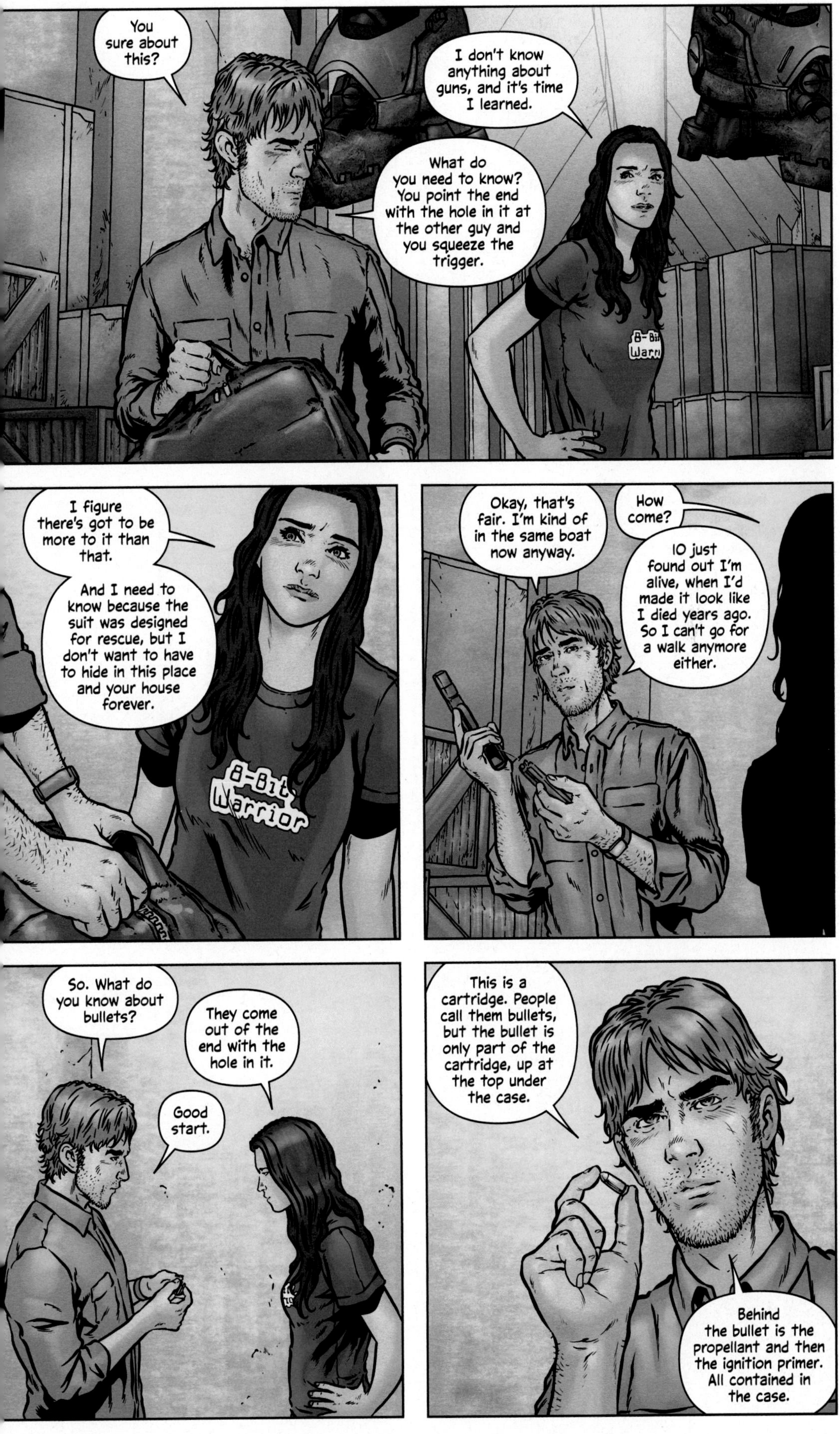
You sure about this?
I don't know anything about guns, and it's time I learned.
What do you need to know? You point the end with the hole in it at the other guy and you squeeze the trigger.
8-Bit Warri
I figure there's got to be more to it than that.
And I need to know because the suit was designed for rescue, but I don't want to have to hide in this place and your house forever.
8-Bit Warrior
Okay, that's fair. I'm kind of in the same boat now anyway.
How come?
IO just found out I'm alive, when I'd made it look like I died years ago. So I can't go for a walk anymore either.
So. What do you know about bullets?
They come out of the end with the hole in it.
Good start.
This is a cartridge. People call them bullets, but the bullet is only part of the cartridge, up at the top under the case.
Behind the bullet is the propellant and then the ignition primer. All contained in the case.

The rim at the back lets the pistol grab the fired case and eject it.

Can you take it apart? So I can see all the bits?

Why?

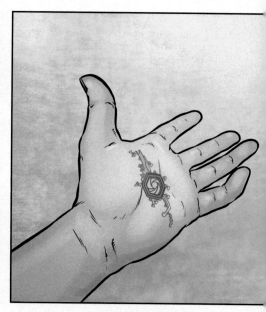

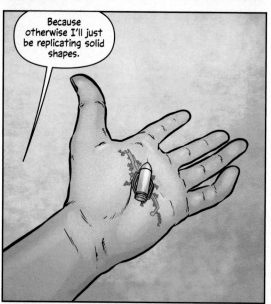

Because otherwise I'll just be replicating solid shapes.

Damn.

I didn't know you could do that.

I couldn't. Not until a day or two ago.

How about this?

Pull apart the bullet. Then pull apart the gun. Let me scan it all.

I'm done hiding.

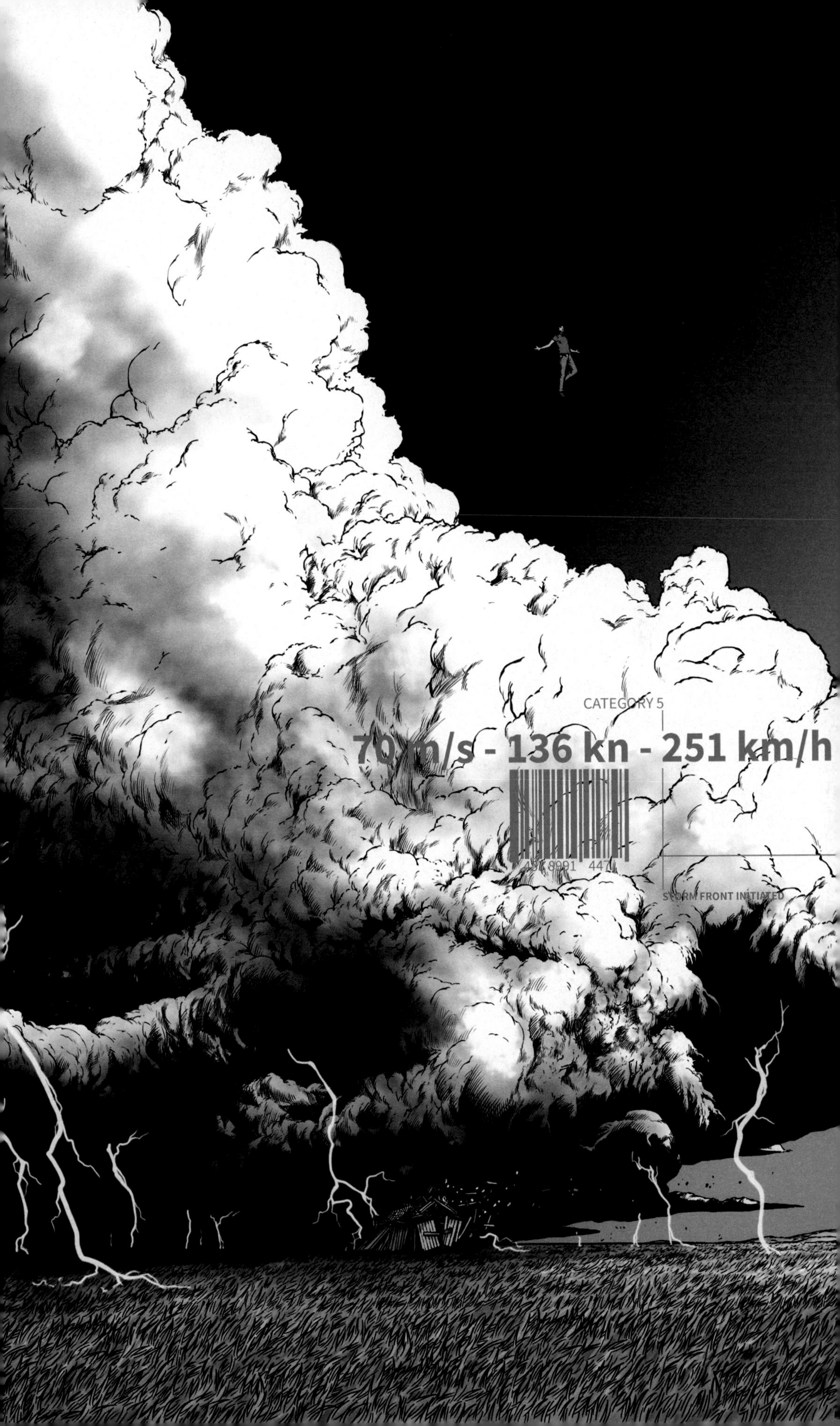
CATEGORY 5
70 m/s - 136 kn - 251 km/h
STORM FRONT INITIATED

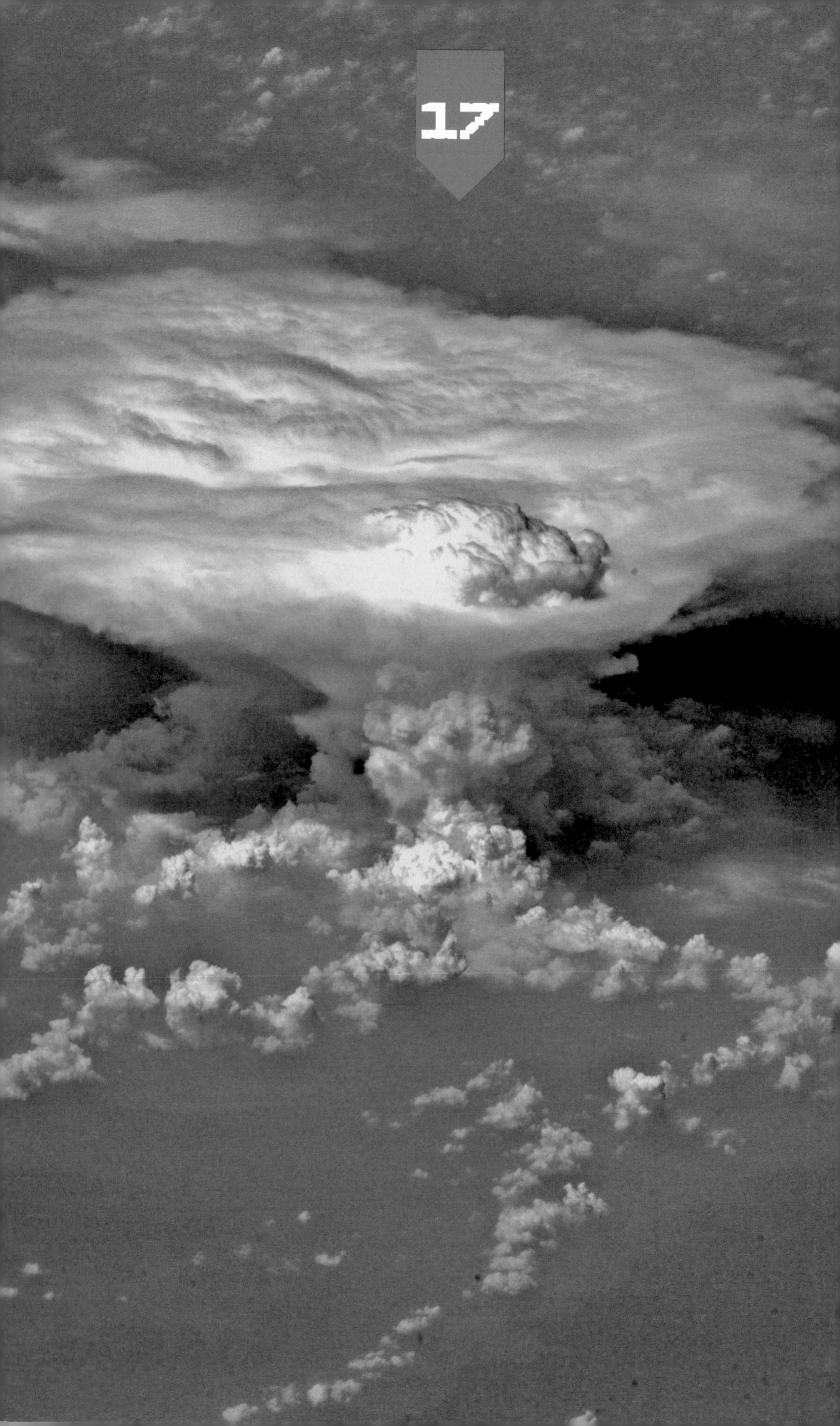
17

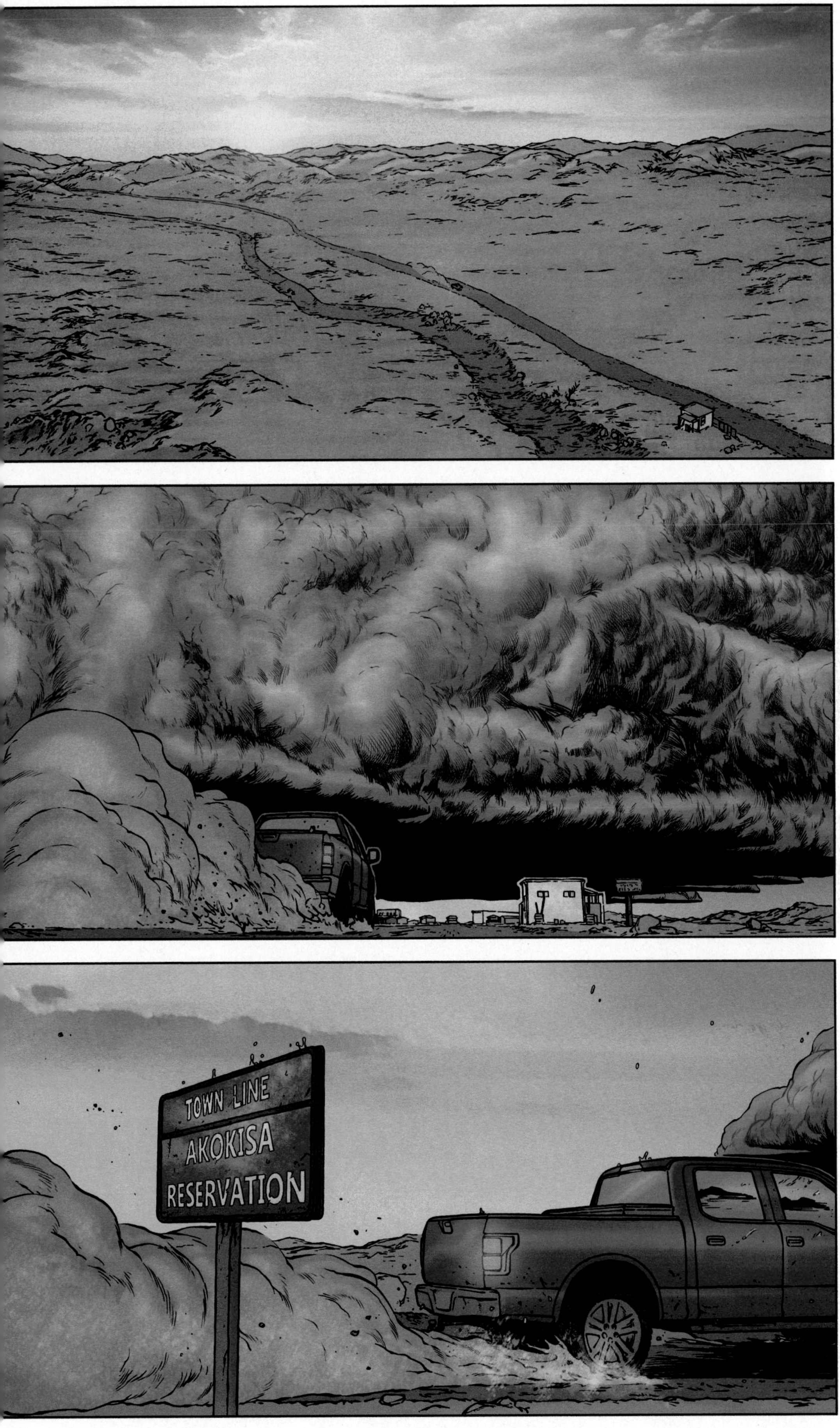
TOWN LINE
AKOKISA
RESERVATION

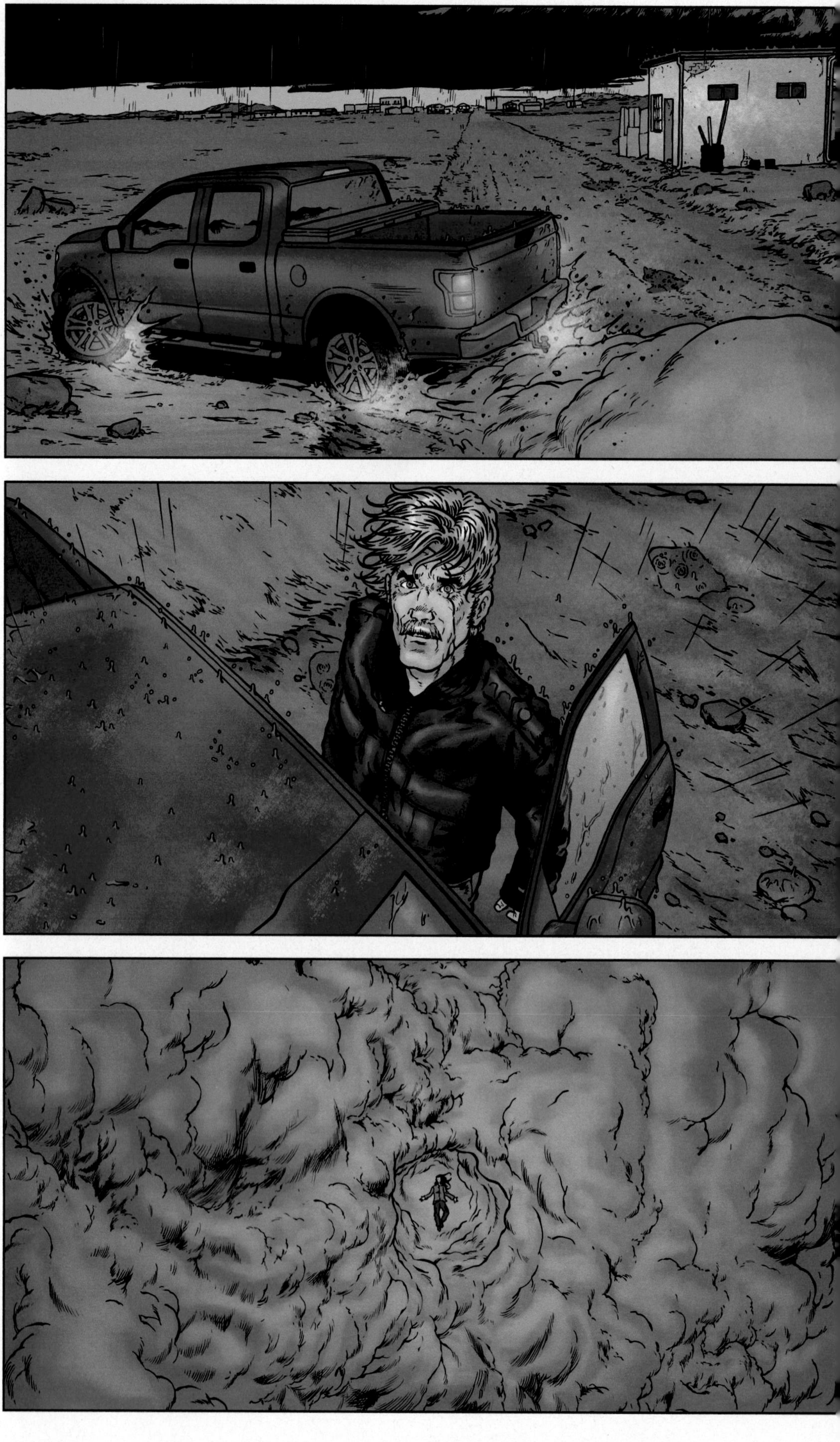

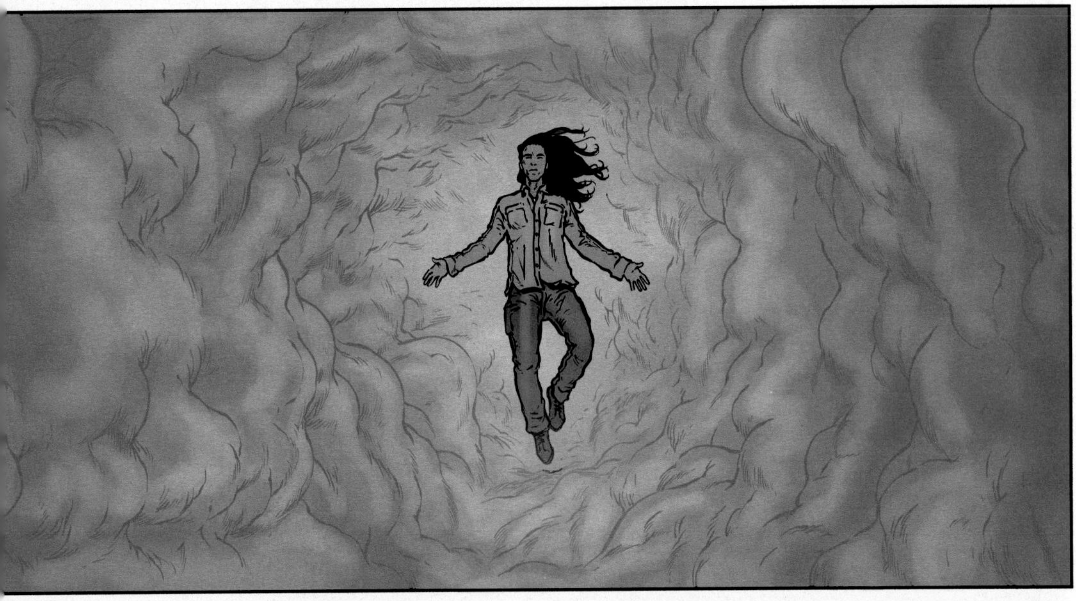
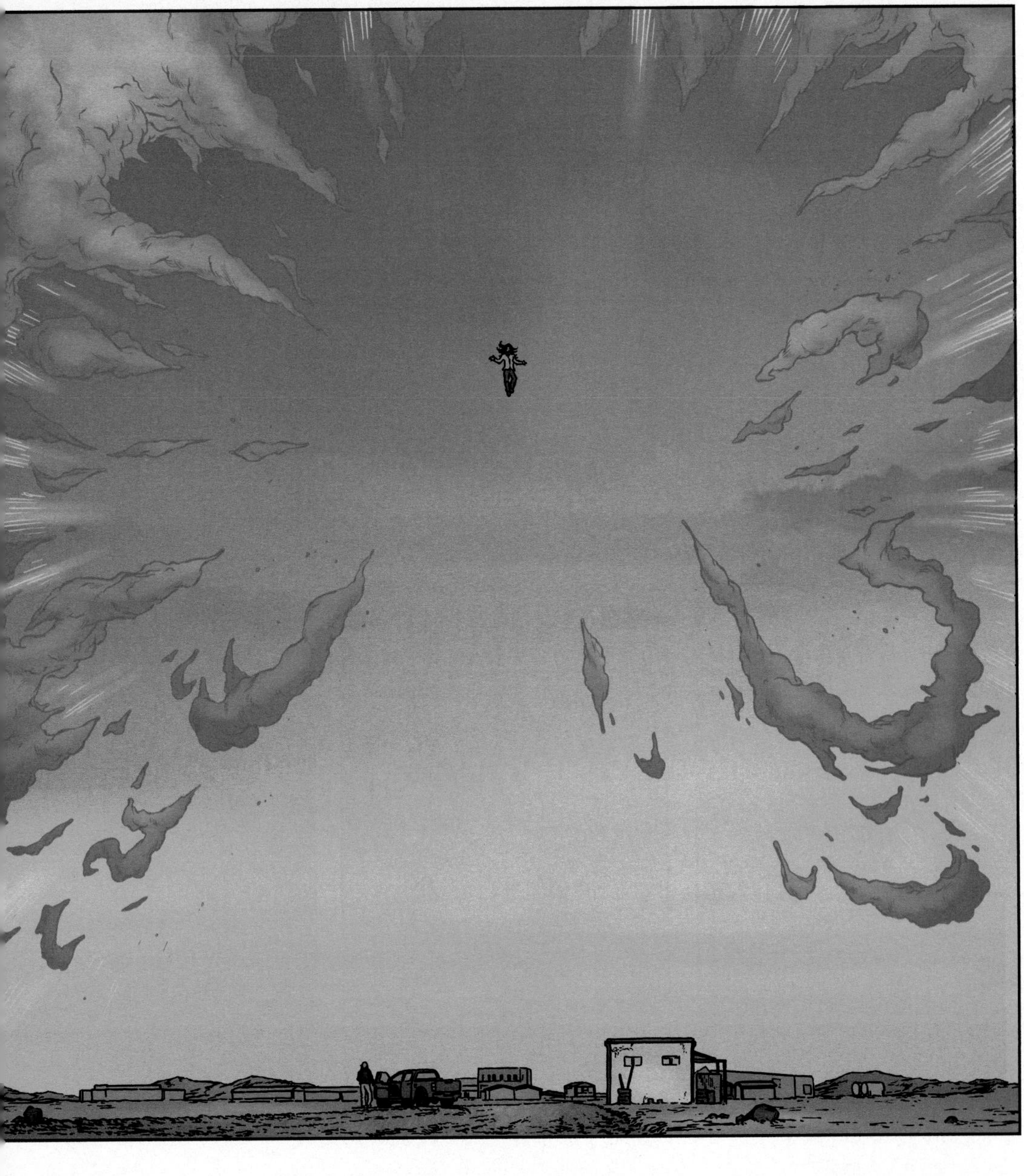

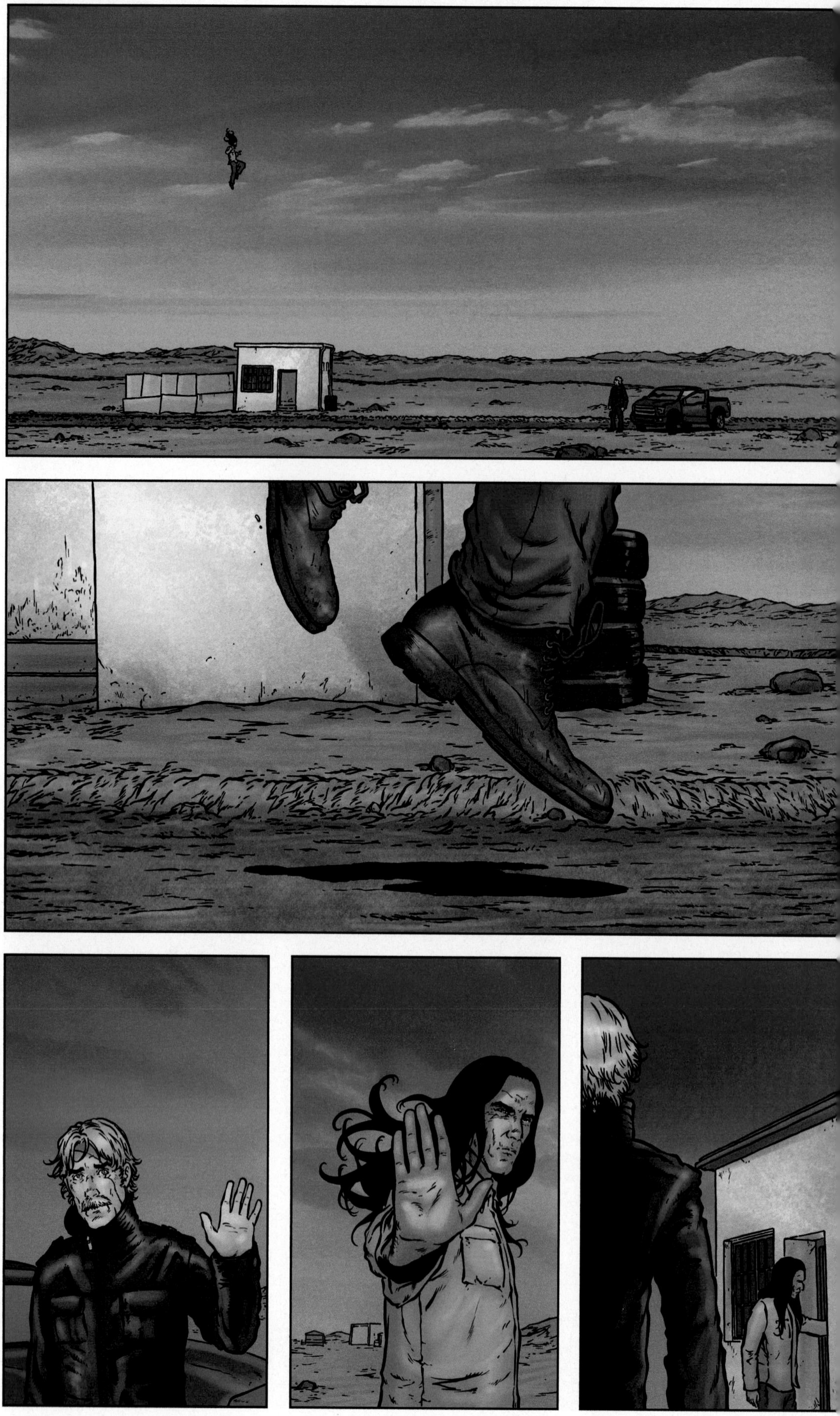

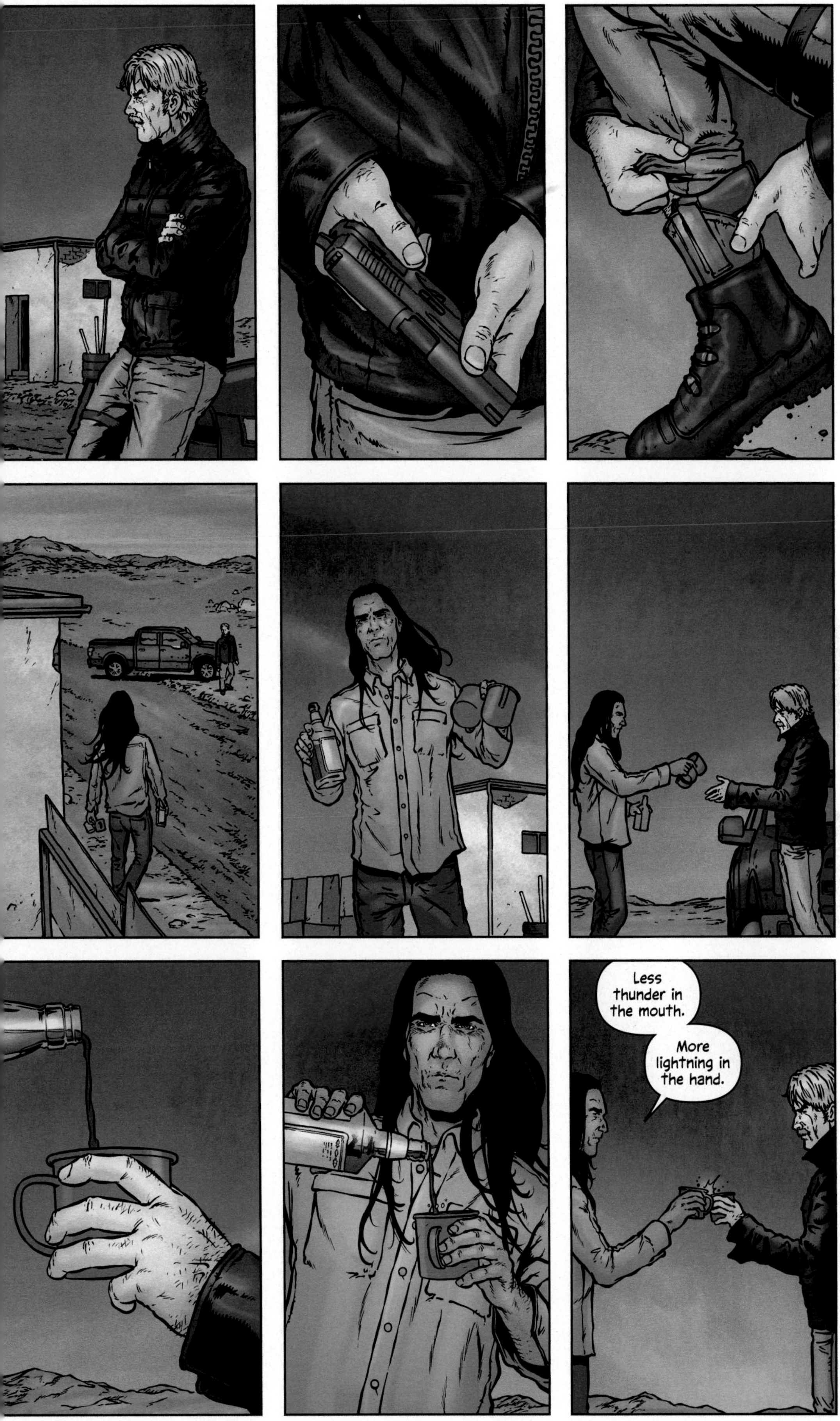
Less thunder in the mouth.
More lightning in the hand.

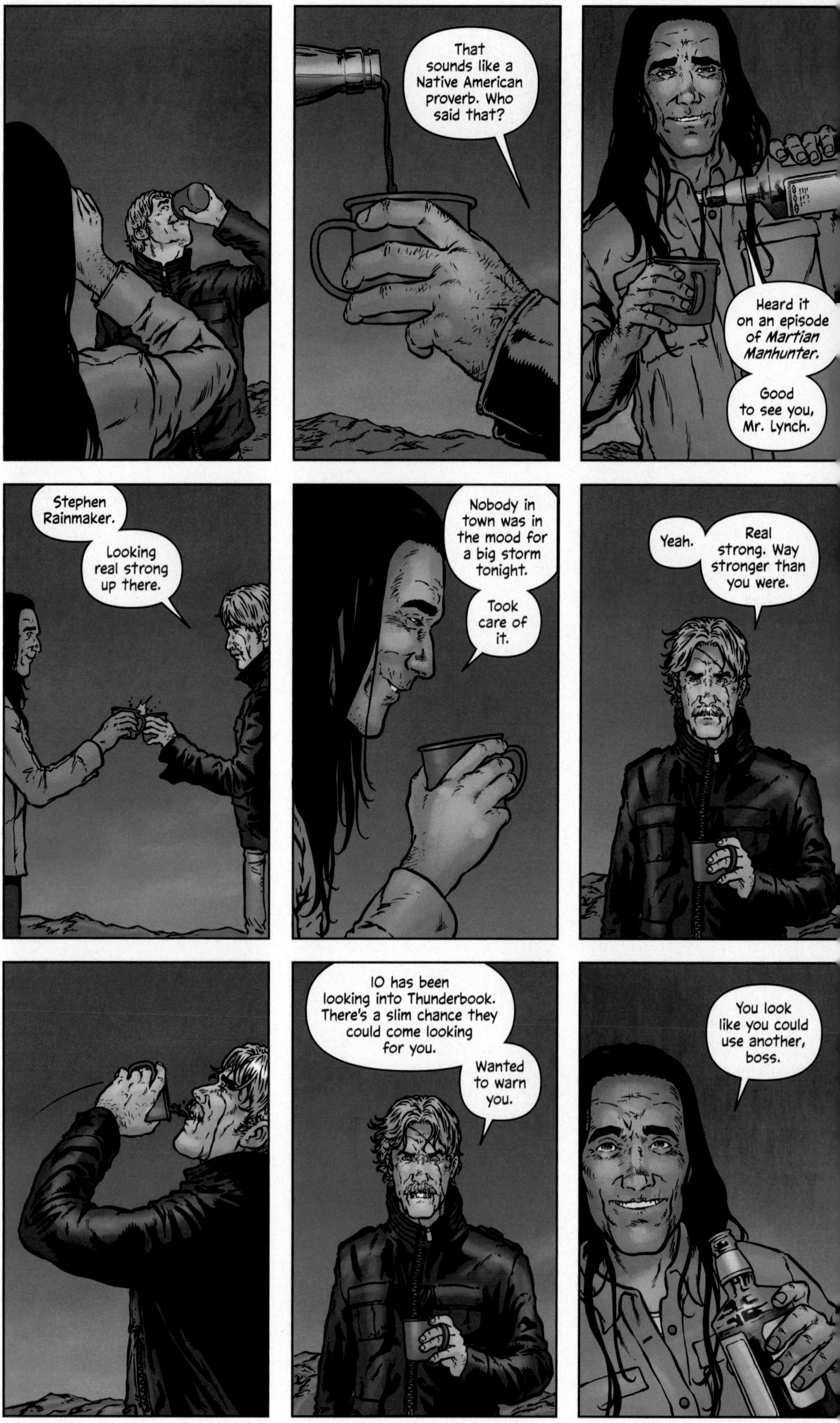
That sounds like a Native American proverb. Who said that?
Heard it on an episode of *Martian Manhunter*.
Good to see you, Mr. Lynch.
Stephen Rainmaker.
Looking real strong up there.
Nobody in town was in the mood for a big storm tonight.
Took care of it.
Yeah.
Real strong. Way stronger than you were.
IO has been looking into Thunderbook. There's a slim chance they could come looking for you.
Wanted to warn you.
You look like you could use another, boss.

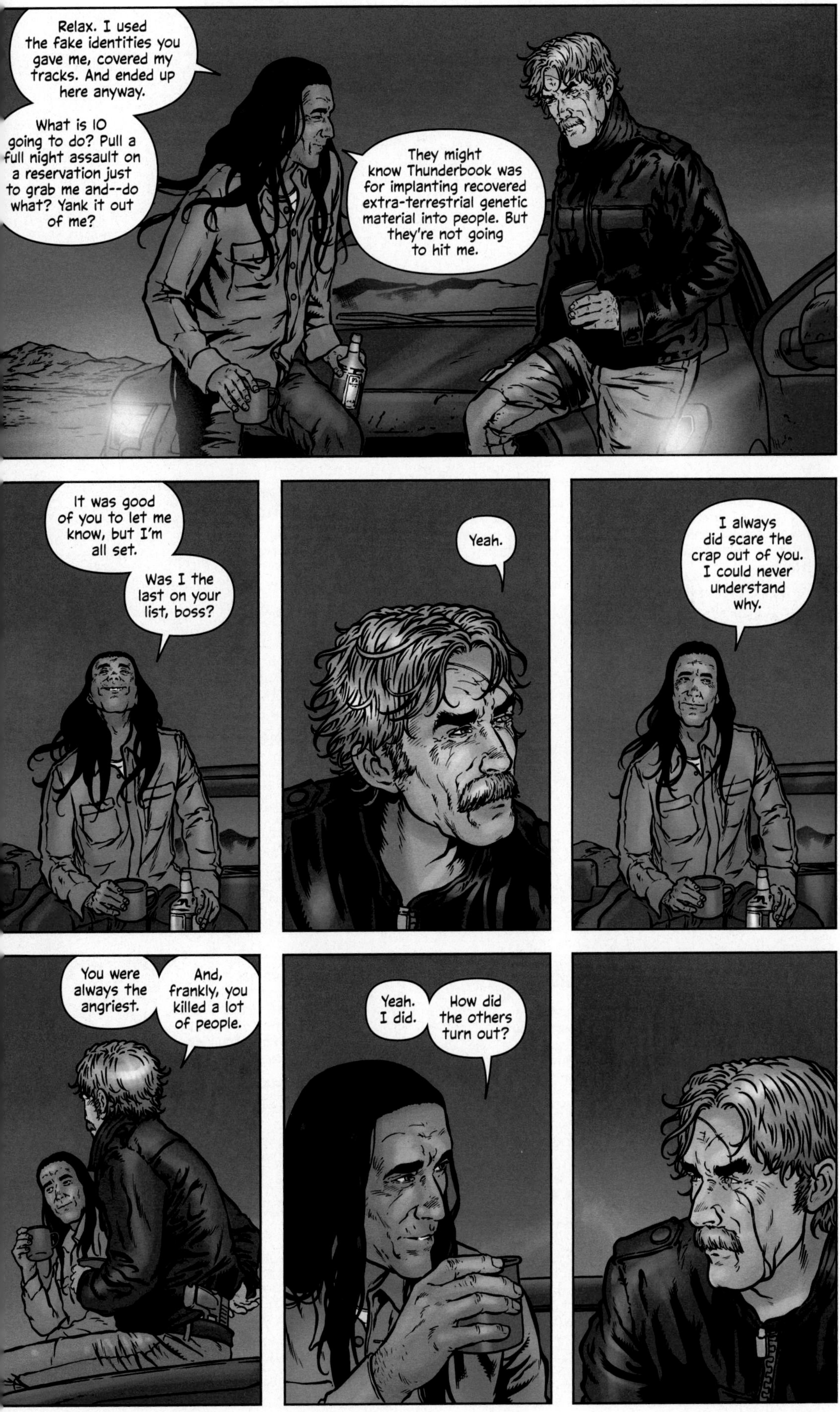
Relax. I used the fake identities you gave me, covered my tracks. And ended up here anyway.
What is IO going to do? Pull a full night assault on a reservation just to grab me and--do what? Yank it out of me?
They might know Thunderbook was for implanting recovered extra-terrestrial genetic material into people. But they're not going to hit me.
It was good of you to let me know, but I'm all set.
Was I the last on your list, boss?
Yeah.
I always did scare the crap out of you. I could never understand why.
You were always the angriest.
And, frankly, you killed a lot of people.
Yeah. I did.
How did the others turn out?

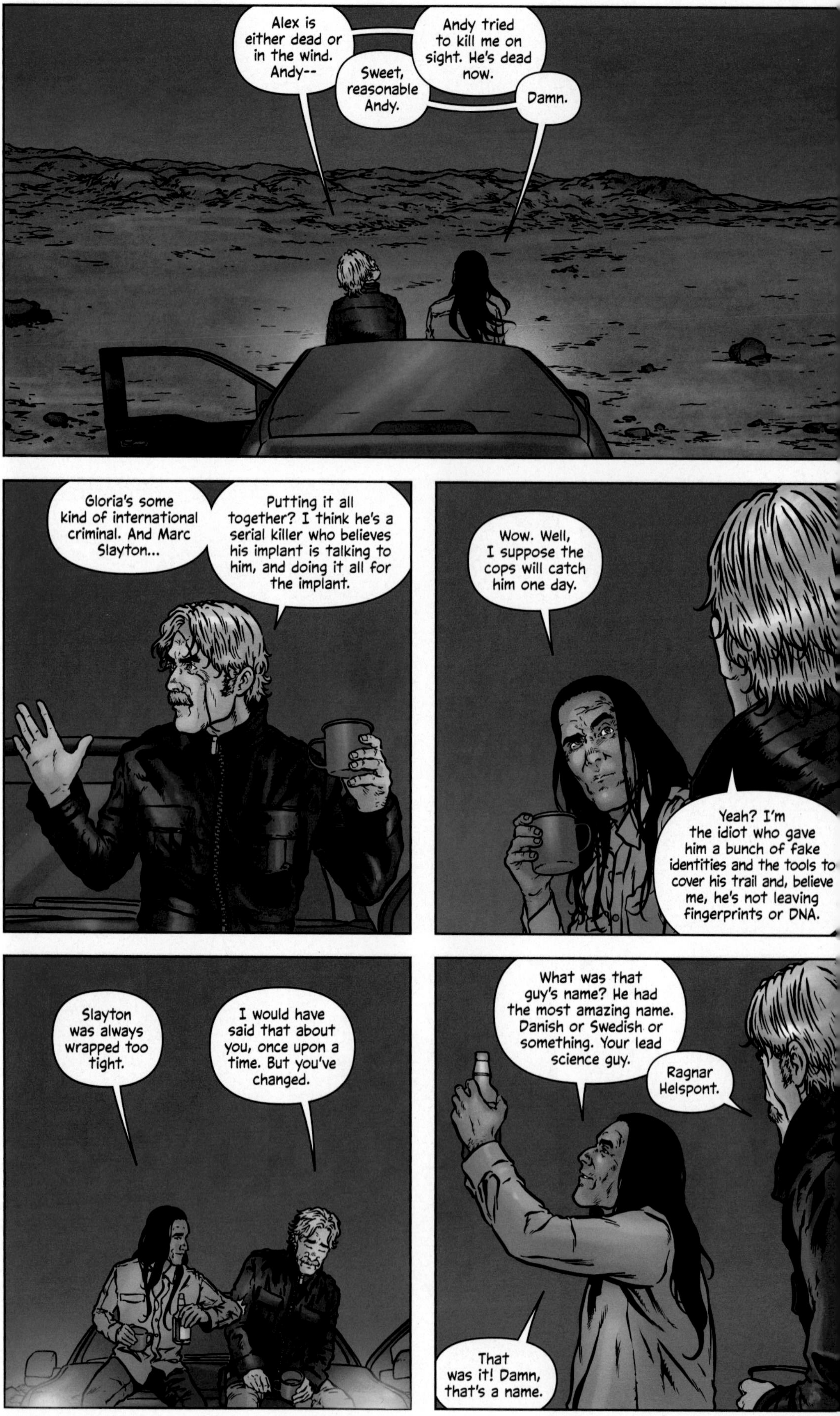
Alex is either dead or in the wind. Andy--
Andy tried to kill me on sight. He's dead now.
Sweet, reasonable Andy.
Damn.
Gloria's some kind of international criminal. And Marc Slayton...
Putting it all together? I think he's a serial killer who believes his implant is talking to him, and doing it all for the implant.
Wow. Well, I suppose the cops will catch him one day.
Yeah? I'm the idiot who gave him a bunch of fake identities and the tools to cover his trail and, believe me, he's not leaving fingerprints or DNA.
Slayton was always wrapped too tight.
I would have said that about you, once upon a time. But you've changed.
What was that guy's name? He had the most amazing name. Danish or Swedish or something. Your lead science guy.
Ragnar Helspont.
That was it! Damn, that's a name.

Helspont was always going on about how we needed to command the implant, control the implant, all that.

And the more I went through the protocol, the more it seemed to take over.

I'd catch myself doing things I wouldn't normally do, you know? But after the fact.

And every time I got angry, there was this reinforcement loop, like I was relishing it? It pleased me?

So I stopped pushing. I decided to just roll with it, instead.

I'm not at war with myself anymore. And I'm not at war with the thing. Turns out peace is good for trade.

Do you have kids, by any chance?

One.

This will sound weird, but was it like a compulsion?

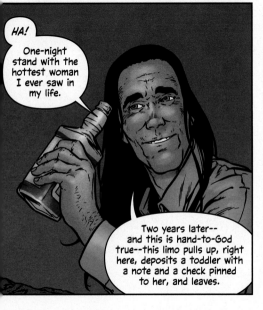

HA!

One-night stand with the hottest woman I ever saw in my life.

Two years later-- and this is hand-to-God true--this limo pulls up, right here, deposits a toddler with a note and a check pinned to her, and leaves.

Just as well I didn't have any plans for the rest of my life, right?

What's the kid's name?

Sarah.

And, yeah, the thing copied over into her.

The thing... it's strong in her. She's traveling right now.

I would have thought she was young to be doing that.

I think she was born old.

She wants to straighten out who she is and who she wants to be. She is absolutely amazing. You'd like her.

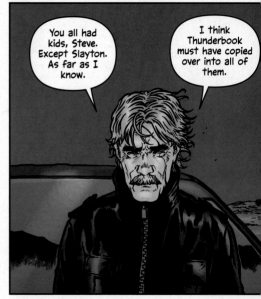

You all had kids, Steve. Except Slayton. As far as I know.

I think Thunderbook must have copied over into all of them.

I want to find them.

Huh.

Guess I'm not the only one who's *"changed."*

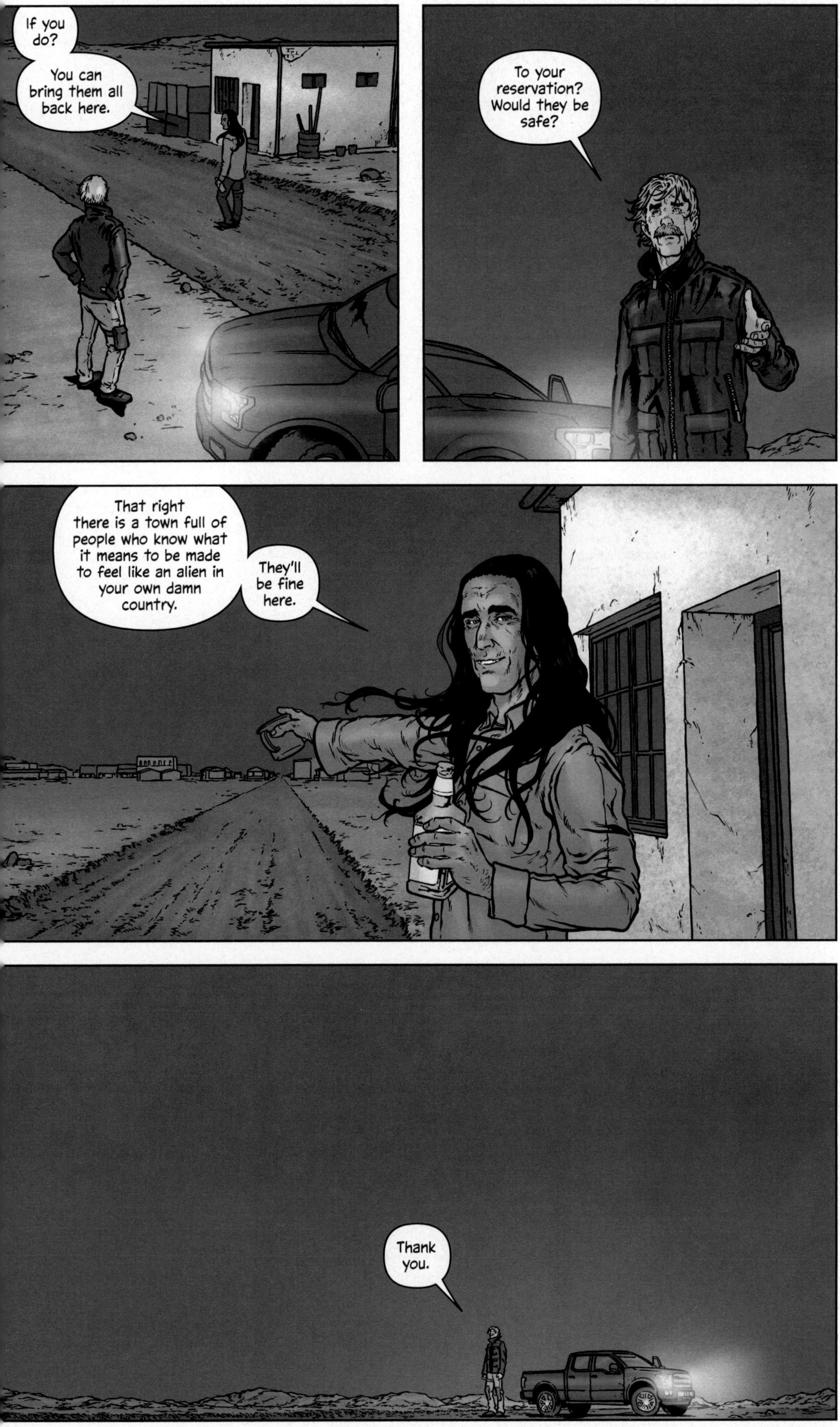
If you do?
You can bring them all back here.
To your reservation? Would they be safe?
That right there is a town full of people who know what it means to be made to feel like an alien in your own damn country.
They'll be fine here.
Thank you.

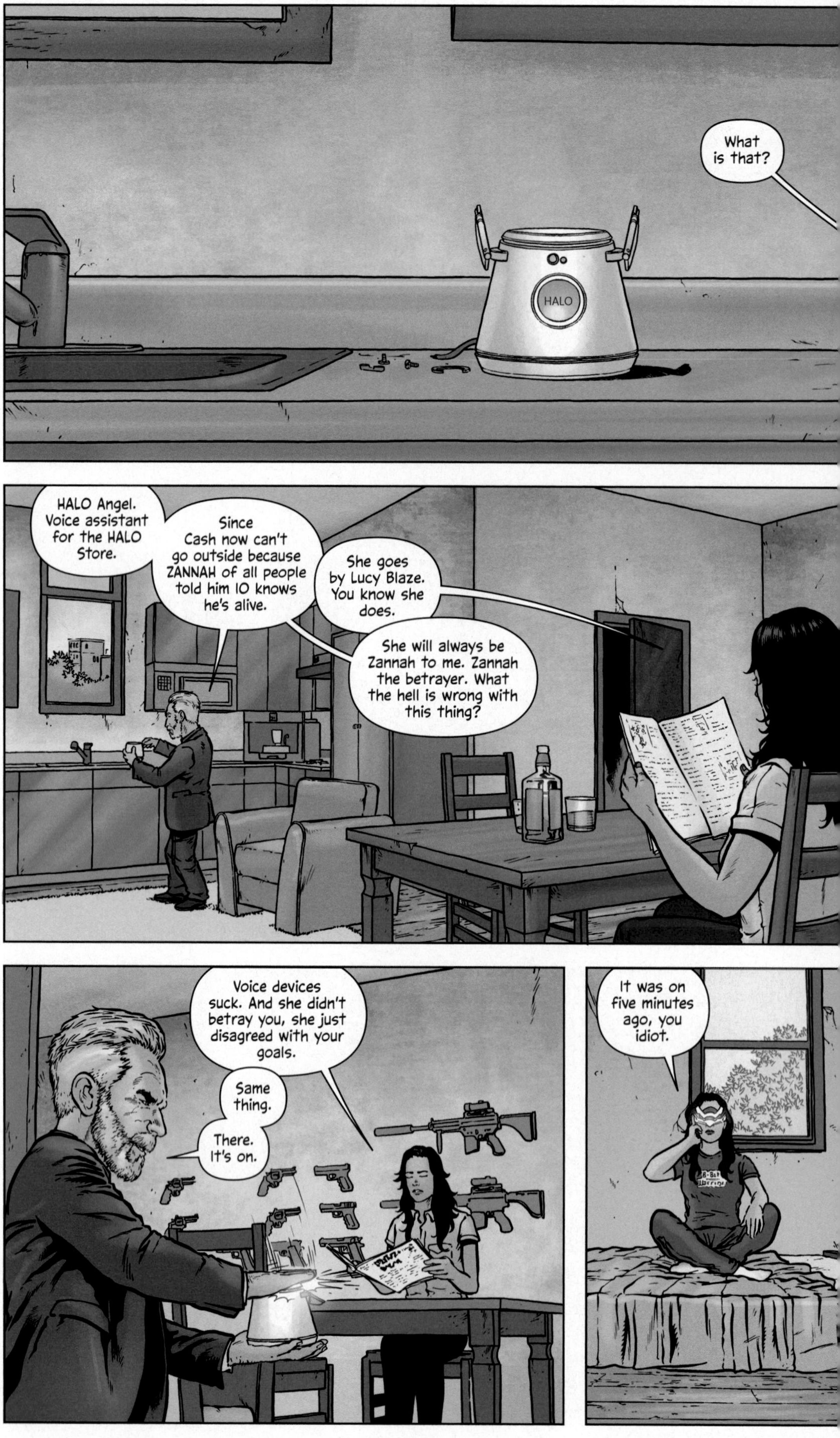
What is that?
HALO
HALO Angel. Voice assistant for the HALO Store.
Since Cash now can't go outside because ZANNAH of all people told him IO knows he's alive.
She goes by Lucy Blaze. You know she does.
She will always be Zannah to me. Zannah the betrayer. What the hell is wrong with this thing?
Voice devices suck. And she didn't betray you, she just disagreed with your goals.
Same thing.
There. It's on.
It was on five minutes ago, you idiot.

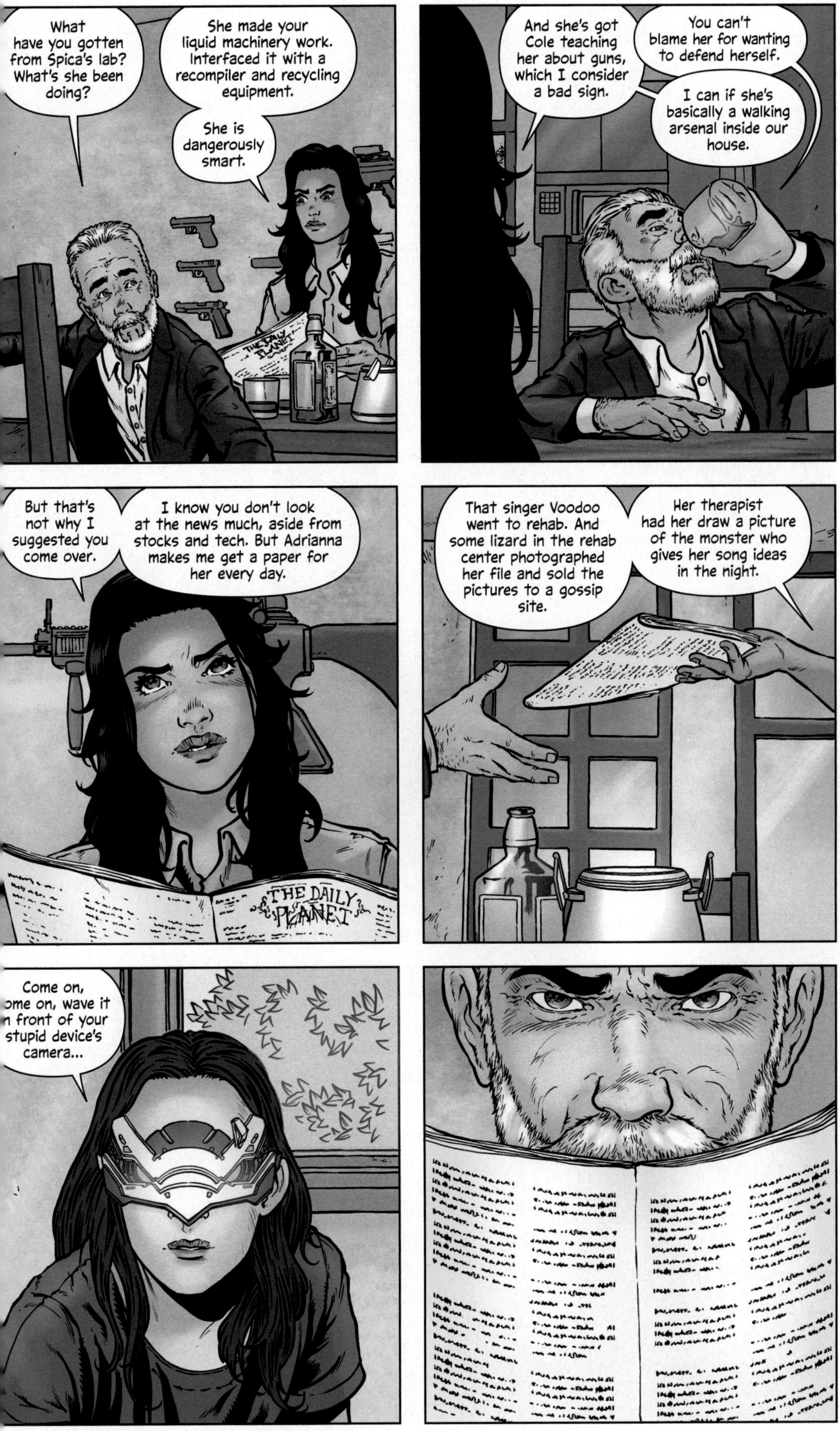
What have you gotten from Spica's lab? What's she been doing?
She made your liquid machinery work. Interfaced it with a recompiler and recycling equipment.
She is dangerously smart.
THE DAILY PLANET
And she's got Cole teaching her about guns, which I consider a bad sign.
You can't blame her for wanting to defend herself.
I can if she's basically a walking arsenal inside our house.
But that's not why I suggested you come over.
I know you don't look at the news much, aside from stocks and tech. But Adrianna makes me get a paper for her every day.
THE DAILY PLANET
That singer Voodoo went to rehab. And some lizard in the rehab center photographed her file and sold the pictures to a gossip site.
Her therapist had her draw a picture of the monster who gives her song ideas in the night.
Come on, ome on, wave it n front of your stupid device's camera...

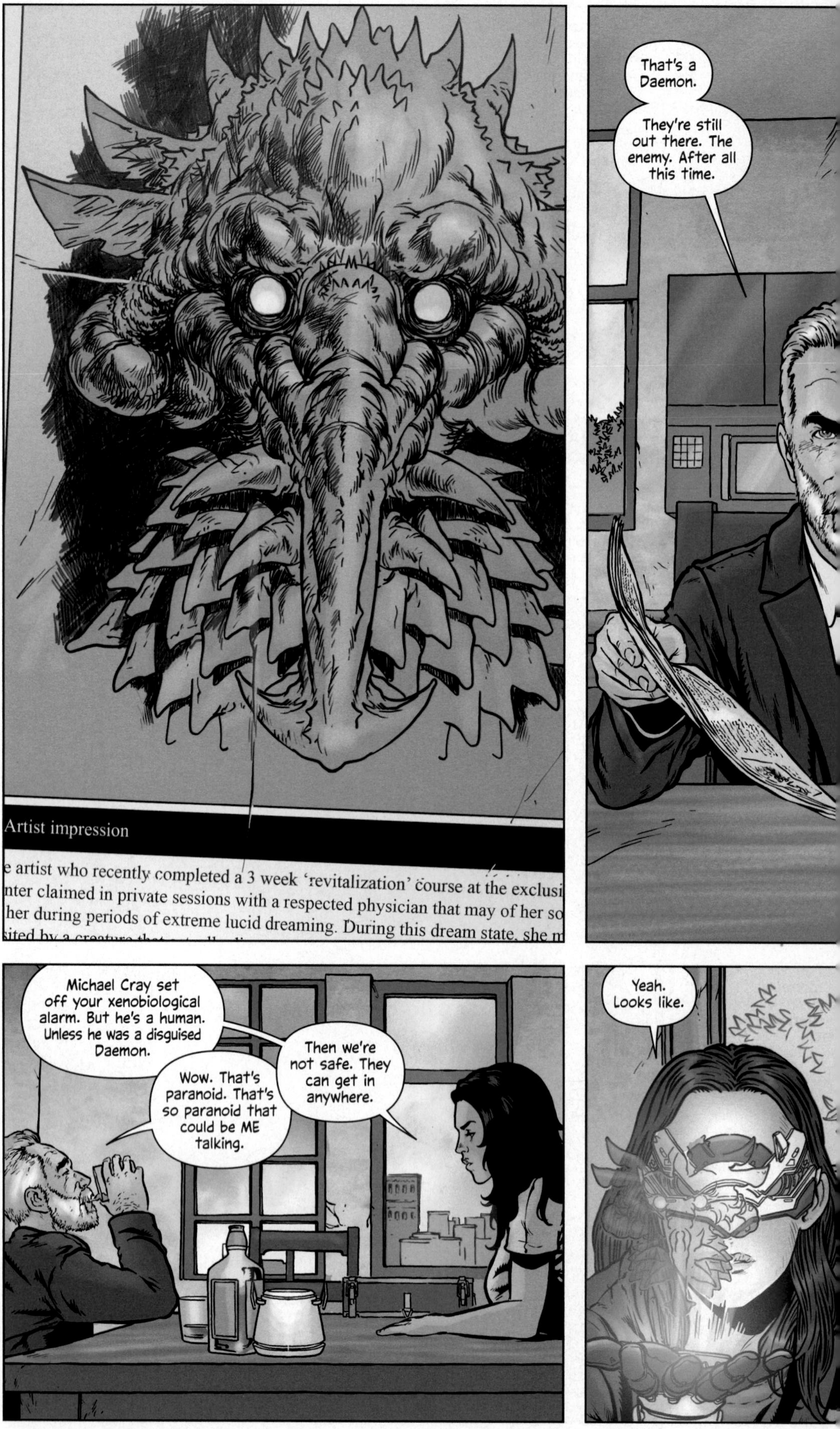
Artist impression
e artist who recently completed a 3 week 'revitalization' course at the exclusi
nter claimed in private sessions with a respected physician that may of her so
her during periods of extreme lucid dreaming. During this dream state, she m
That's a Daemon.
They're still out there. The enemy. After all this time.
Michael Cray set off your xenobiological alarm. But he's a human. Unless he was a disguised Daemon.
Then we're not safe. They can get in anywhere.
Wow. That's paranoid. That's so paranoid that could be ME talking.
Yeah. Looks like.

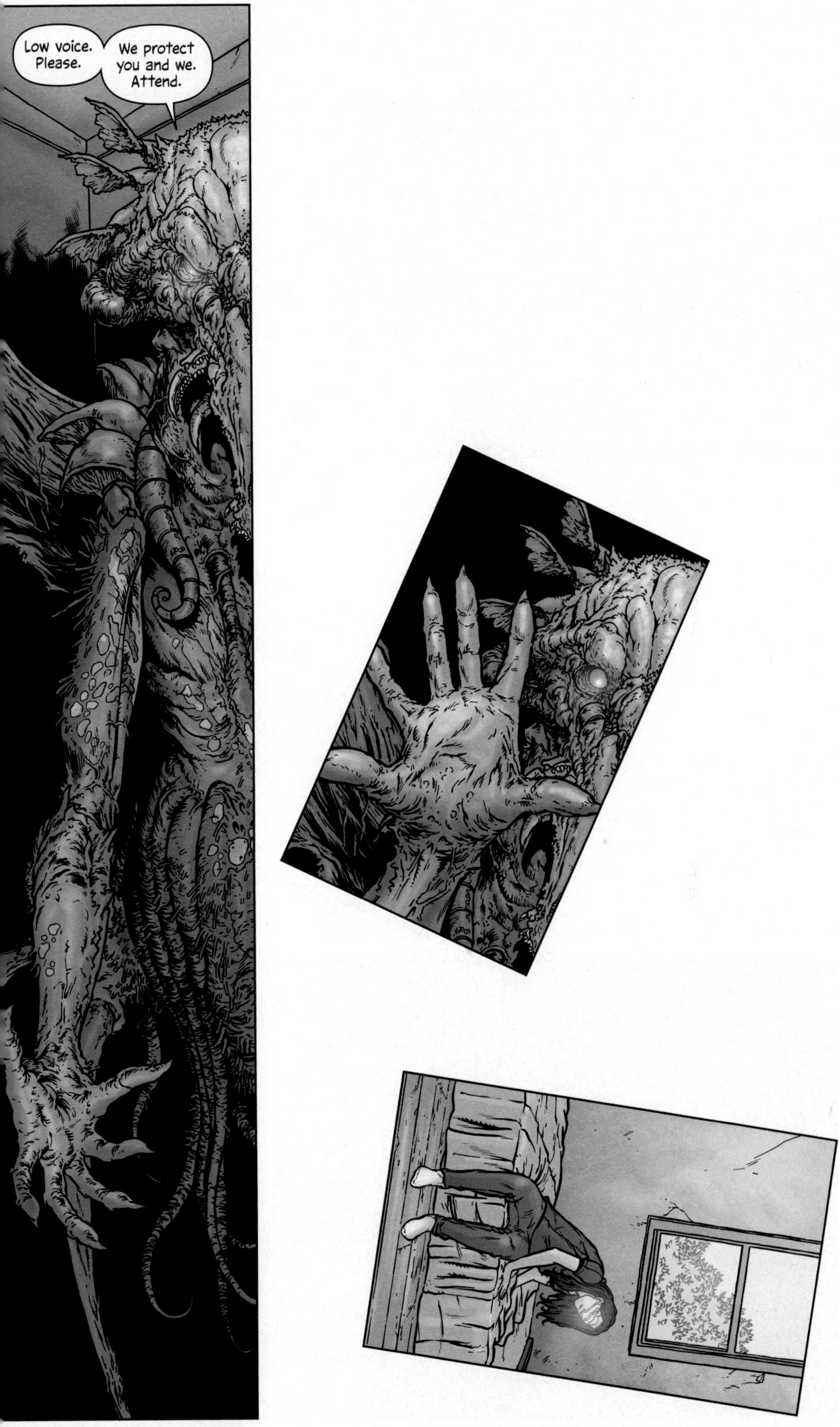
Low voice. Please.
We protect you and we. Attend.

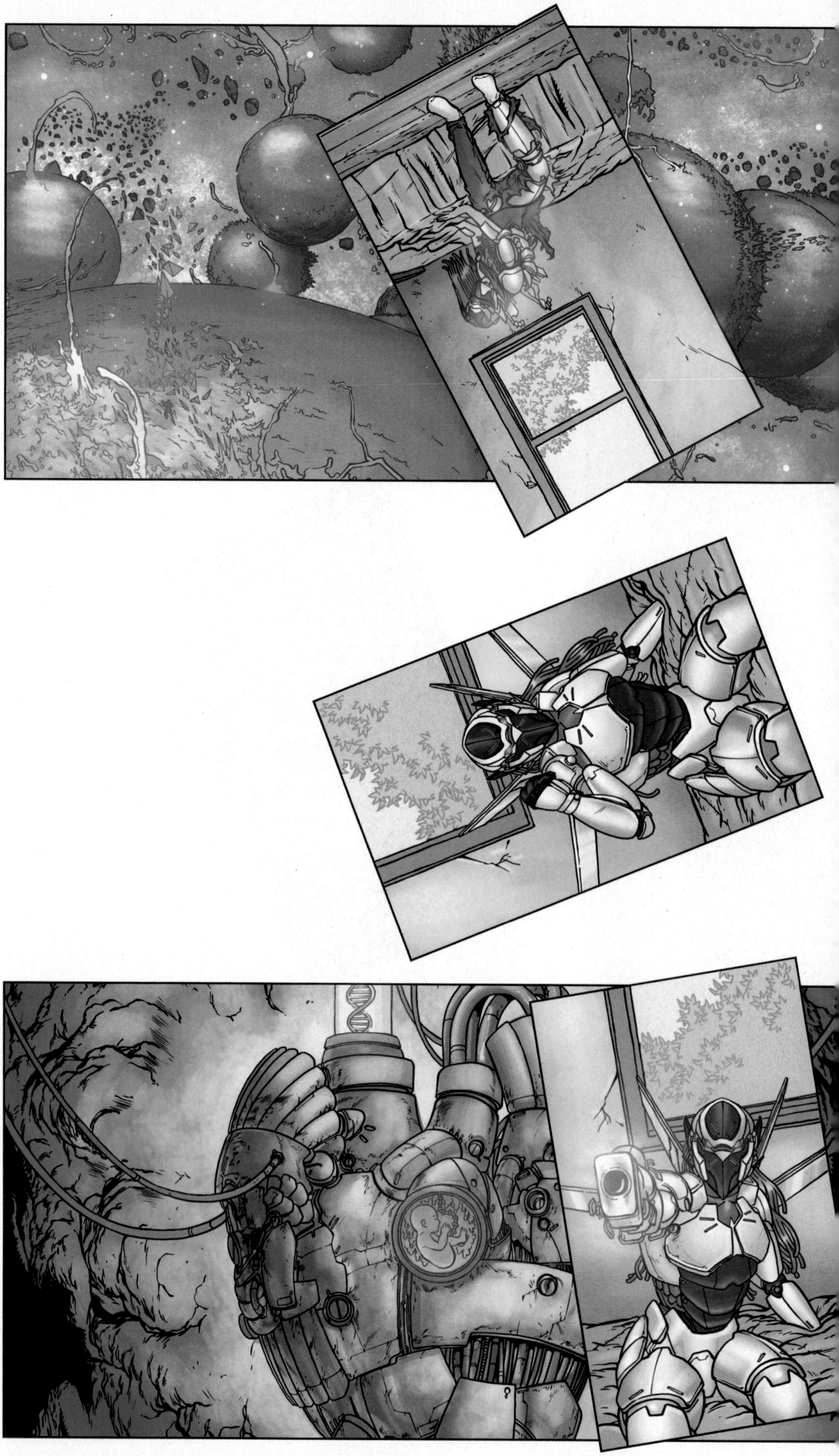

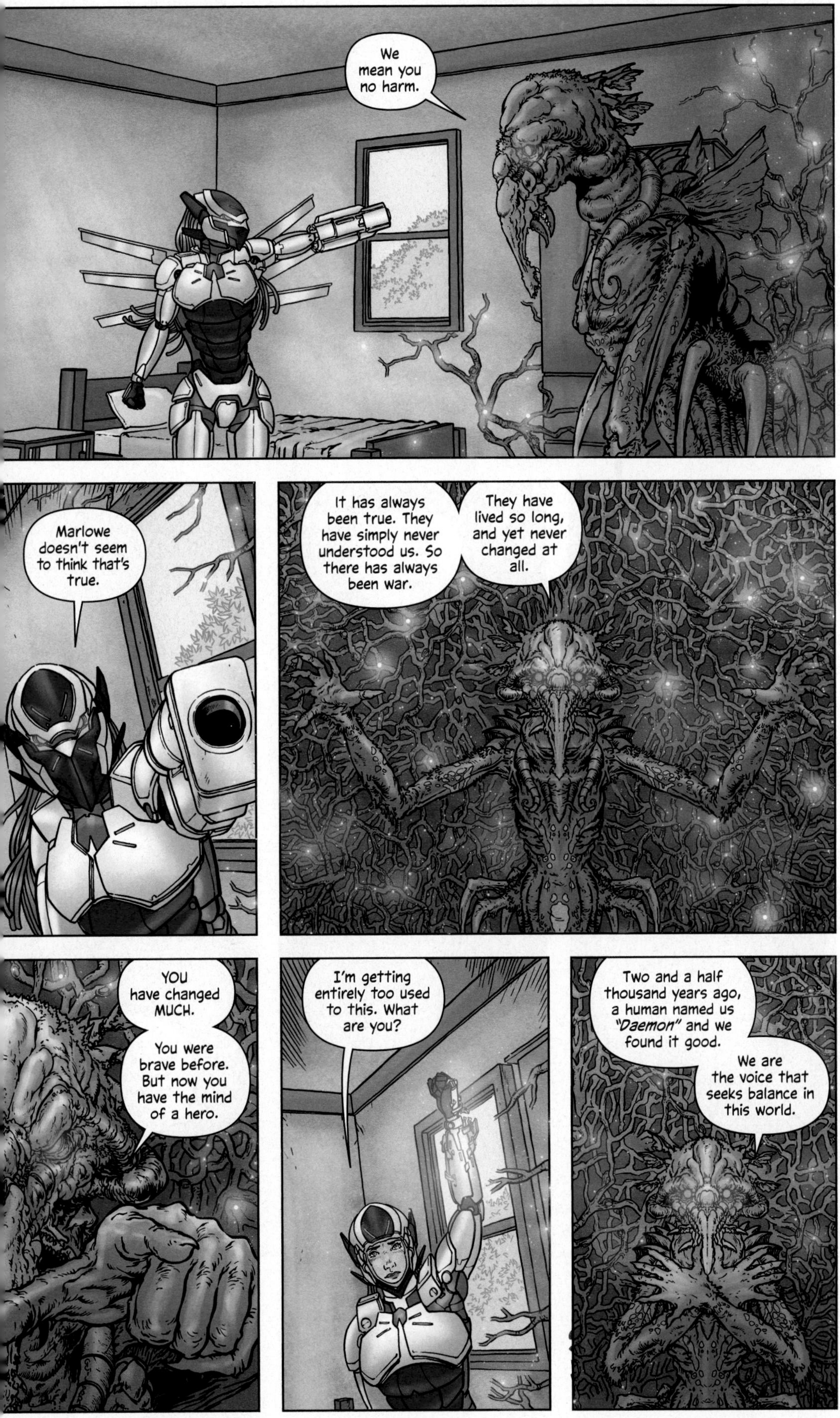
We mean you no harm.
Marlowe doesn't seem to think that's true.
It has always been true. They have simply never understood us. So there has always been war.
They have lived so long, and yet never changed at all.
YOU have changed MUCH.
You were brave before. But now you have the mind of a hero.
I'm getting entirely too used to this. What are you?
Two and a half thousand years ago, a human named us *"Daemon"* and we found it good.
We are the voice that seeks balance in this world.

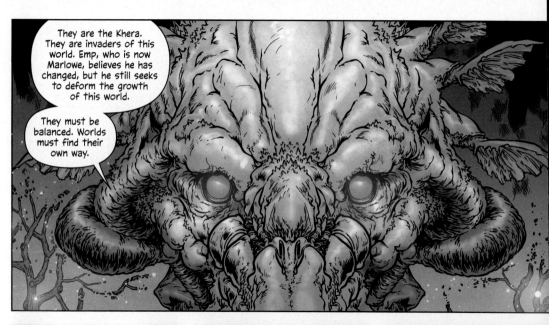

They are the Khera. They are invaders of this world. Emp, who is now Marlowe, believes he has changed, but he still seeks to deform the growth of this world.

They must be balanced. Worlds must find their own way.

But a storm has come. This world has lost its way. And balance is lost.

Your act of altruism changed the world, but the world was already deformed. So now we must speak.

When the time comes, call to the Sparks.

The Sparks is the defense mechanism.

The Sparks has the authority to take action to restore the balance.

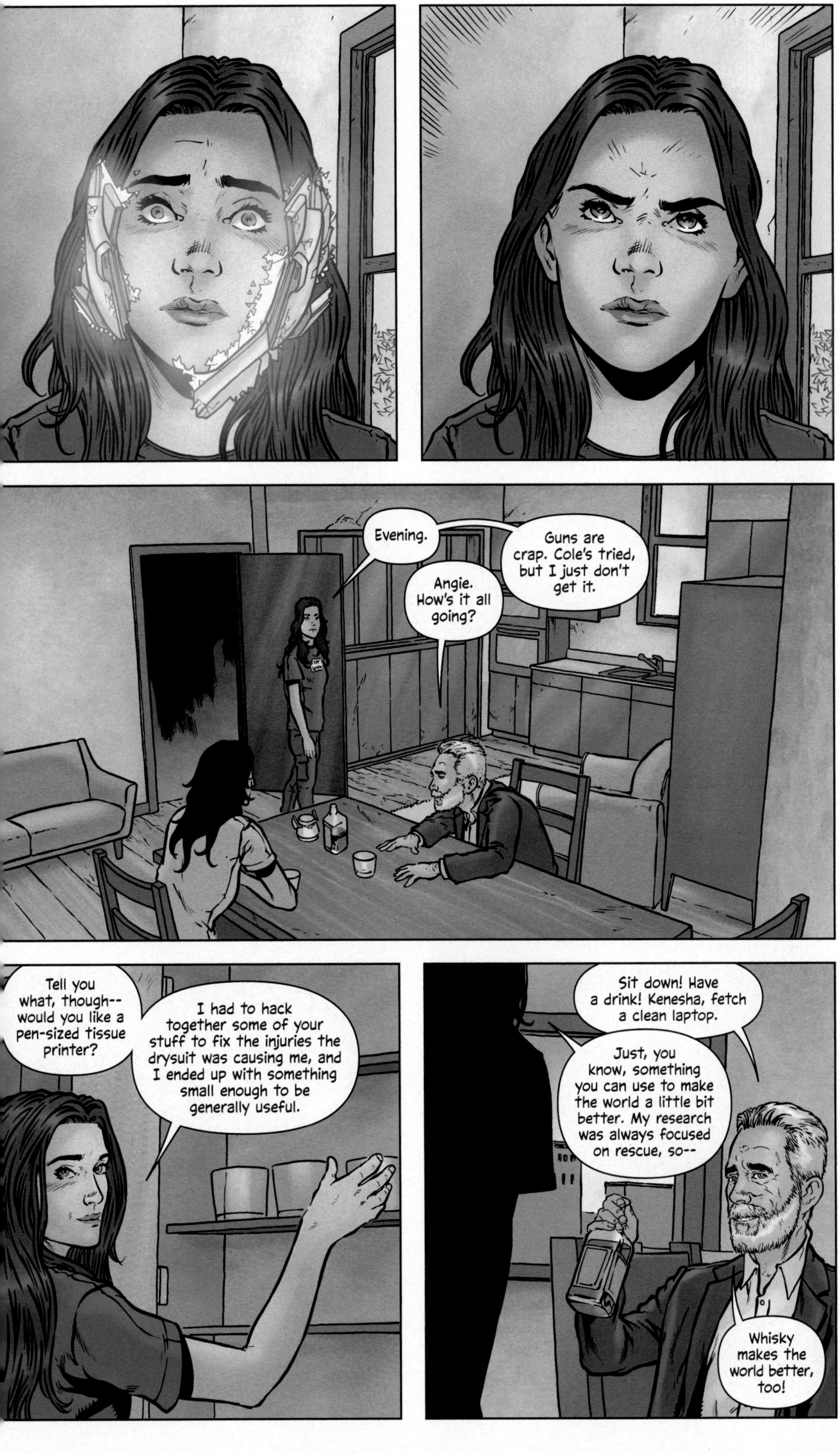
Evening.
Angie. How's it all going?
Guns are crap. Cole's tried, but I just don't get it.
Tell you what, though-- would you like a pen-sized tissue printer?
I had to hack together some of your stuff to fix the injuries the drysuit was causing me, and I ended up with something small enough to be generally useful.
Sit down! Have a drink! Kenesha, fetch a clean laptop.
Just, you know, something you can use to make the world a little bit better. My research was always focused on rescue, so--
Whisky makes the world better, too!

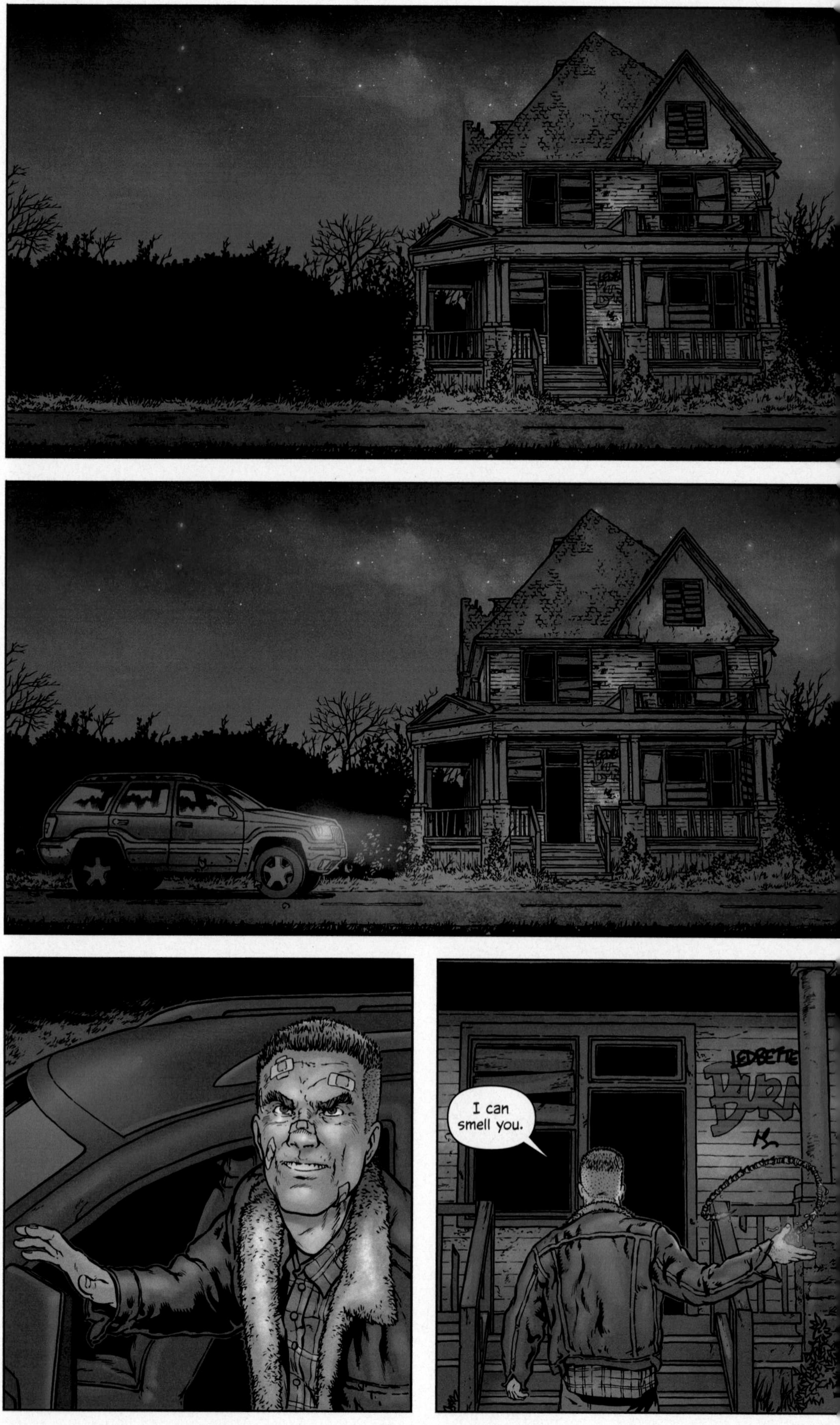
I can smell you.

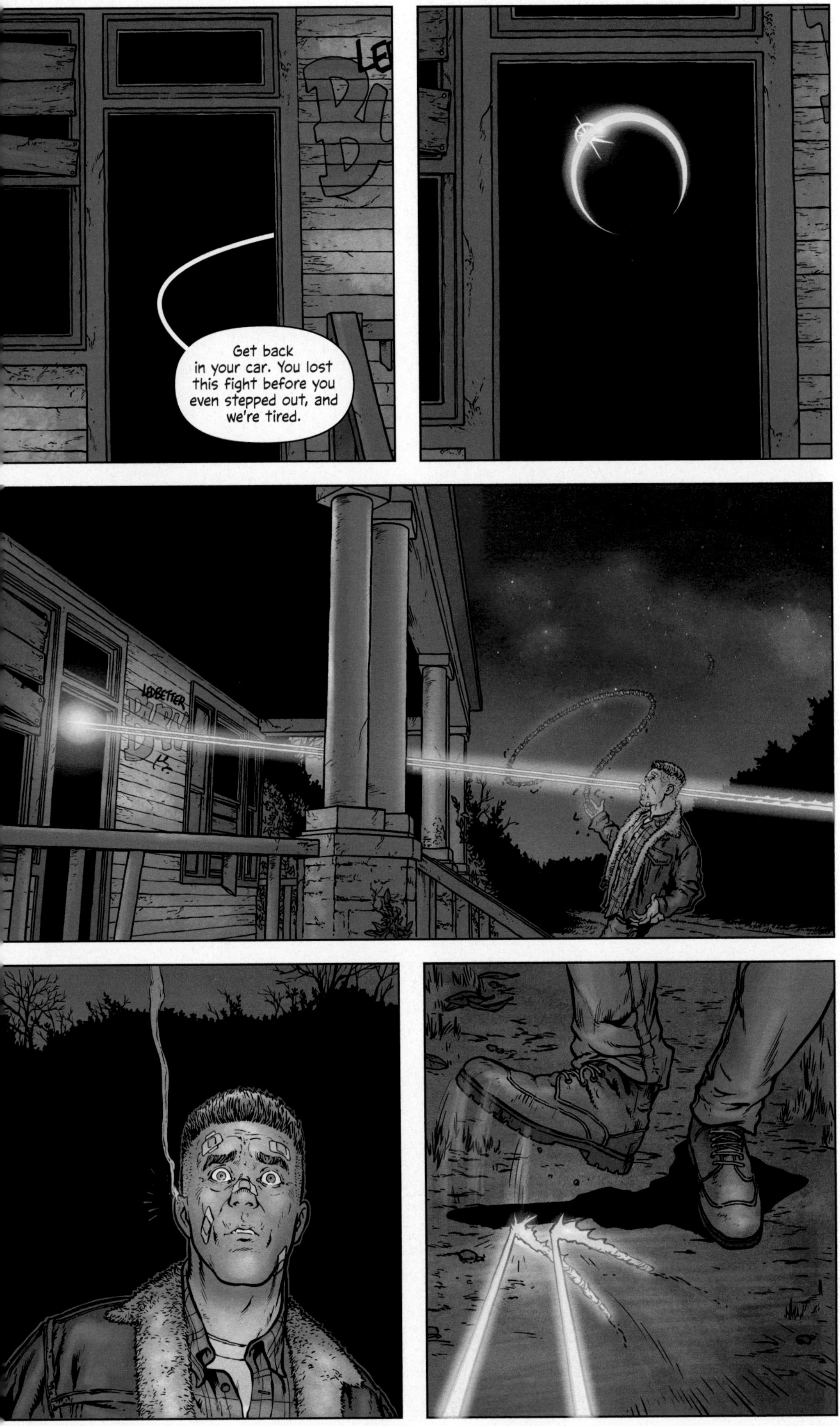
Get back in your car. You lost this fight before you even stepped out, and we're tired.
LEDBETTER

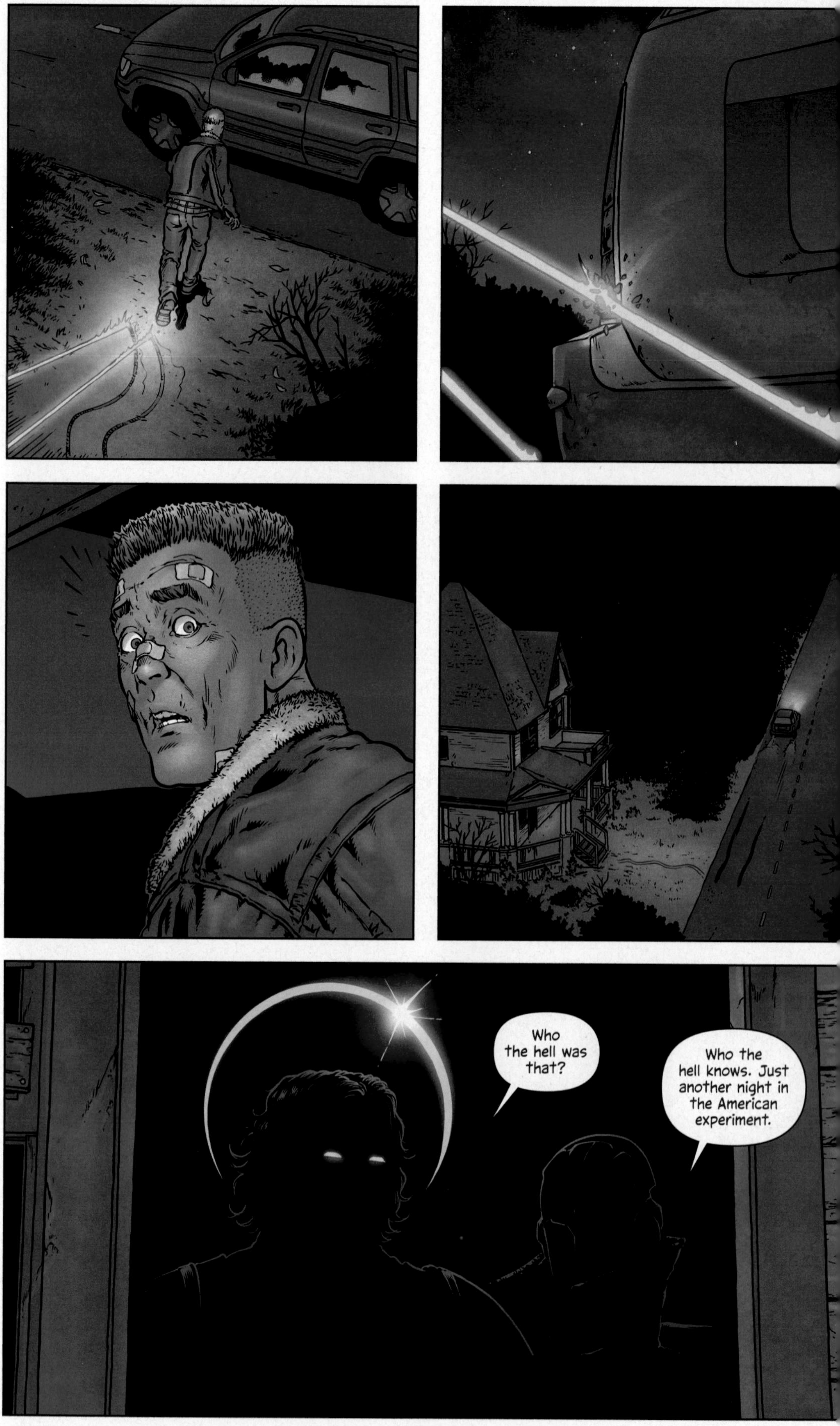
Who the hell was that?
Who the hell knows. Just another night in the American experiment.

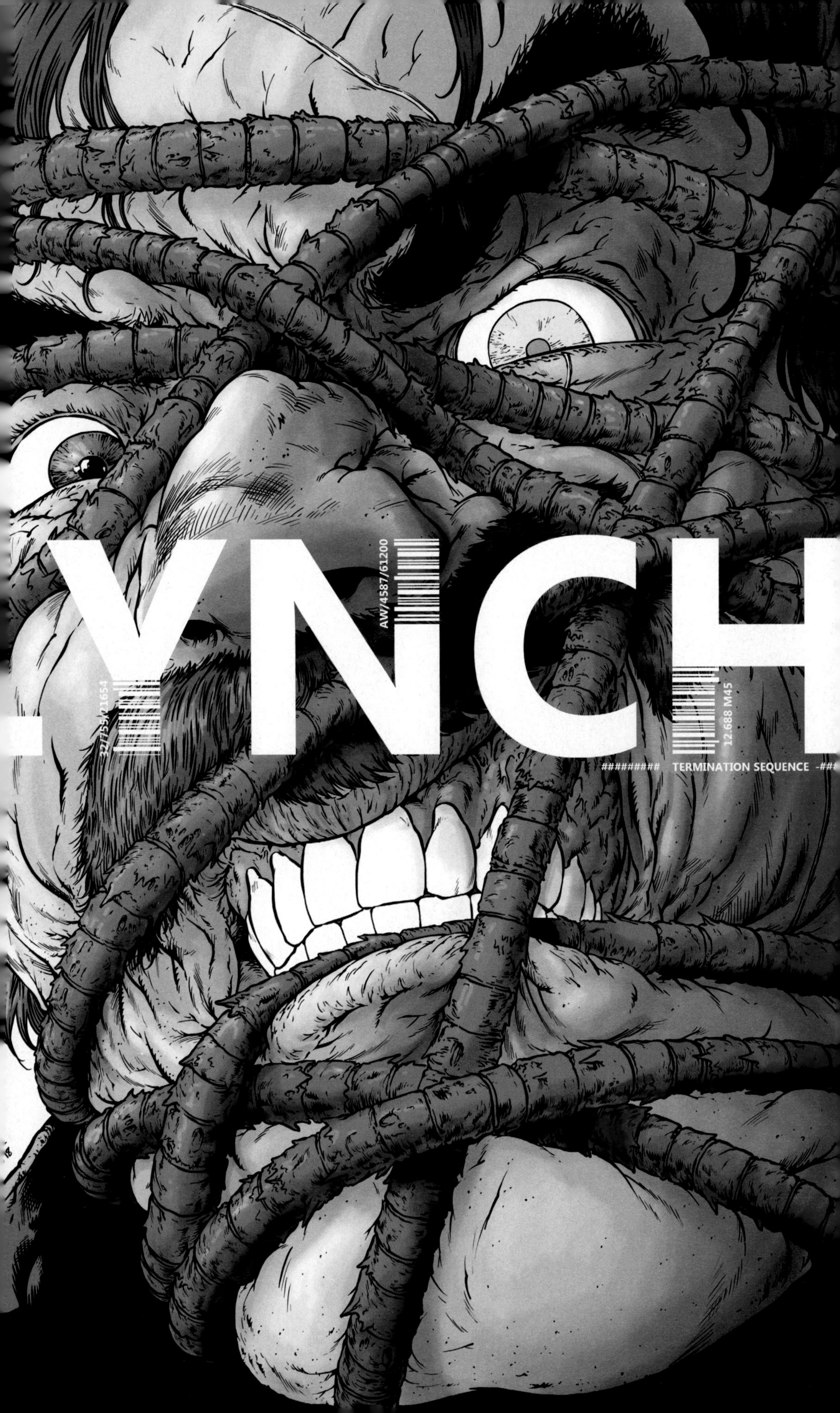
YNCH
AW/4587/61200
12.688 M45
######### TERMINATION SEQUENCE -##

18

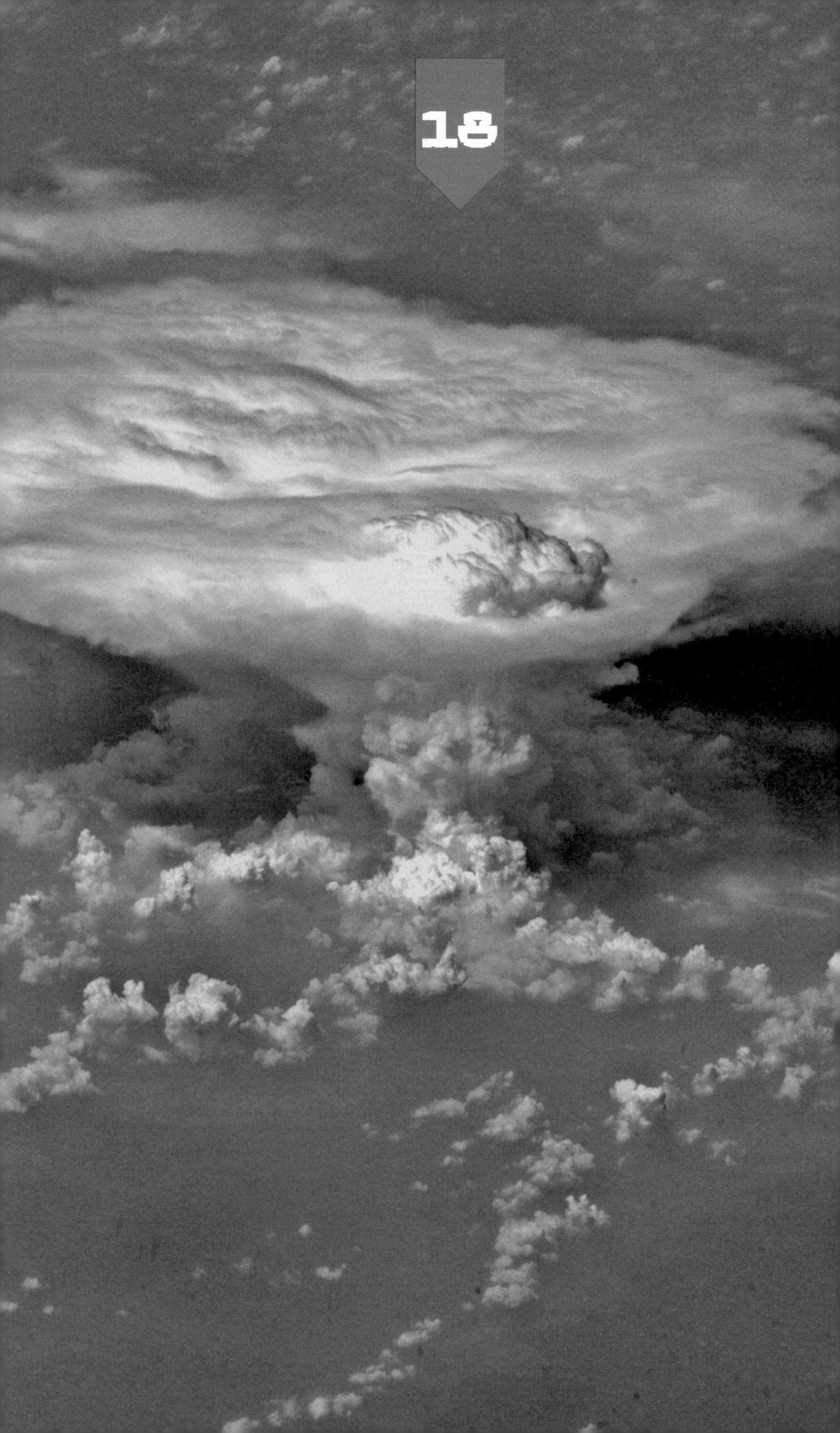

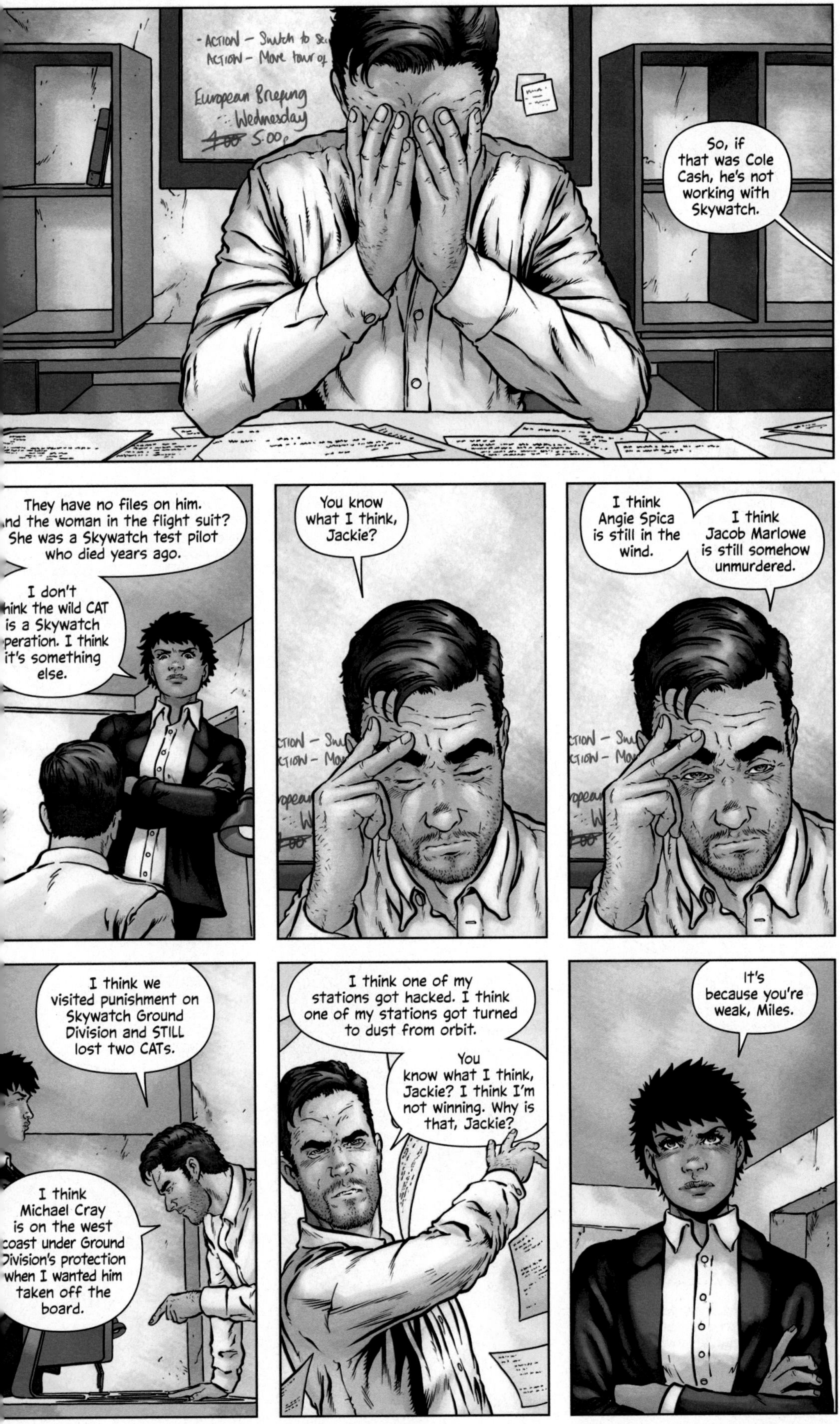

European Briefing
Wednesday
So, if that was Cole Cash, he's not working with Skywatch.
They have no files on him. nd the woman in the flight suit? She was a Skywatch test pilot who died years ago.
I don't hink the wild CAT is a Skywatch peration. I think it's something else.
You know what I think, Jackie?
I think Angie Spica is still in the wind.
I think Jacob Marlowe is still somehow unmurdered.
I think we visited punishment on Skywatch Ground Division and STILL lost two CATs.
I think Michael Cray is on the west coast under Ground Division's protection when I wanted him taken off the board.
I think one of my stations got hacked. I think one of my stations got turned to dust from orbit.
You know what I think, Jackie? I think I'm not winning. Why is that, Jackie?
It's because you're weak, Miles.

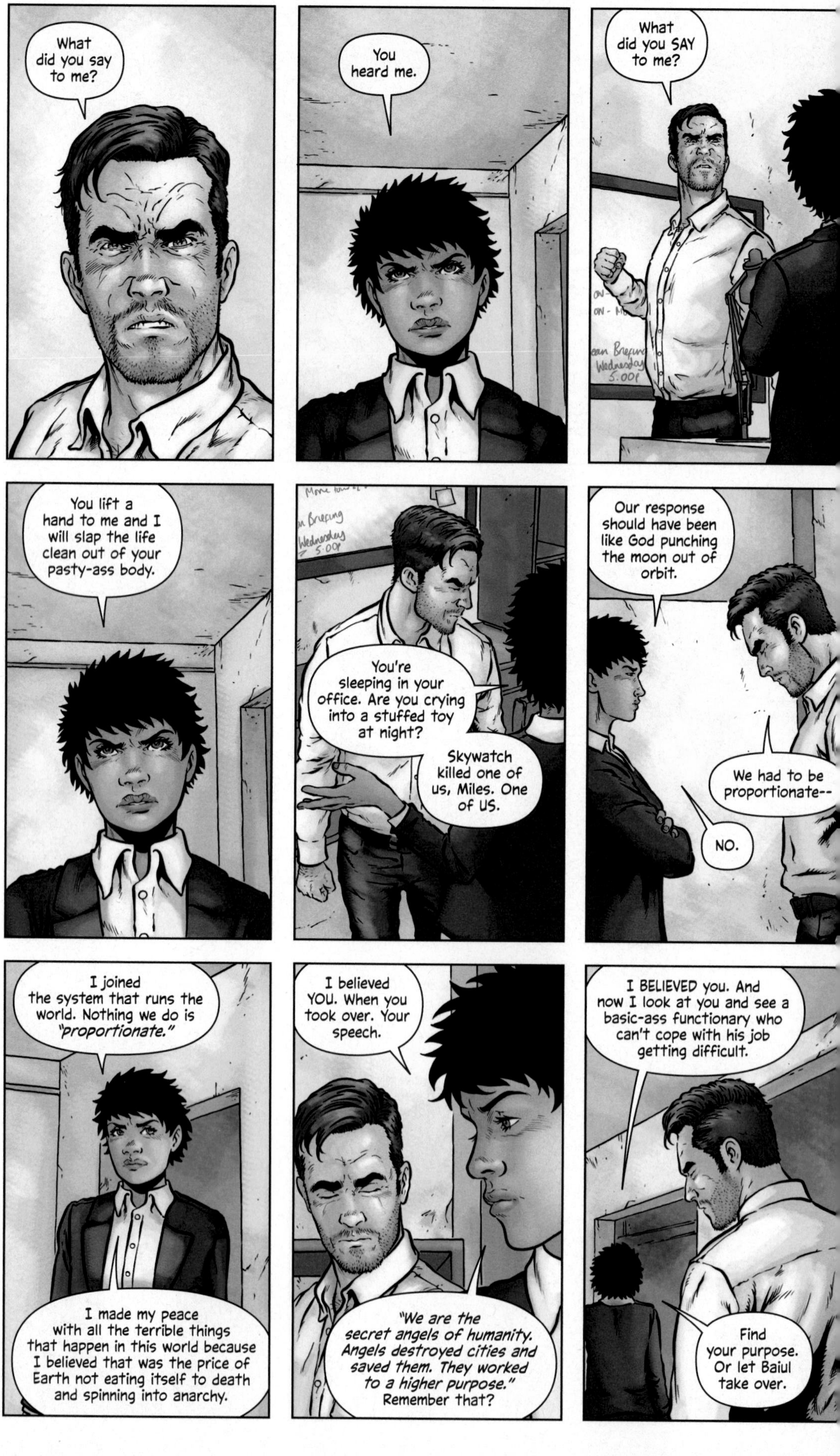

What did you say to me?
You heard me.
What did you SAY to me?
You lift a hand to me and I will slap the life clean out of your pasty-ass body.
You're sleeping in your office. Are you crying into a stuffed toy at night?
Skywatch killed one of us, Miles. One of US.
Our response should have been like God punching the moon out of orbit.
We had to be proportionate--
NO.
I joined the system that runs the world. Nothing we do is *"proportionate."*
I made my peace with all the terrible things that happen in this world because I believed that was the price of Earth not eating itself to death and spinning into anarchy.
I believed YOU. When you took over. Your speech.
"We are the secret angels of humanity. Angels destroyed cities and saved them. They worked to a higher purpose." Remember that?
I BELIEVED you. And now I look at you and see a basic-ass functionary who can't cope with his job getting difficult.
Find your purpose. Or let Baiul take over.

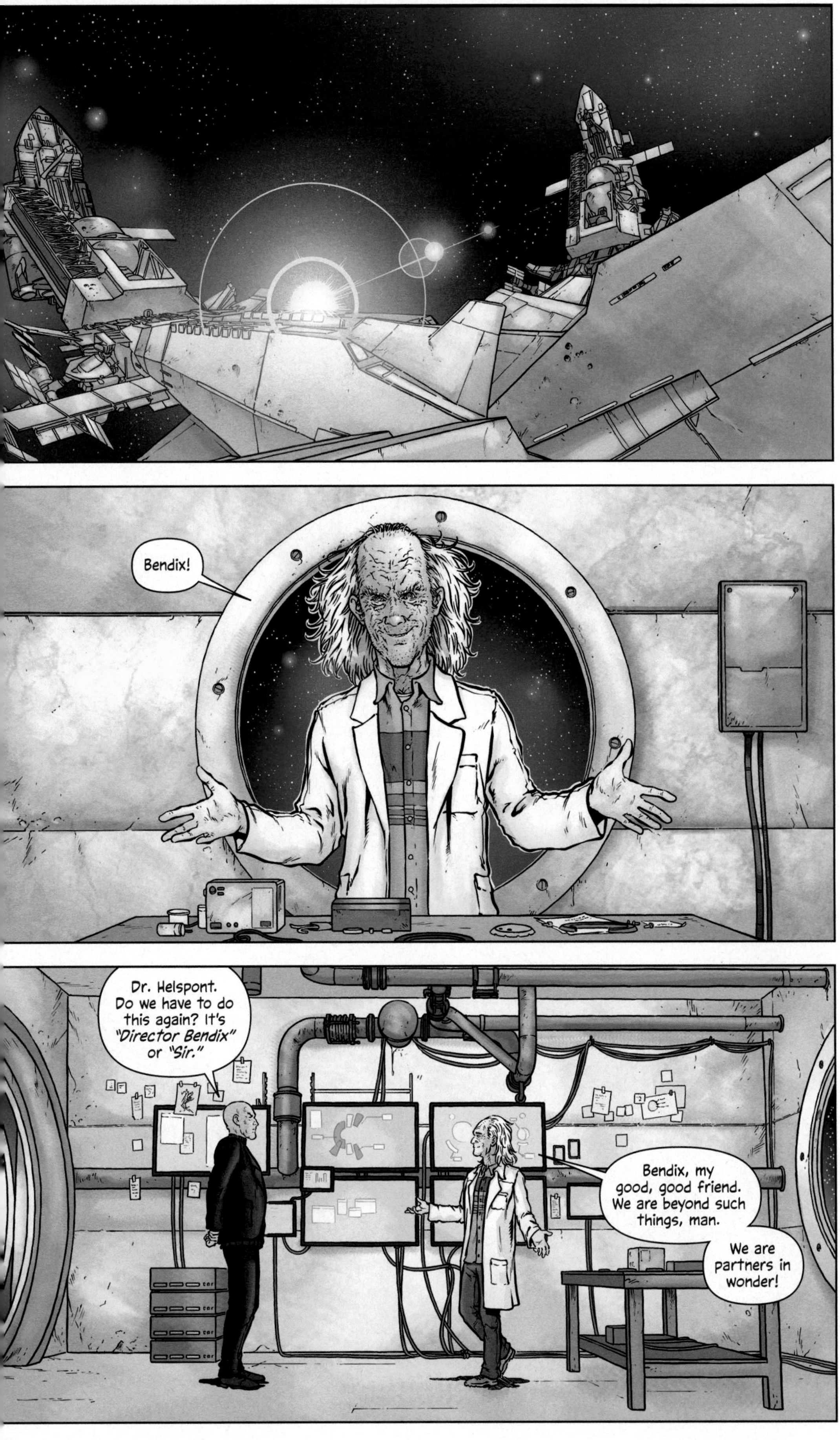
Bendix!
Dr. Helspont. Do we have to do this again? It's *"Director Bendix"* or *"Sir."*
Bendix, my good, good friend. We are beyond such things, man.
We are partners in wonder!

FFFFF.

What are you doing?

I'm processing the data from Trelane's team. Young Michael Cray's implant is fully awake. It's marvelous.

From his debrief to Trelane, I can only speculate that the mysterious electromagnetic discharge he experienced in Marlowe's office somehow kickstarted the implant.

Marvelous.

I'm here to talk about MY experimental subjects.

Yes. Scattered across the Earth, when you could have kept them right here on this fantastic space city to deploy at your whim.

Oh, yes. Great idea. Keeping experimental transhumans that could conceivably punch through buildings in a giant tin box of air in outer space.

No. I wanted them down on Earth where they couldn't hurt me.

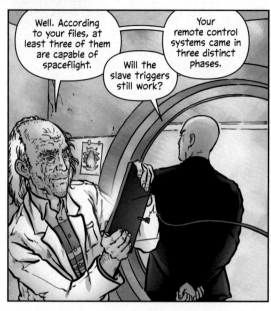

Well. According to your files, at least three of them are capable of spaceflight.

Will the slave triggers still work?

Your remote control systems came in three distinct phases.

Only the latter rollout of the system I designed will be infallible. Even the escapees will submit.

Why were you never worried about the escapee subjects?

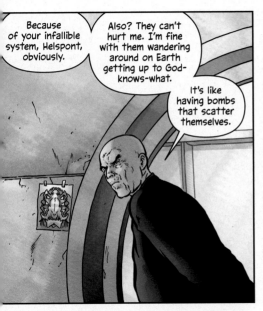

Because of your infallible system, Helspont, obviously.

Also? They can't hurt me. I'm fine with them wandering around on Earth getting up to God-knows-what.

It's like having bombs that scatter themselves.

Mmm. John Lynch had a similar thought, before he retired.

As if Thunderbook belonged to HIM.

Oh, God. Not this again.

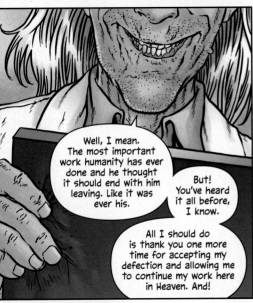

Well, I mean. The most important work humanity has ever done and he thought it should end with him leaving. Like it was ever his.

But! You've heard it all before, I know.

All I should do is thank you one more time for accepting my defection and allowing me to continue my work here in Heaven. And!

Your original control circuits were terrible.

Some of them will burn out, misfire, and cause neural damage.

This will likely induce uncontrollable violence in the subjects.

The follow-up neurochemical gateways will likely work, but they're simple. Specific guidance of the subjects may fail.

MY implants will work perfectly, and they can receive up to twenty lines of code.

Everything in Heaven is fine, Bendix.

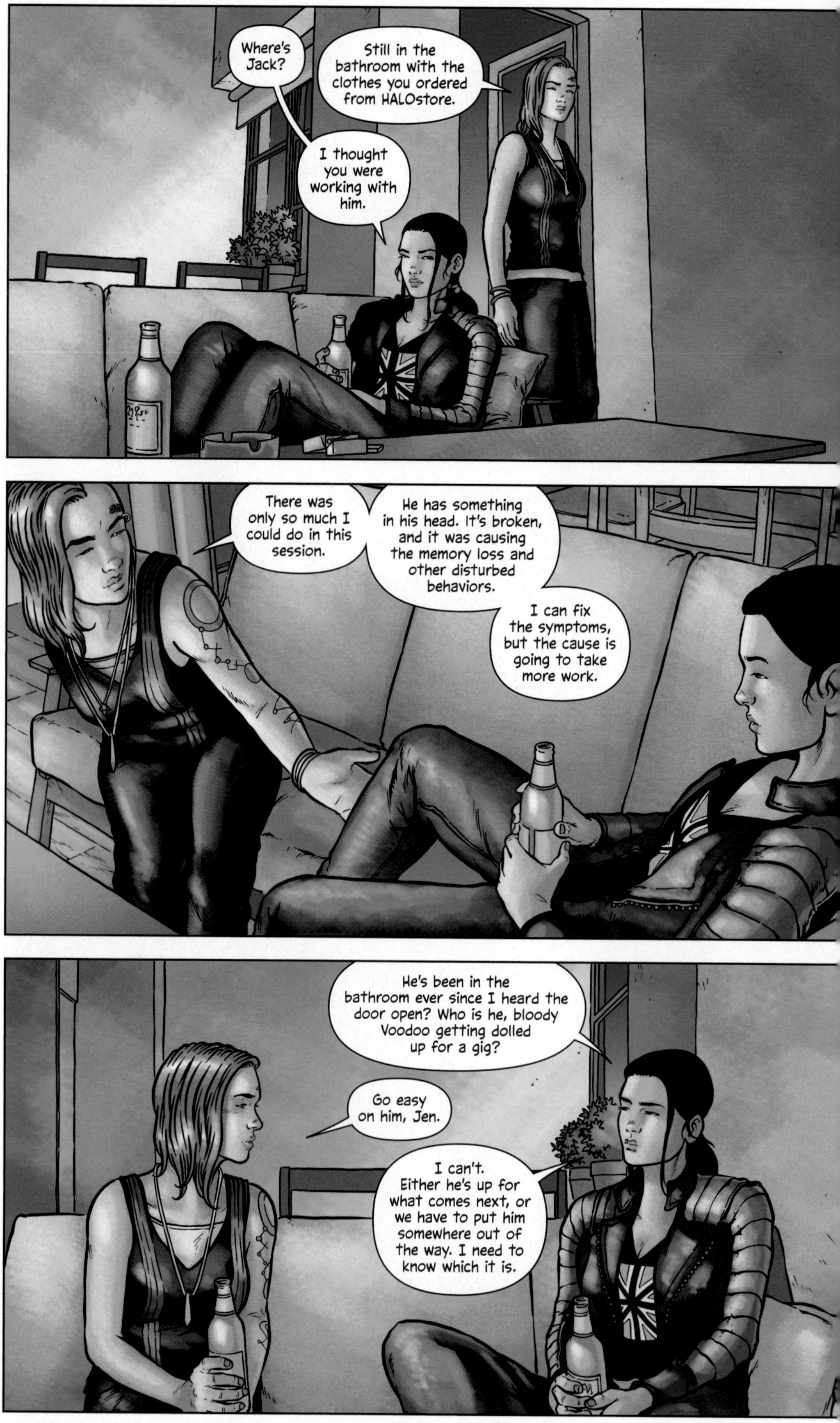
Where's Jack?
Still in the bathroom with the clothes you ordered from HALOstore.
I thought you were working with him.
There was only so much I could do in this session.
He has something in his head. It's broken, and it was causing the memory loss and other disturbed behaviors.
I can fix the symptoms, but the cause is going to take more work.
He's been in the bathroom ever since I heard the door open? Who is he, bloody Voodoo getting dolled up for a gig?
Go easy on him, Jen.
I can't. Either he's up for what comes next, or we have to put him somewhere out of the way. I need to know which it is.

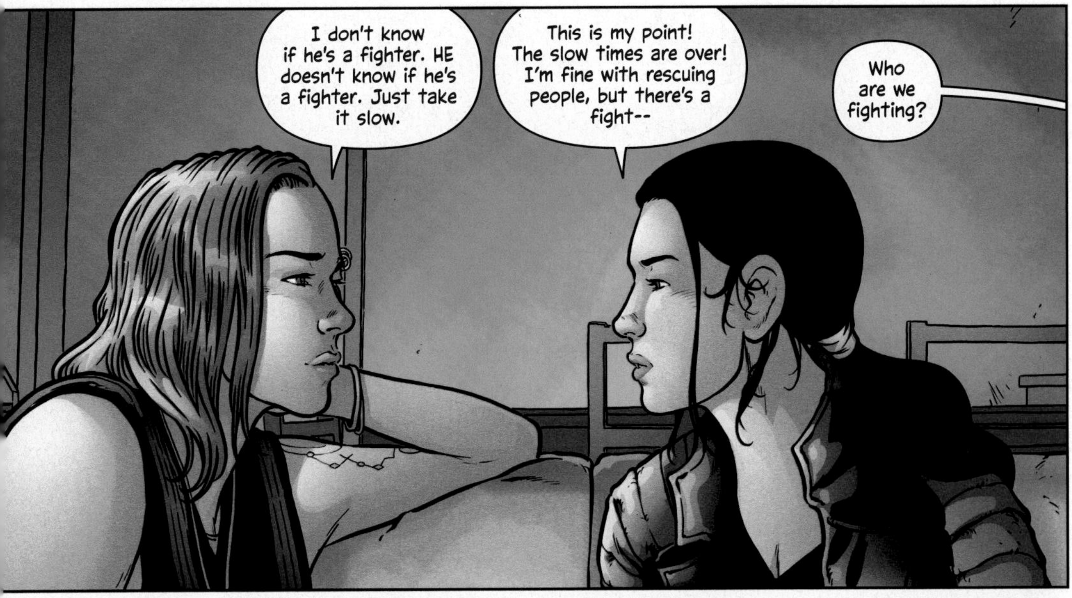
I don't know if he's a fighter. HE doesn't know if he's a fighter. Just take it slow.
This is my point! The slow times are over! I'm fine with rescuing people, but there's a fight--
Who are we fighting?

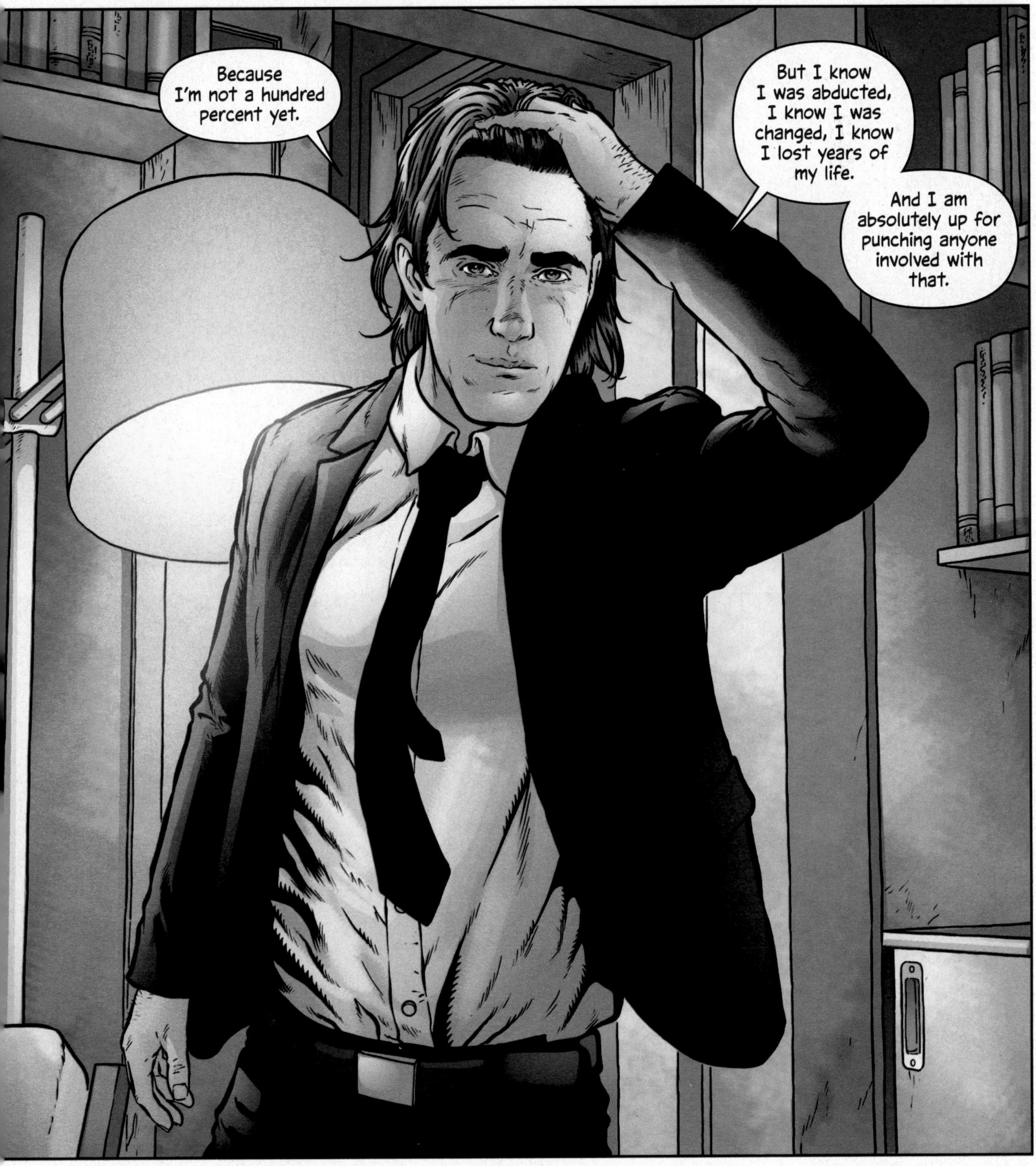
Because I'm not a hundred percent yet.
But I know I was abducted, I know I was changed, I know I lost years of my life.
And I am absolutely up for punching anyone involved with that.

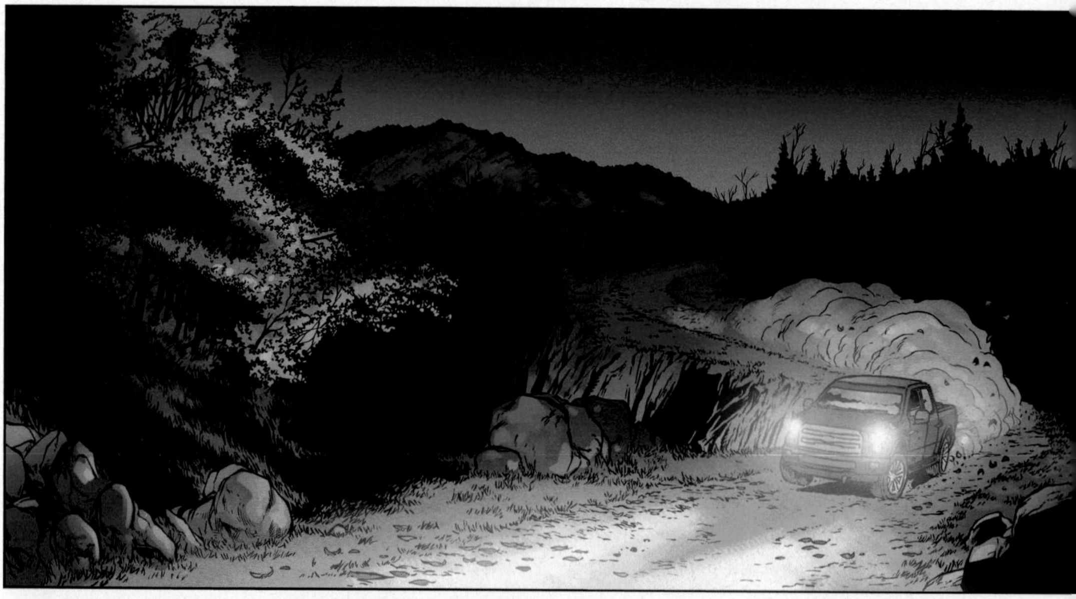

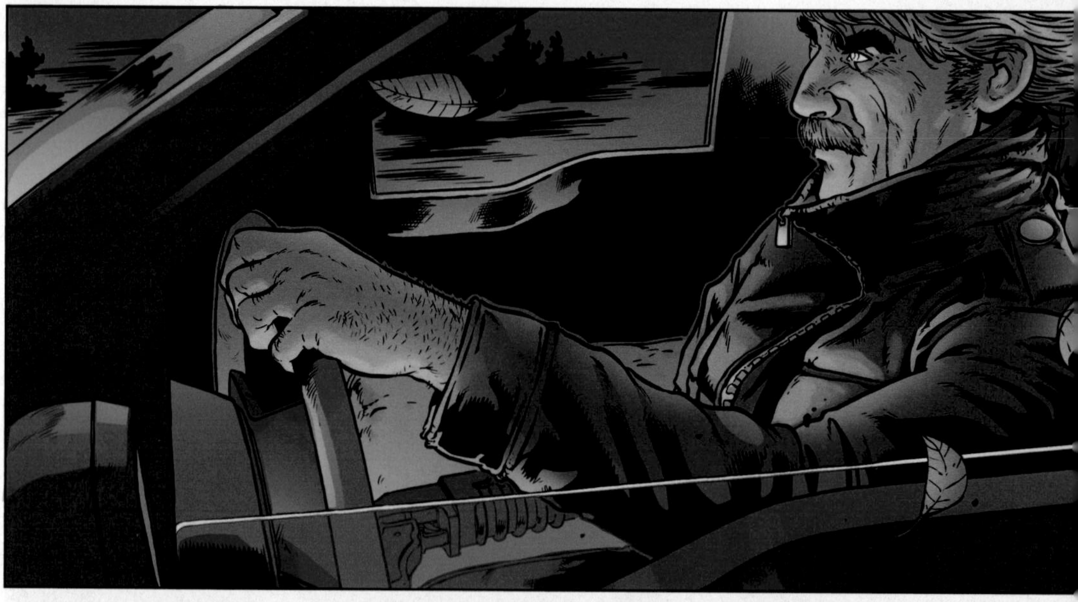

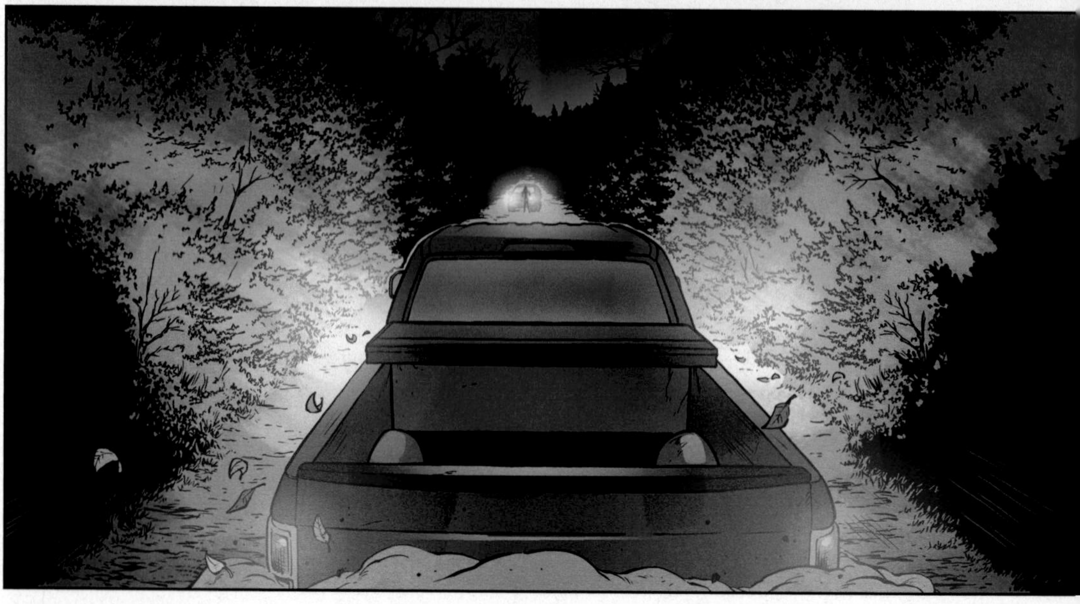

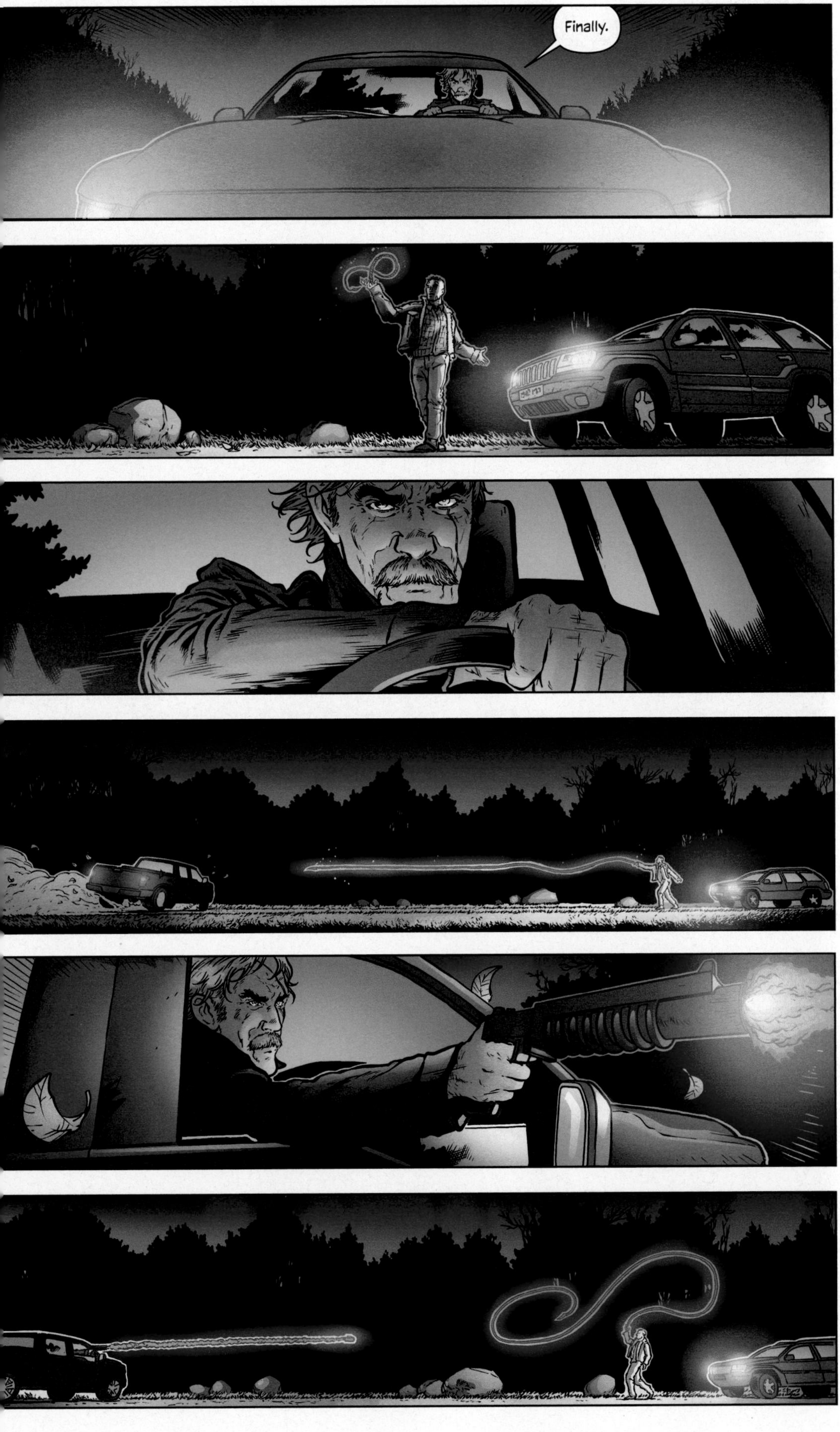
Finally.

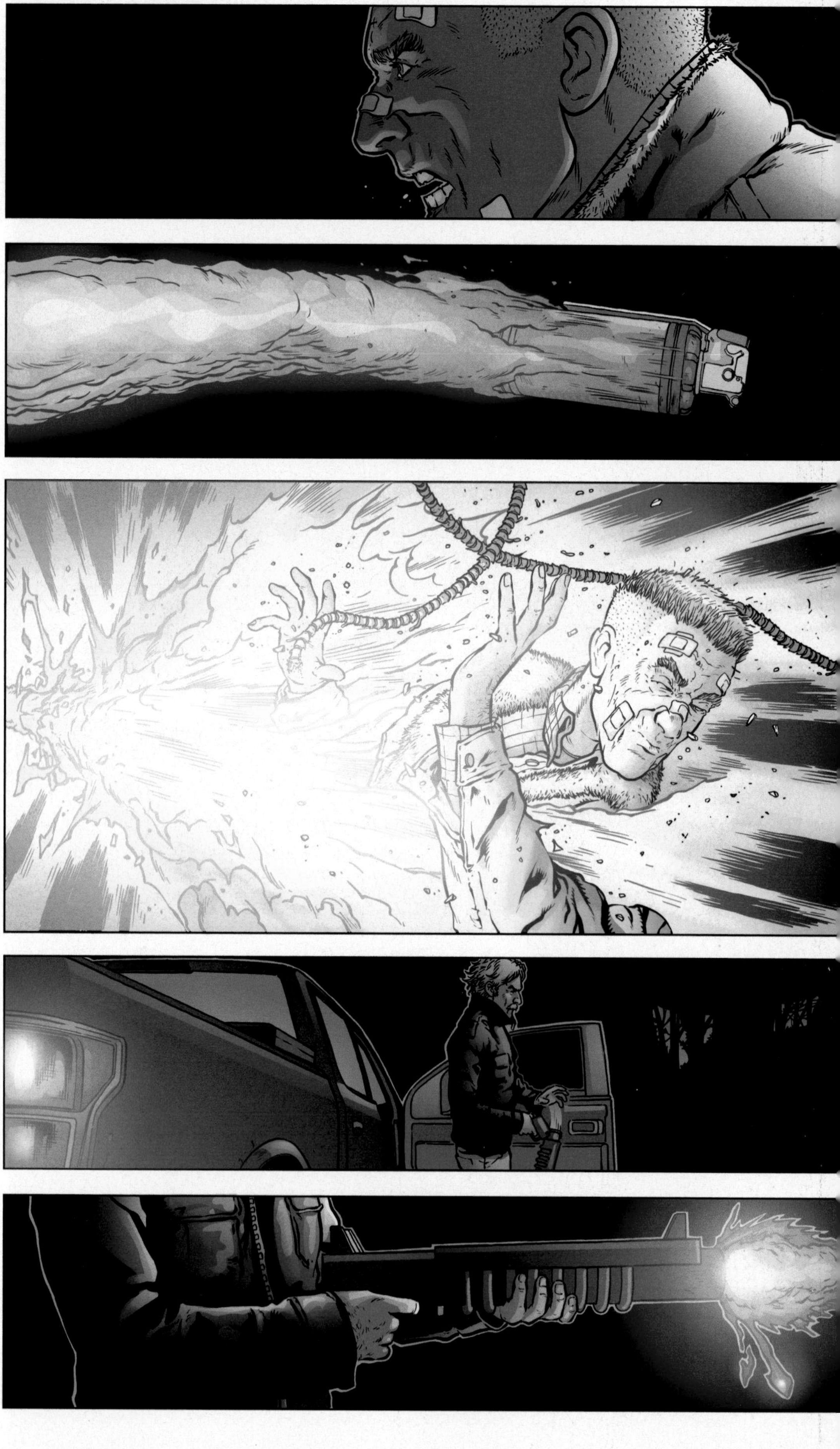

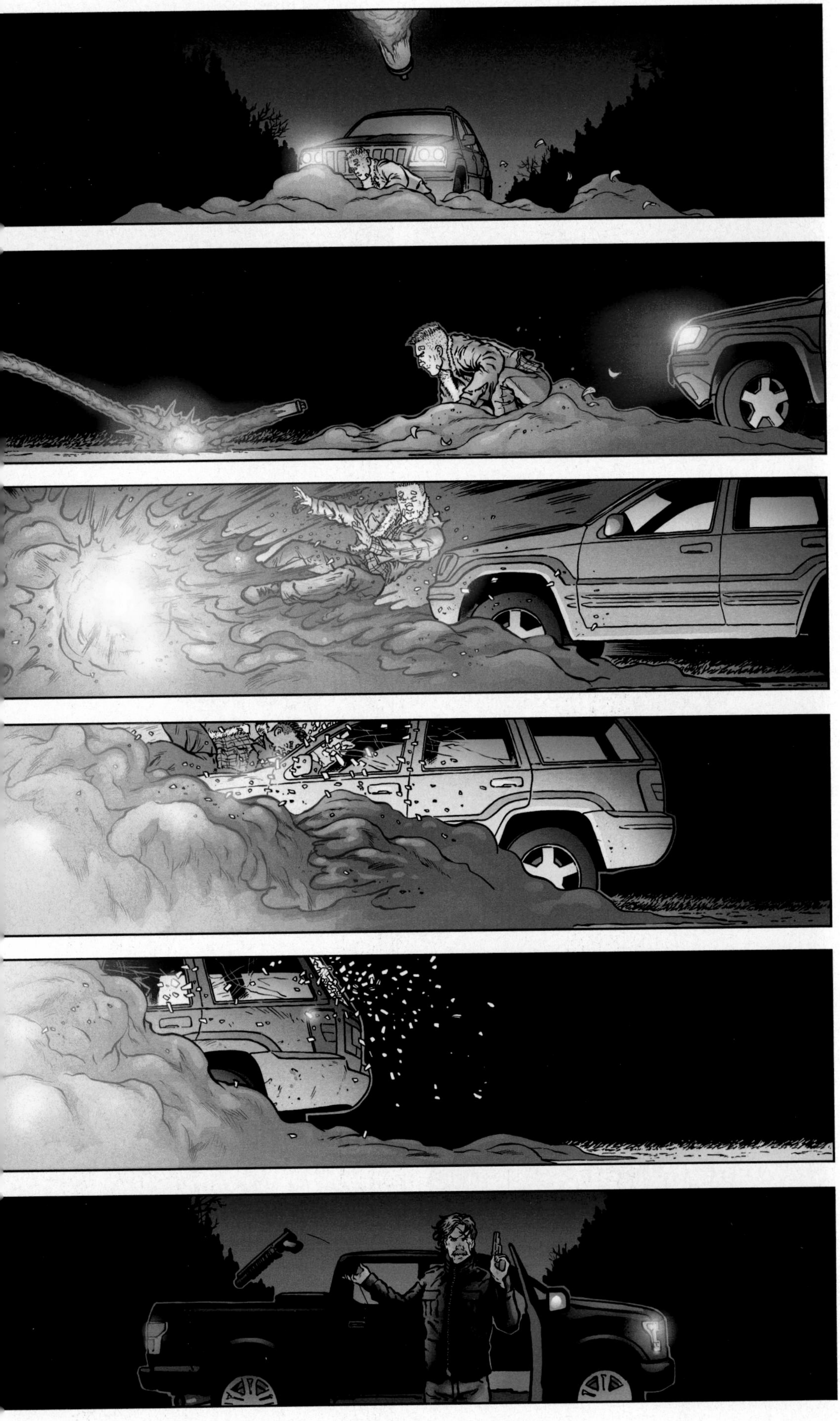

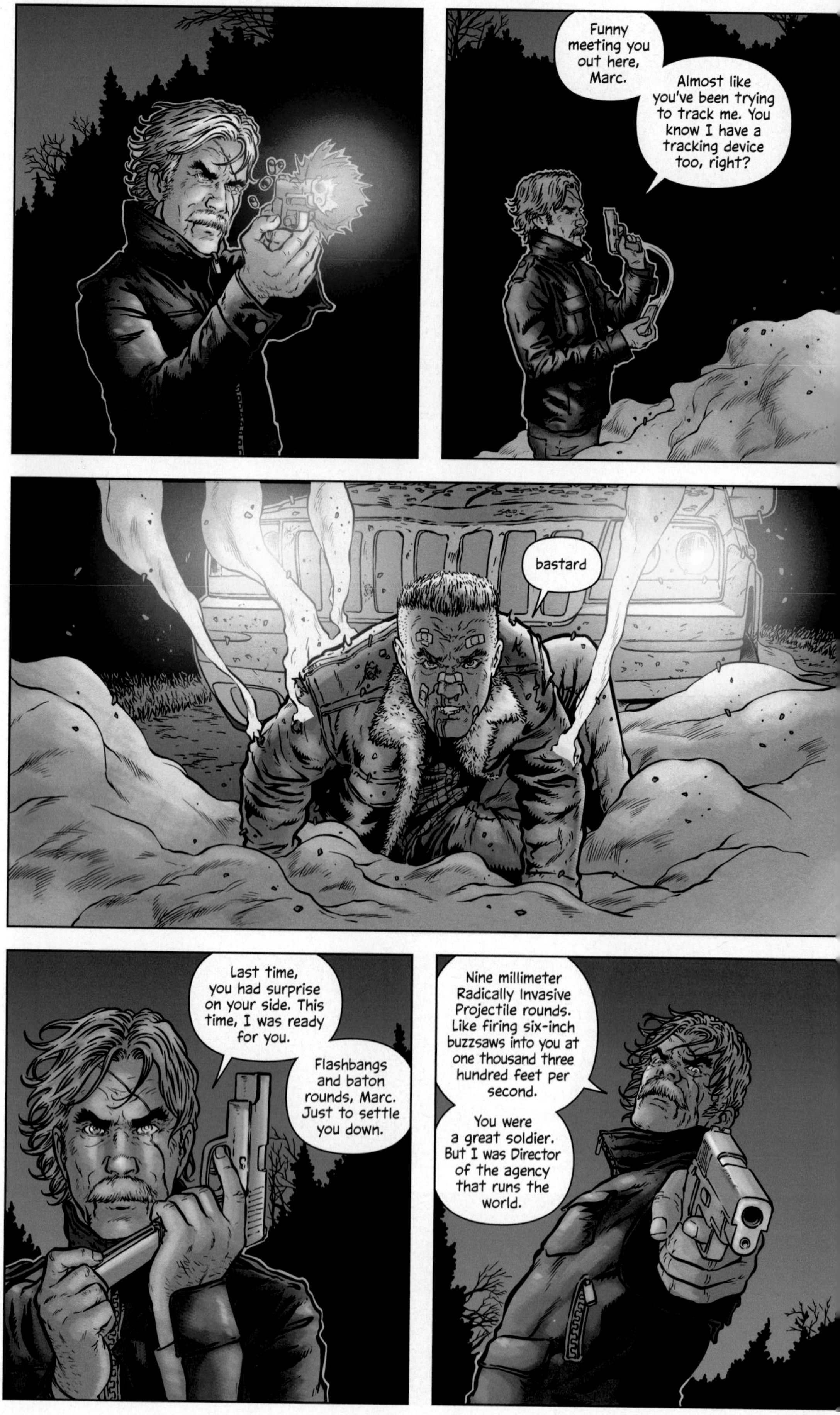
Funny meeting you out here, Marc.
Almost like you've been trying to track me. You know I have a tracking device too, right?
bastard
Last time, you had surprise on your side. This time, I was ready for you.
Flashbangs and baton rounds, Marc. Just to settle you down.
Nine millimeter Radically Invasive Projectile rounds. Like firing six-inch buzzsaws into you at one thousand three hundred feet per second.
You were a great soldier. But I was Director of the agency that runs the world.

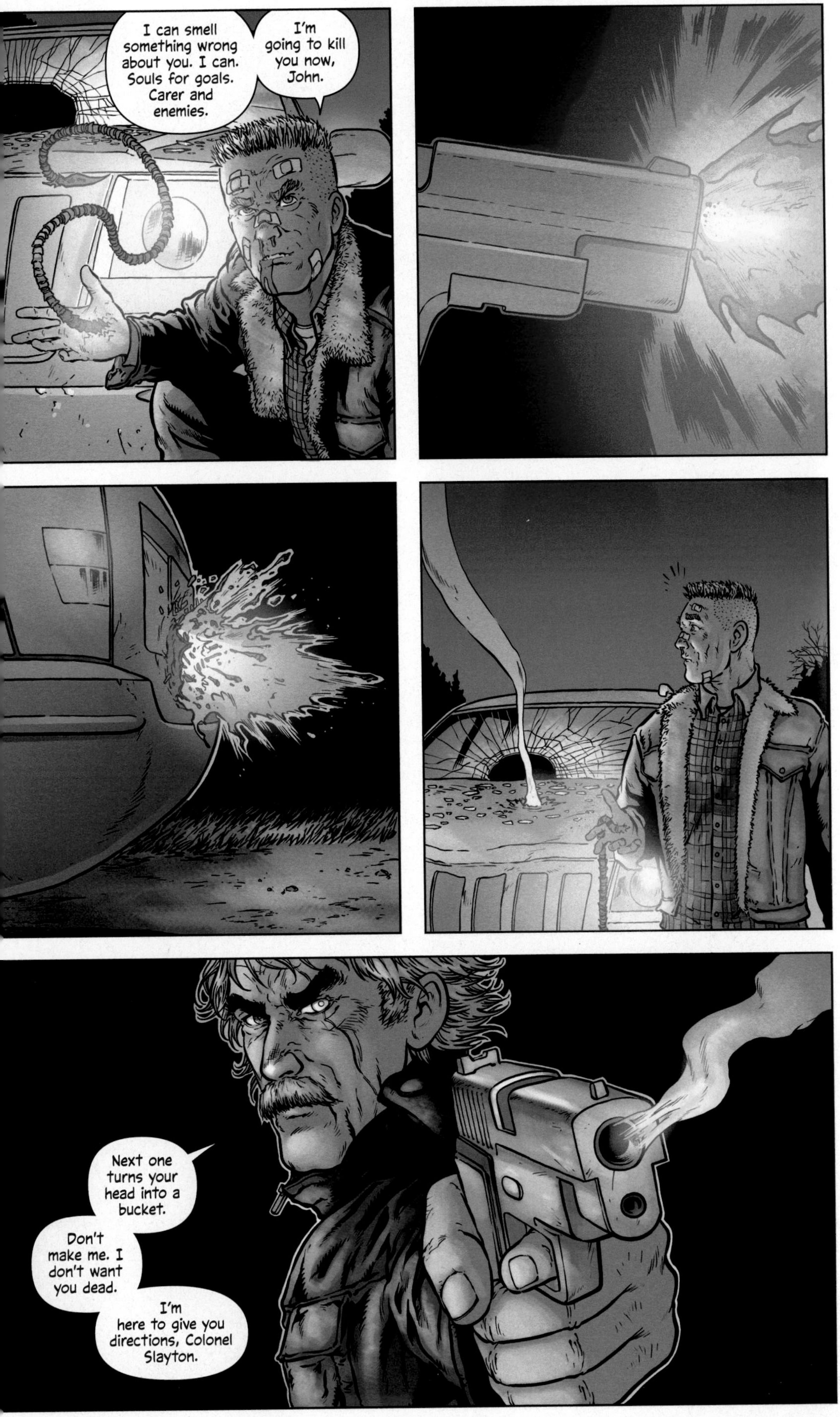
I can smell something wrong about you. I can. Souls for goals. Carer and enemies.
I'm going to kill you now, John.
Next one turns your head into a bucket.
Don't make me. I don't want you dead.
I'm here to give you directions, Colonel Slayton.

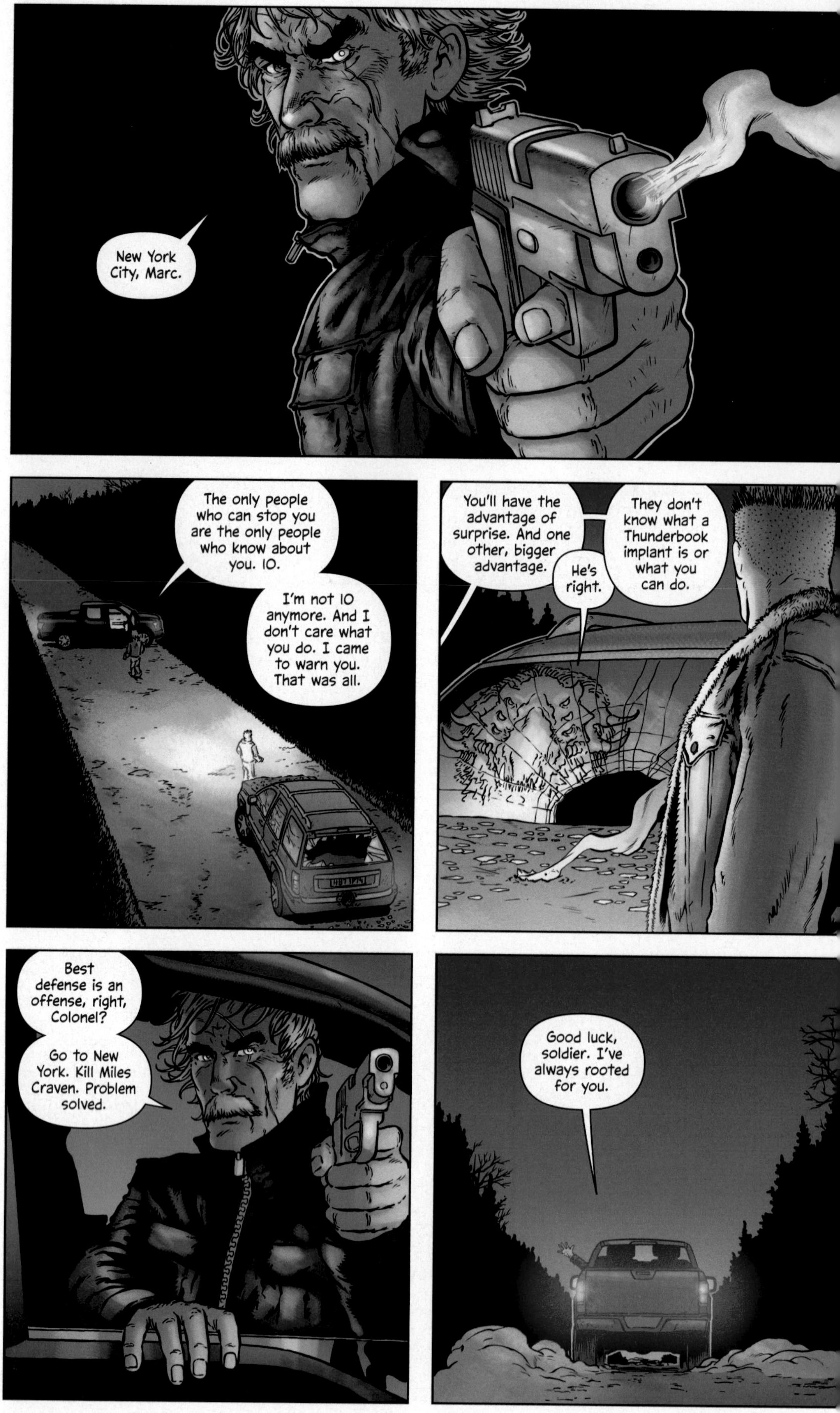
New York City, Marc.
The only people who can stop you are the only people who know about you. 10.
I'm not 10 anymore. And I don't care what you do. I came to warn you. That was all.
You'll have the advantage of surprise. And one other, bigger advantage.
He's right.
They don't know what a Thunderbook implant is or what you can do.
Best defense is an offense, right, Colonel?
Go to New York. Kill Miles Craven. Problem solved.
Good luck, soldier. I've always rooted for you.

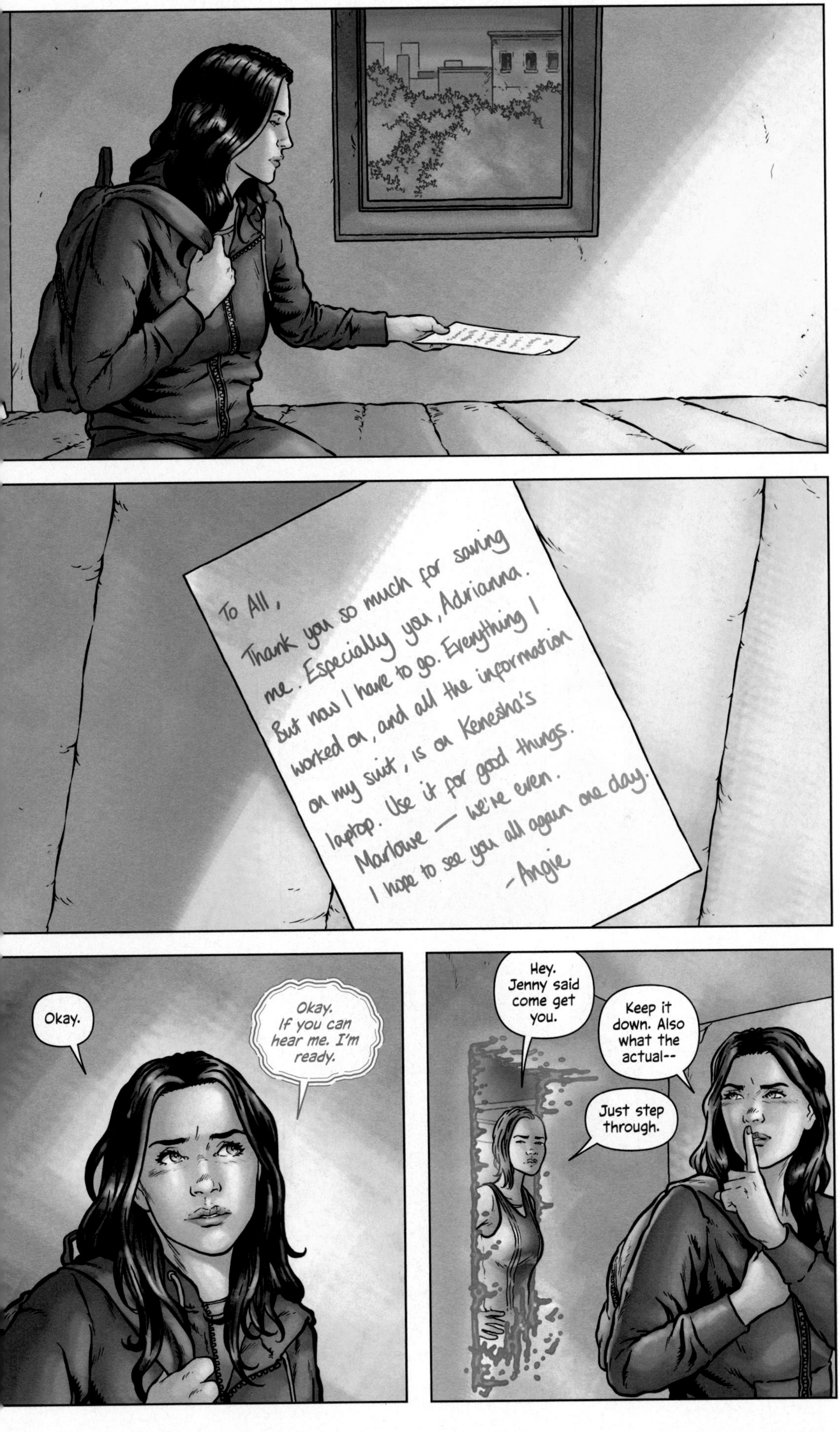
To All,
Thank you so much for saving me. Especially you, Adrianna. But now I have to go. Everything I worked on, and all the information on my suit, is on Kenesha's laptop. Use it for good things. Marlowe — we're even. I hope to see you all again one day.
-Angie
Okay.
Okay. If you can hear me. I'm ready.
Hey. Jenny said come get you.
Keep it down. Also what the actual--
Just step through.

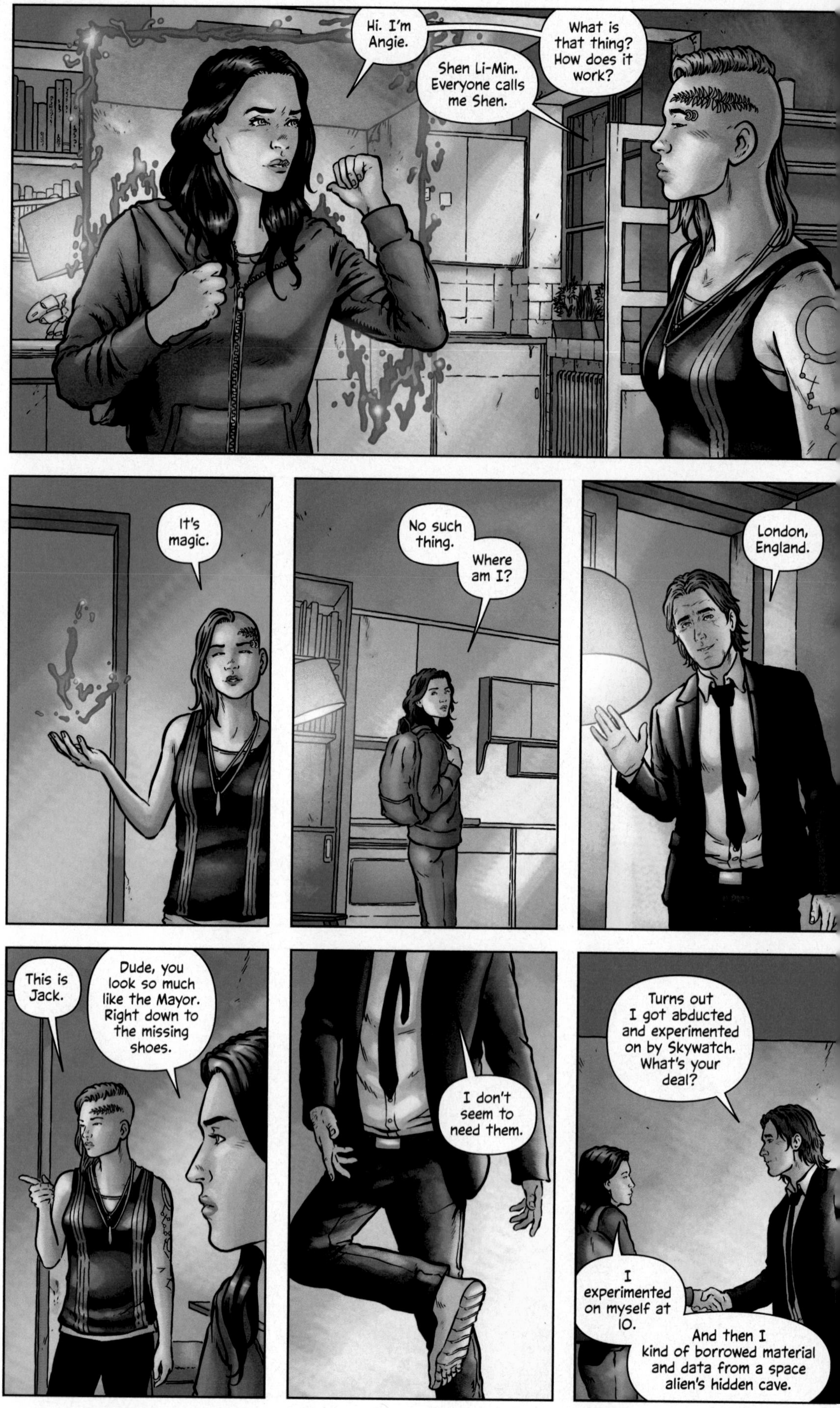

Hi. I'm Angie.
What is that thing? How does it work?
Shen Li-Min. Everyone calls me Shen.
It's magic.
No such thing.
Where am I?
London, England.
This is Jack.
Dude, you look so much like the Mayor. Right down to the missing shoes.
I don't seem to need them.
Turns out I got abducted and experimented on by Skywatch. What's your deal?
I experimented on myself at 10.
And then I kind of borrowed material and data from a space alien's hidden cave.

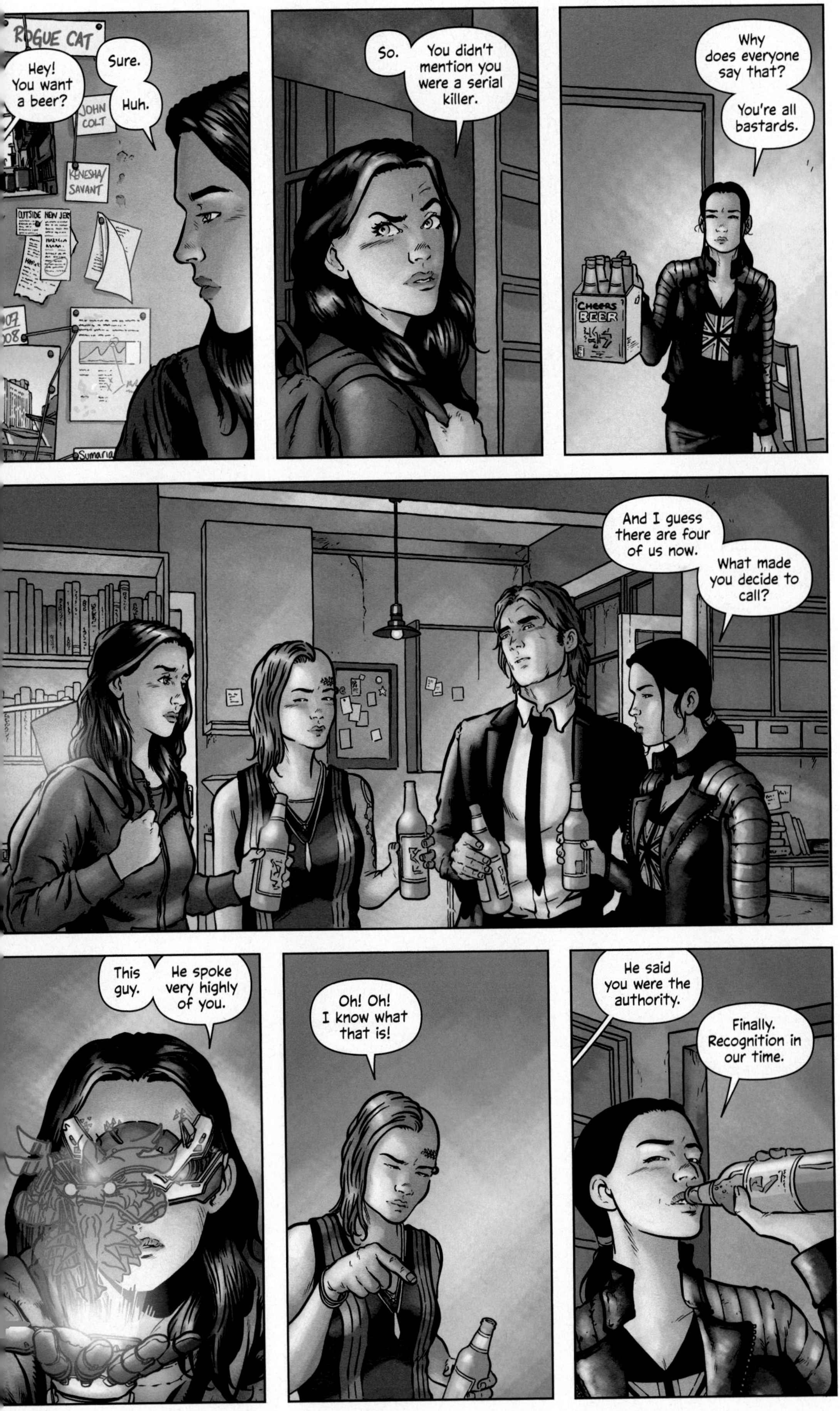
ROGUE CAT
Hey! You want a beer?
Sure.
Huh.
JOHN COLT
KENESHA/ SAVANT
OUTSIDE NEW JERS
Sumaria
So.
You didn't mention you were a serial killer.
Why does everyone say that?
You're all bastards.
CHEERS BEER
And I guess there are four of us now.
What made you decide to call?
This guy.
He spoke very highly of you.
Oh! Oh! I know what that is!
He said you were the authority.
Finally. Recognition in our time.

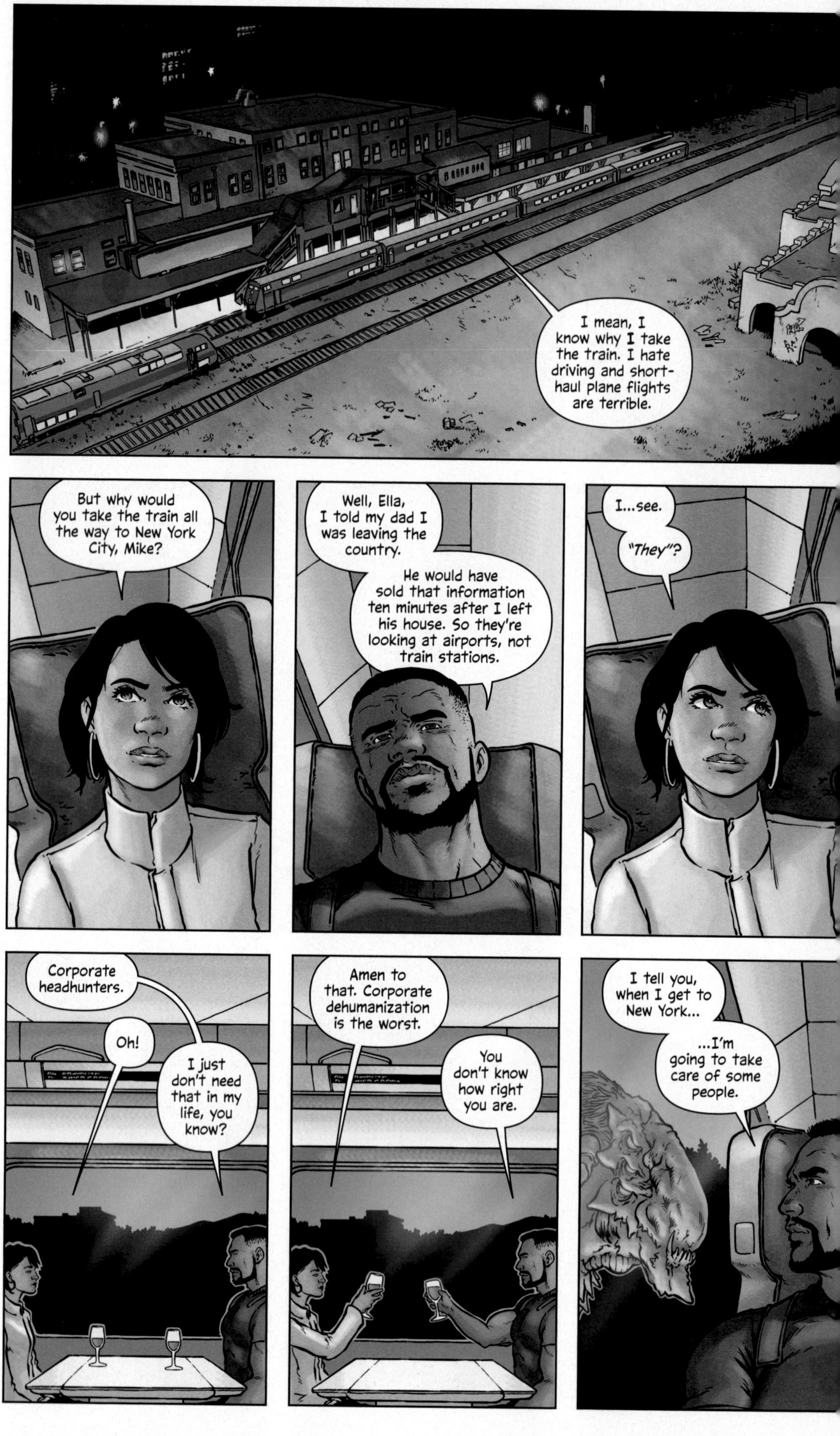
I mean, I know why I take the train. I hate driving and short-haul plane flights are terrible.
But why would you take the train all the way to New York City, Mike?
Well, Ella, I told my dad I was leaving the country.
He would have sold that information ten minutes after I left his house. So they're looking at airports, not train stations.
I...see.
"They"?
Corporate headhunters.
Oh!
I just don't need that in my life, you know?
Amen to that. Corporate dehumanization is the worst.
You don't know how right you are.
I tell you, when I get to New York...
...I'm going to take care of some people.

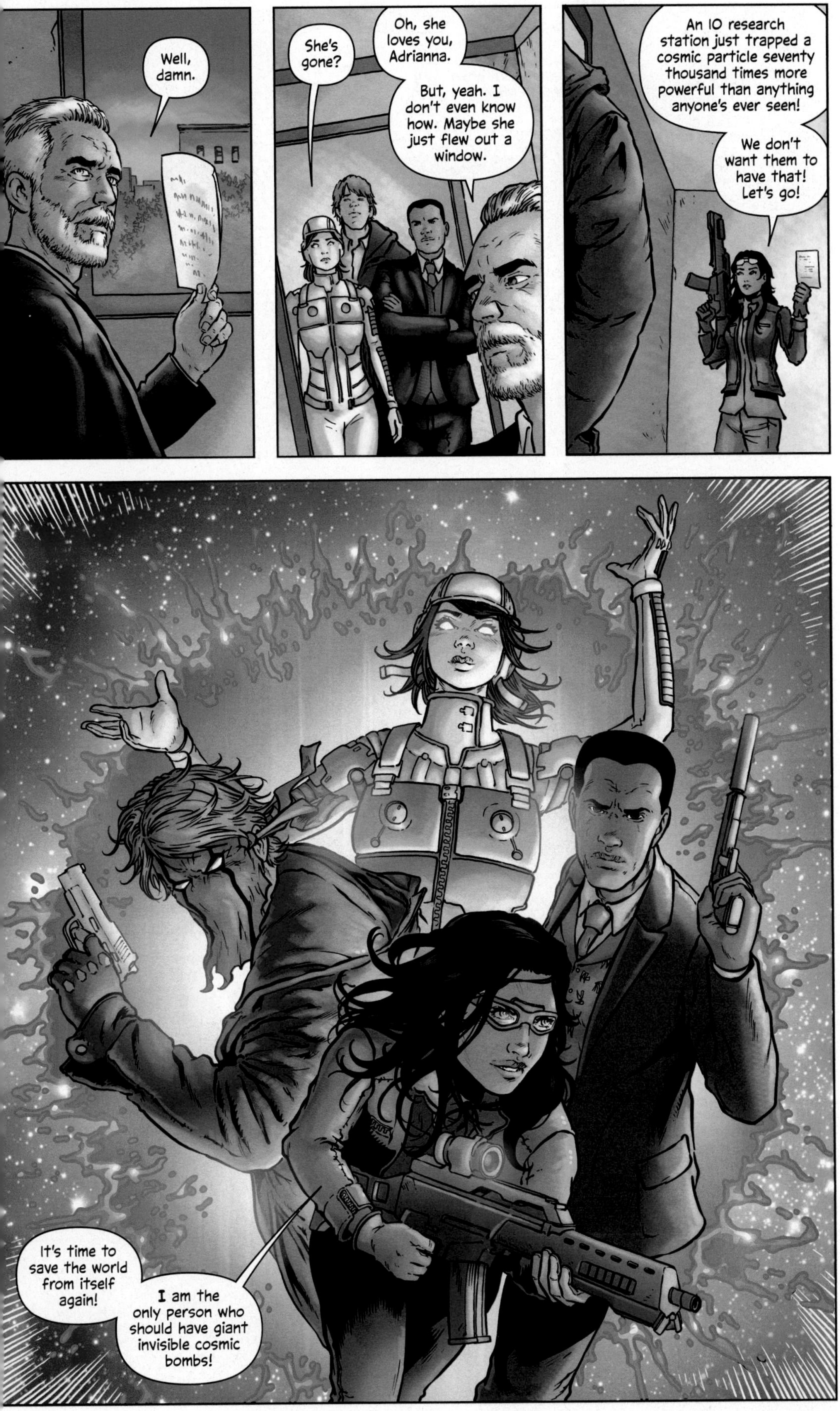

Well, damn.
She's gone?
Oh, she loves you, Adrianna.
But, yeah. I don't even know how. Maybe she just flew out a window.
An IO research station just trapped a cosmic particle seventy thousand times more powerful than anything anyone's ever seen!
We don't want them to have that! Let's go!
It's time to save the world from itself again!
I am the only person who should have giant invisible cosmic bombs!

Why is English so stupidly hard? I always sound like a prophet with brain damage when I speak it.

"We protect you and we." English makes no damn sense.

Now French. That's a language. There is no sound in French that is not designed to be beautiful. That's how you do a language.

Oh. Hey. Isn't that Zannah of the Khera? She can't hear us, can she?

Nah. I'm disguising us and overlaying noise. I don't want to have to speak to her in English. It'd ruin my night. Besides, I don't like her.

They hate us, I know, I get it. But Zannah works with the humans.

Listen, umpty-thousand years ago Emp says, I don't agree with the Kheran plan to turn this planet into a slave camp, right?

And it's ZANNAH who goes "Die in a fire, Emp" and takes off.

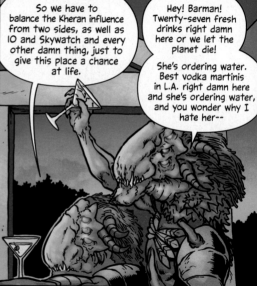

So we have to balance the Kheran influence from two sides, as well as IO and Skywatch and every other damn thing, just to give this place a chance at life.

Hey! Barman! Twenty-seven fresh drinks right damn here or we let the planet die!

She's ordering water. Best vodka martinis in L.A. right damn here and she's ordering water, and you wonder why I hate her--

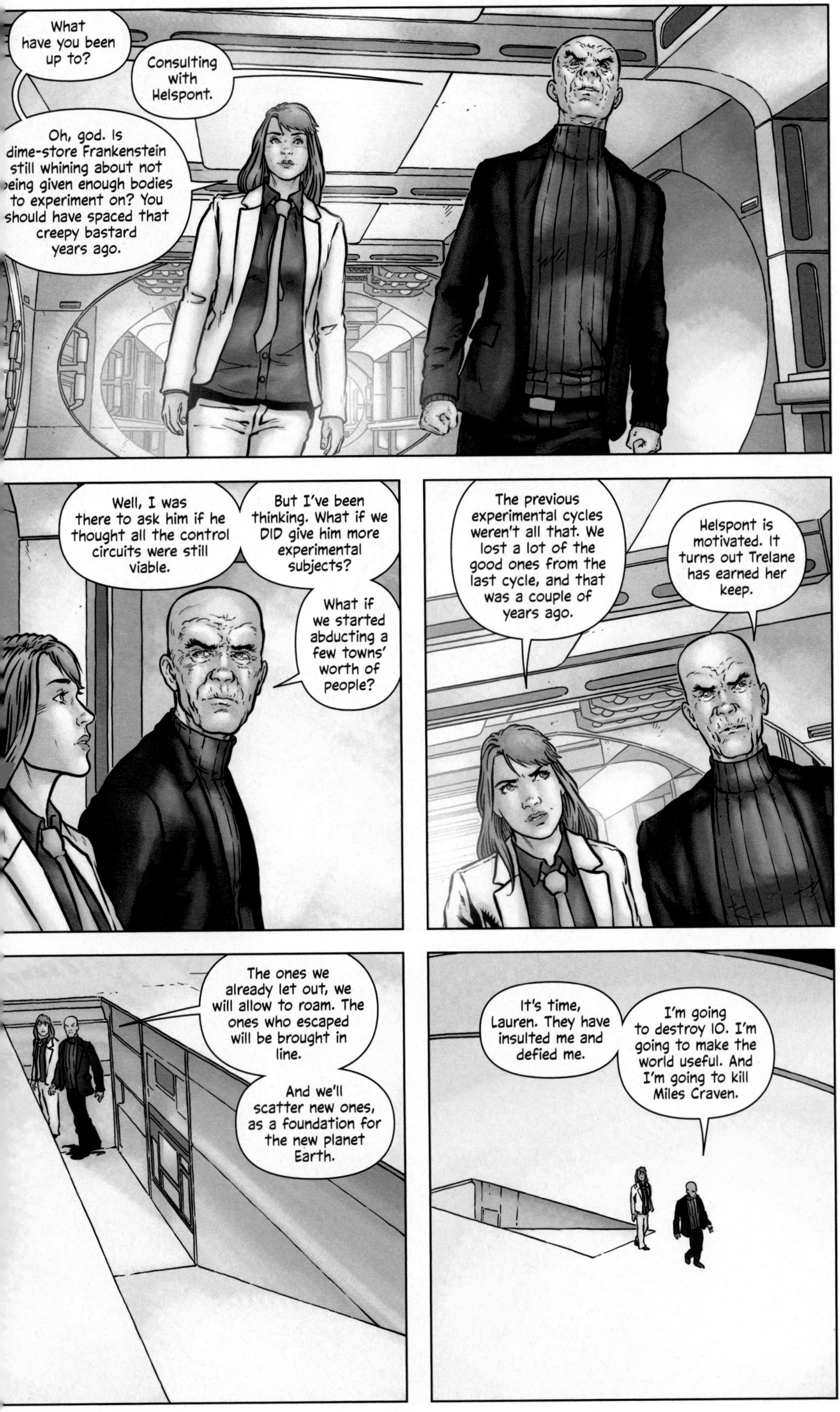
What have you been up to?
Consulting with Helspont.
Oh, god. Is dime-store Frankenstein still whining about not being given enough bodies to experiment on? You should have spaced that creepy bastard years ago.
Well, I was there to ask him if he thought all the control circuits were still viable.
But I've been thinking. What if we DID give him more experimental subjects?
What if we started abducting a few towns' worth of people?
The previous experimental cycles weren't all that. We lost a lot of the good ones from the last cycle, and that was a couple of years ago.
Helspont is motivated. It turns out Trelane has earned her keep.
The ones we already let out, we will allow to roam. The ones who escaped will be brought in line.
And we'll scatter new ones, as a foundation for the new planet Earth.
It's time, Lauren. They have insulted me and defied me.
I'm going to destroy IO. I'm going to make the world useful. And I'm going to kill Miles Craven.

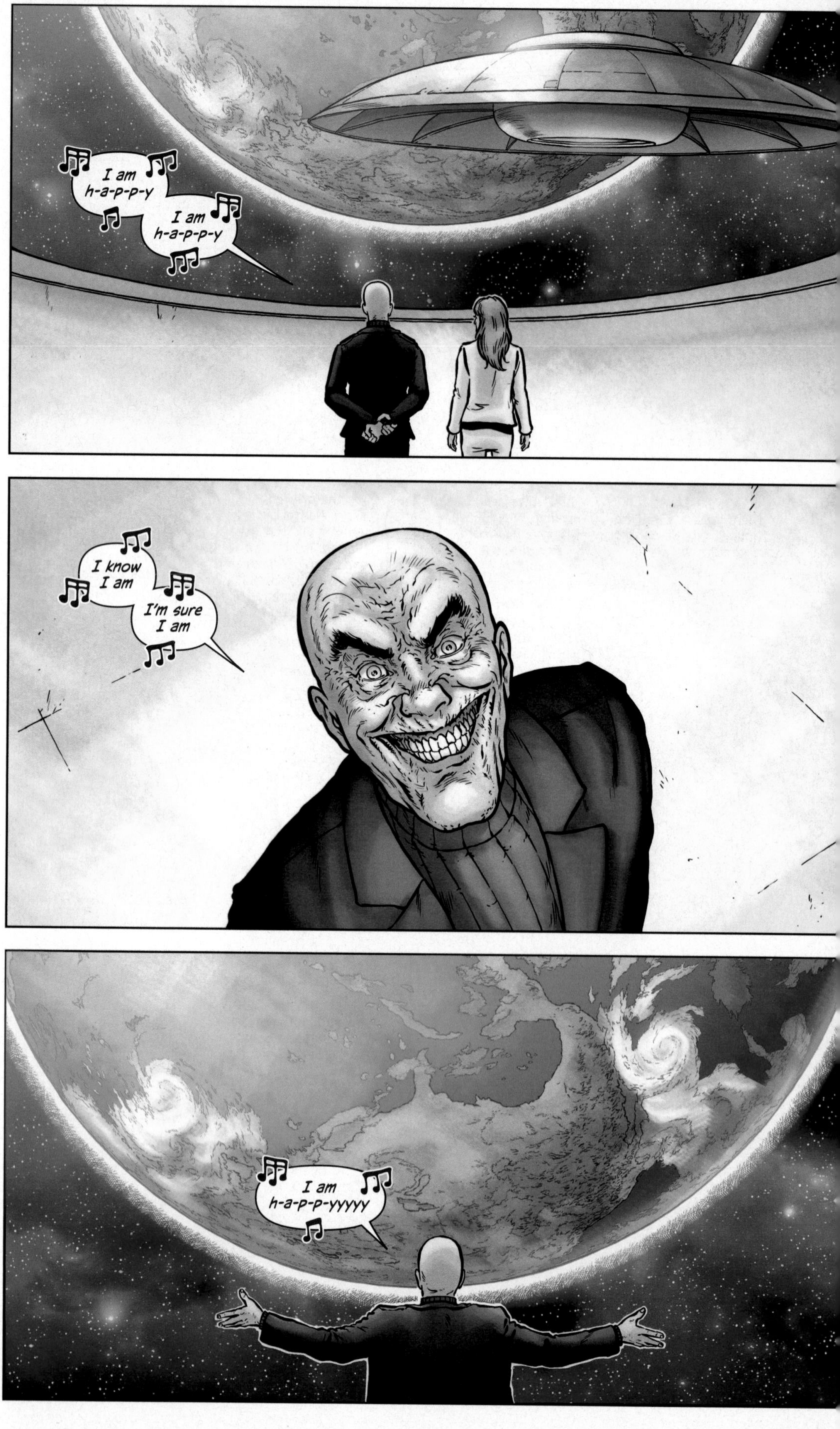
I am h-a-p-p-y
I am h-a-p-p-y
I know I am
I'm sure I am
I am h-a-p-p-yyyyy

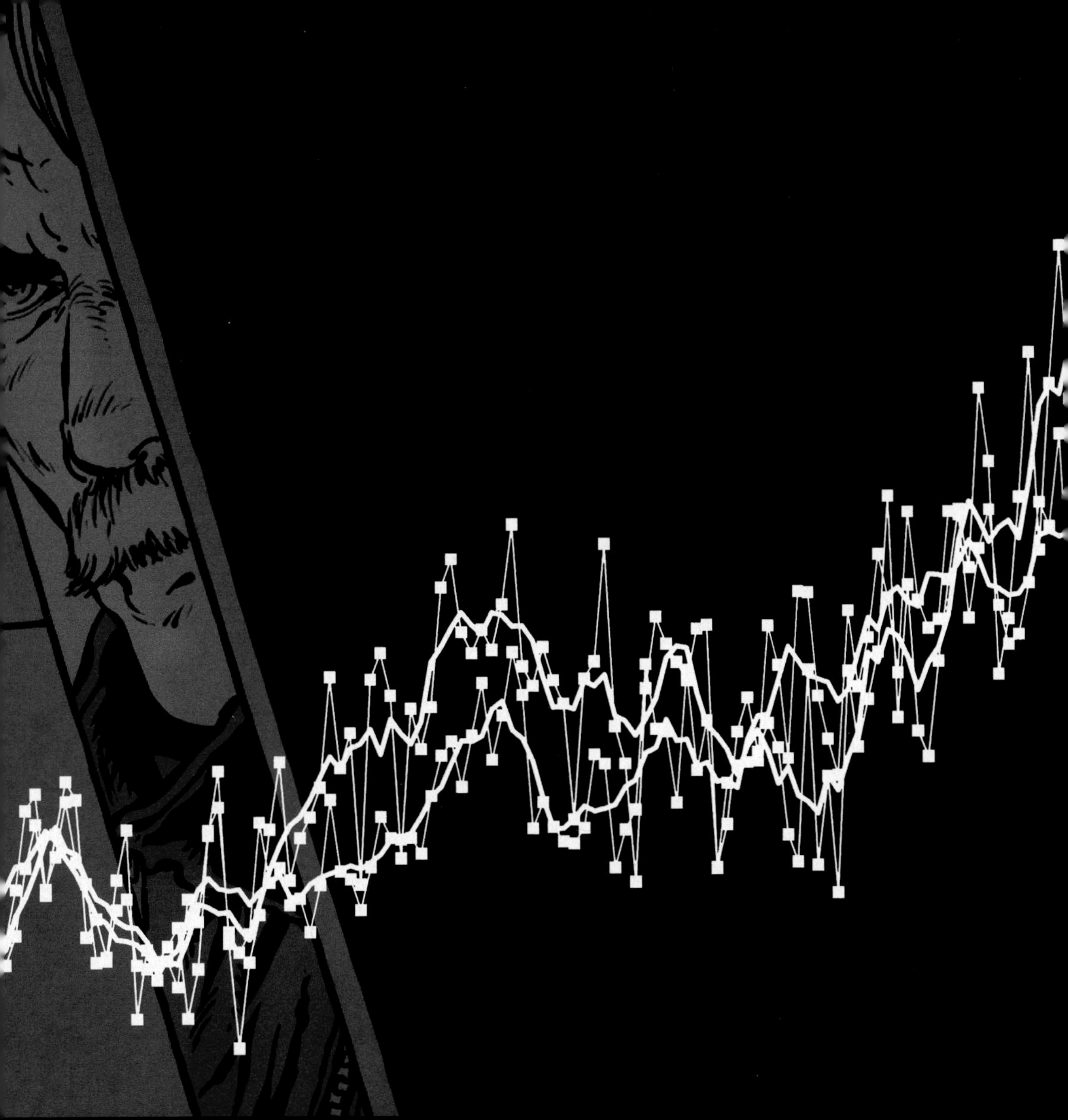

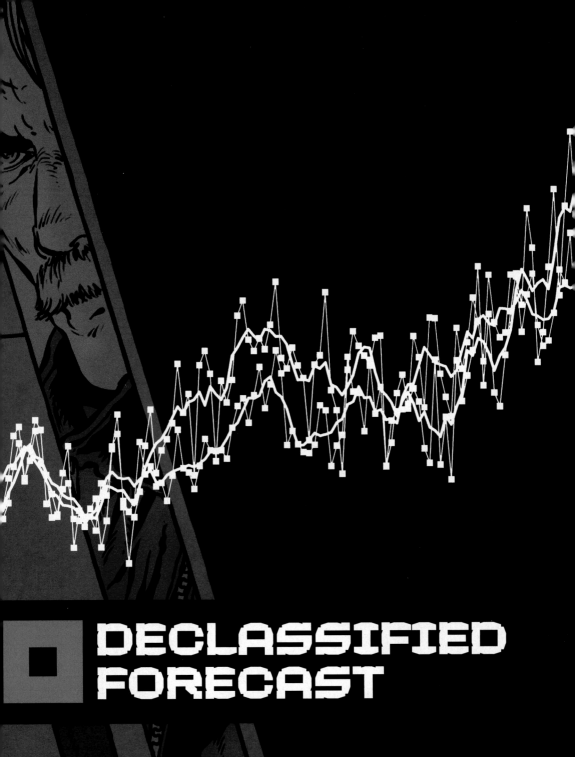

DECLASSIFIED FORECAST

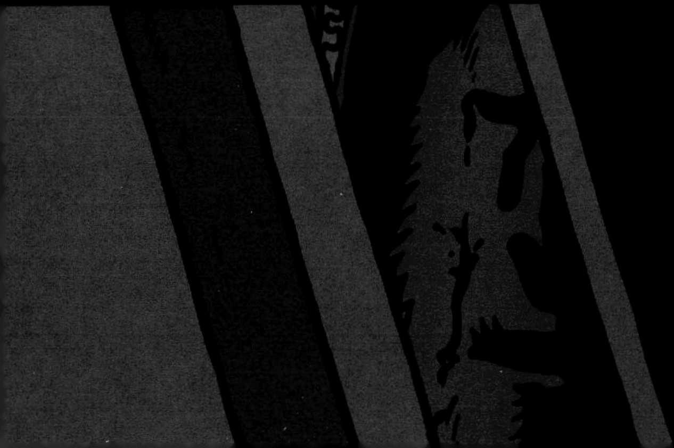

THE WILD STORM #13
Variant Cover by
FRANCESCO FRANCAVILLA

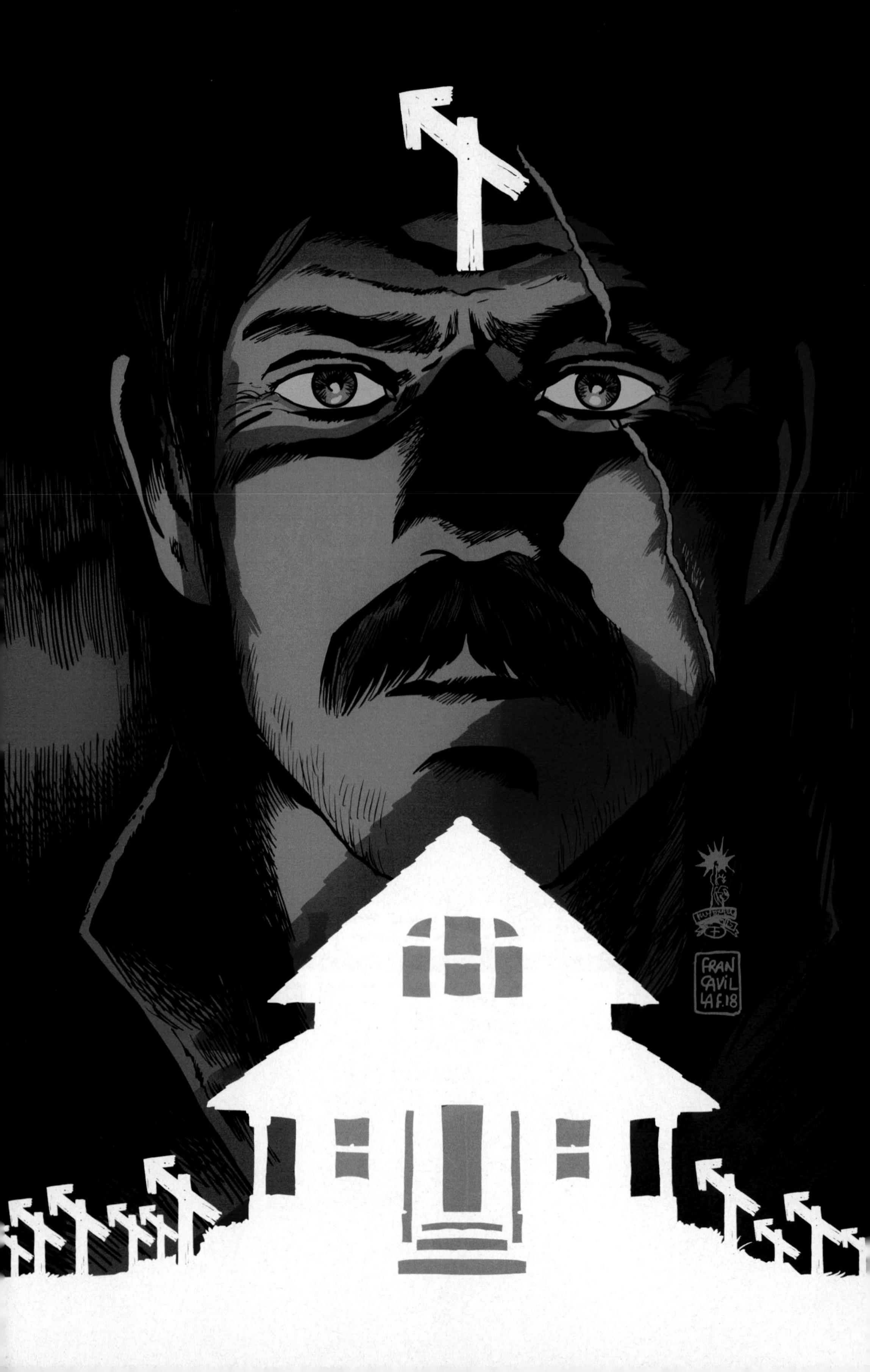

FRAN
CAVIL
LA F.18

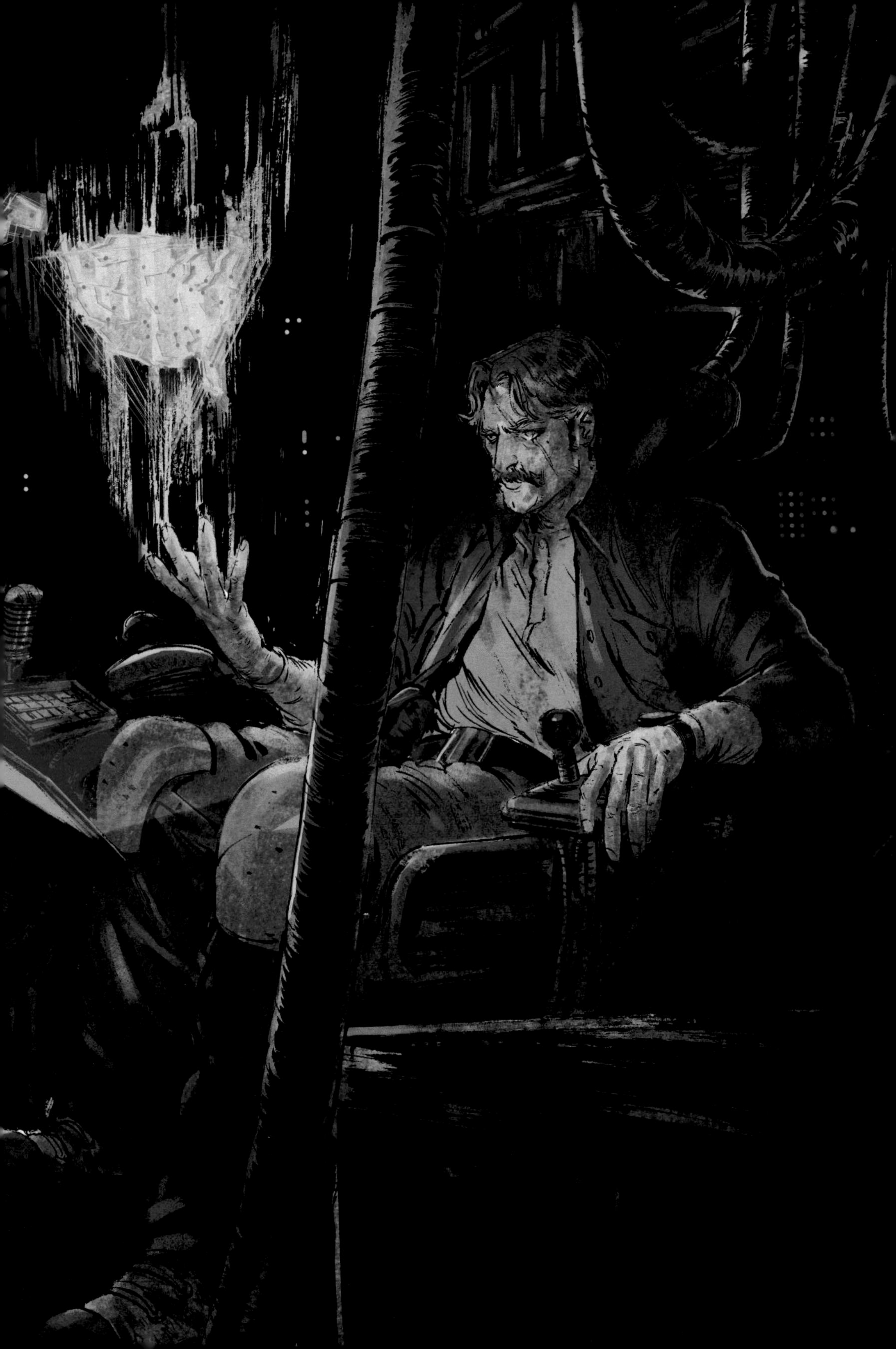

THE WILD STORM #15
Variant Cover by
VALENTINE DE LANDRO

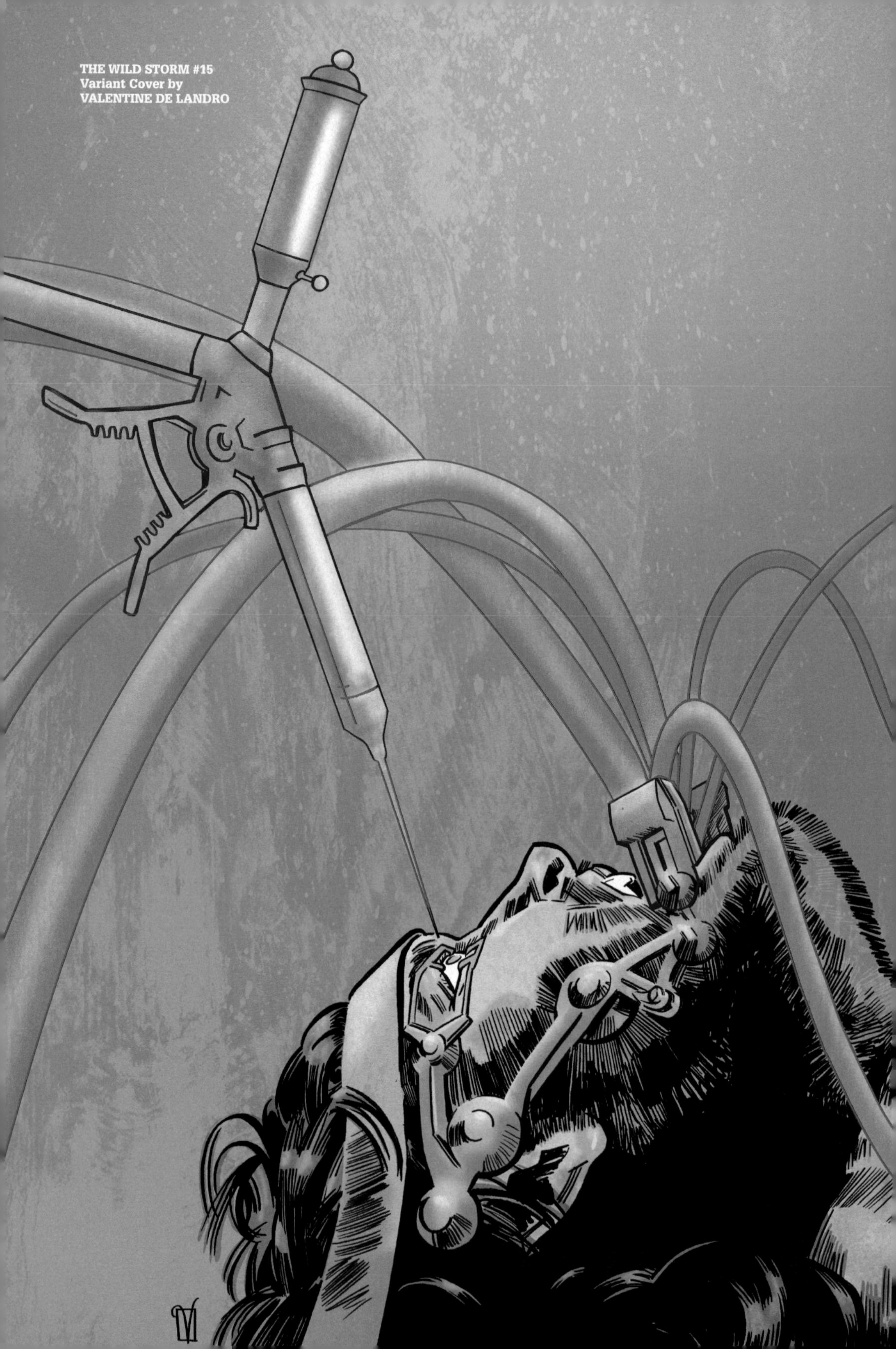

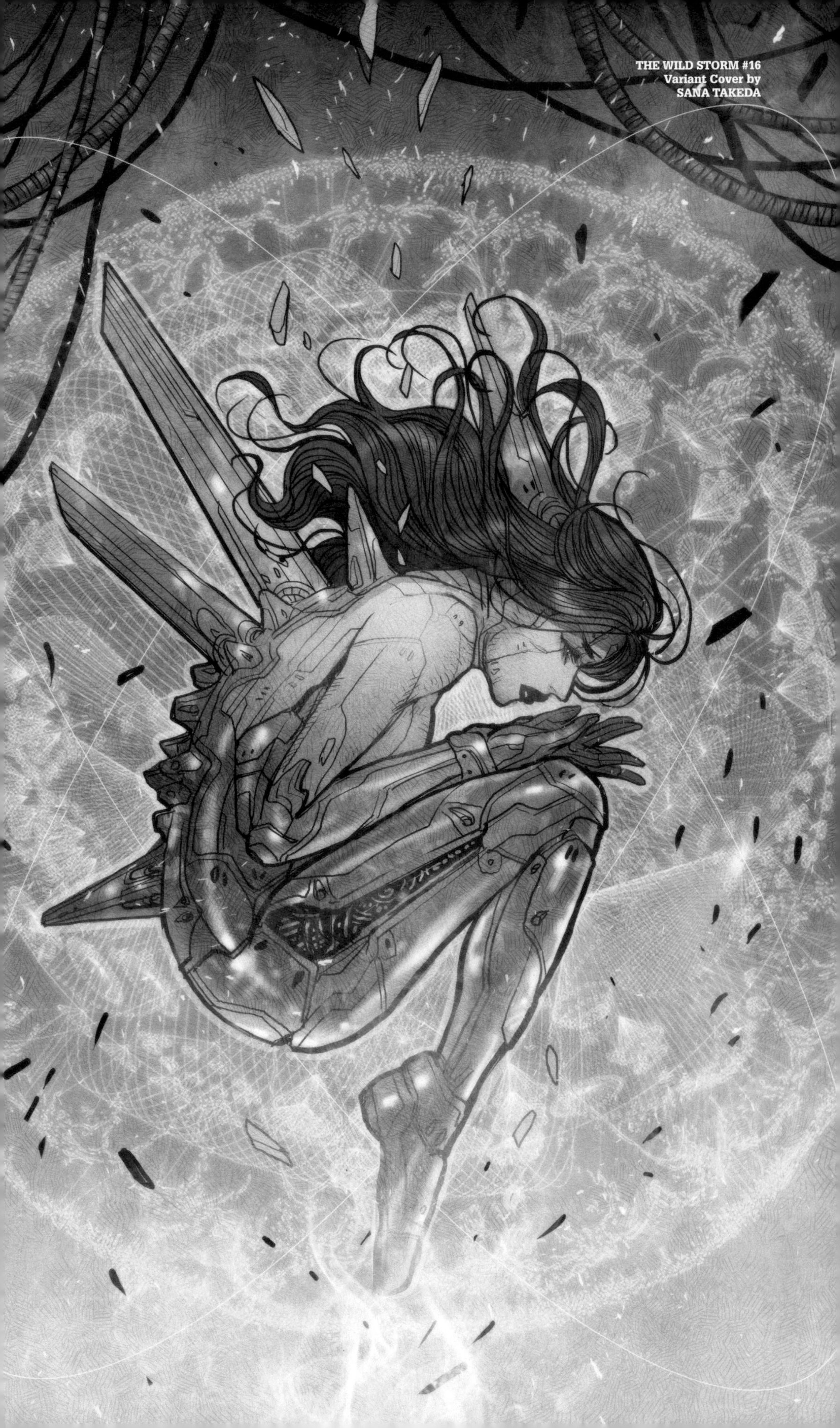

THE WILD STORM #16
Variant Cover by
SANA TAKEDA

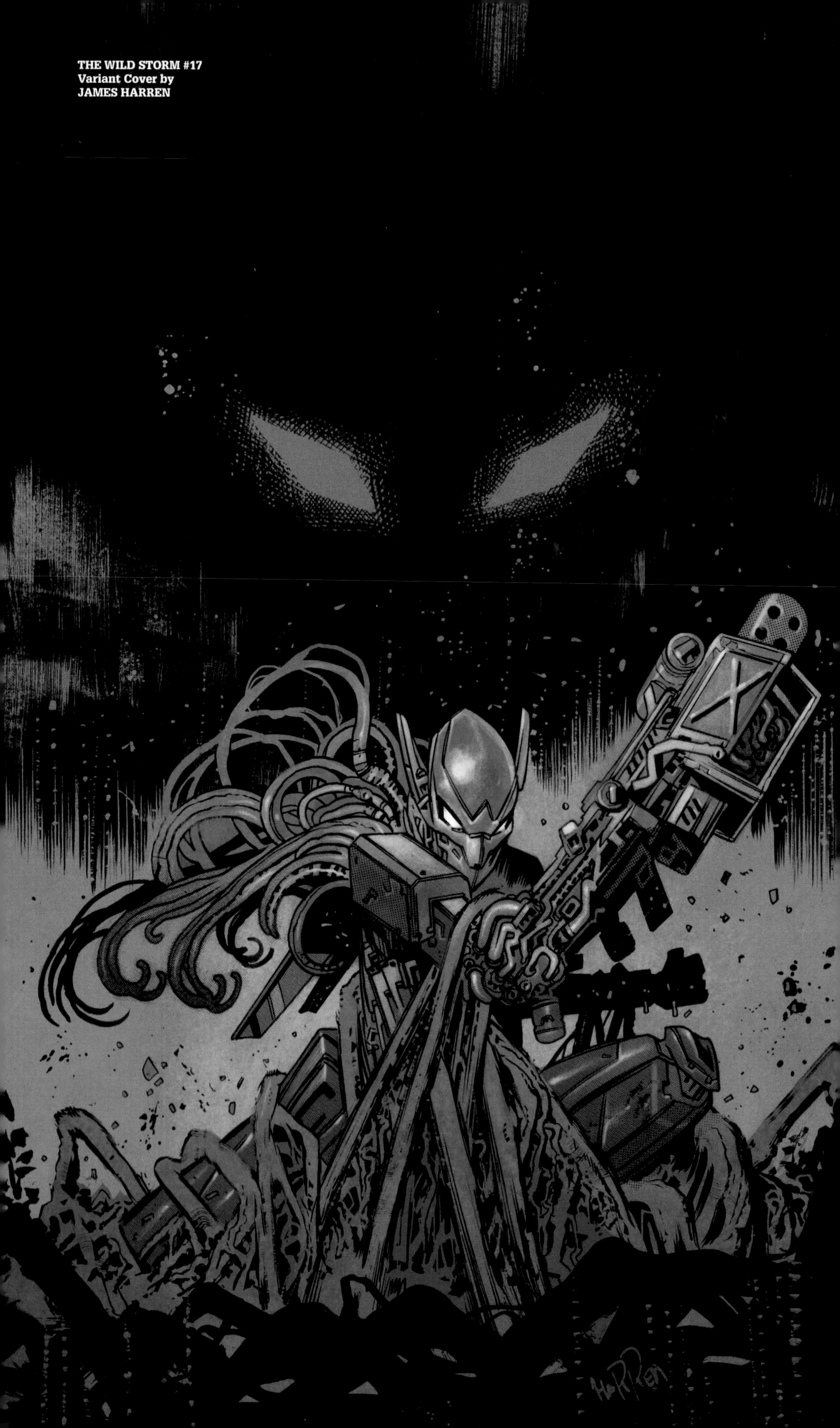

THE WILD STORM #17
Variant Cover by
JAMES HARREN

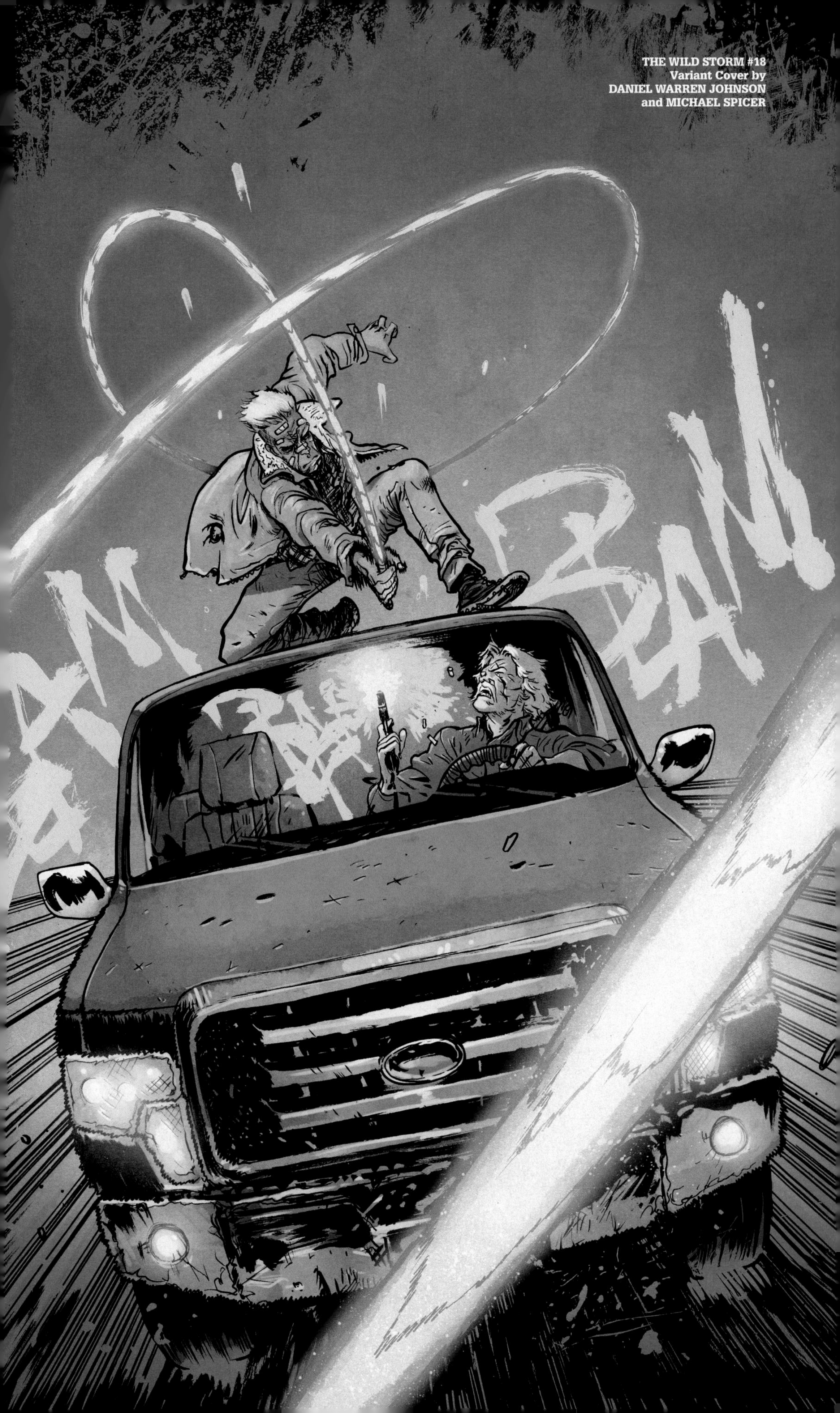

THE WILD STORM #18
Variant Cover by
DANIEL WARREN JOHNSON
and MICHAEL SPICER

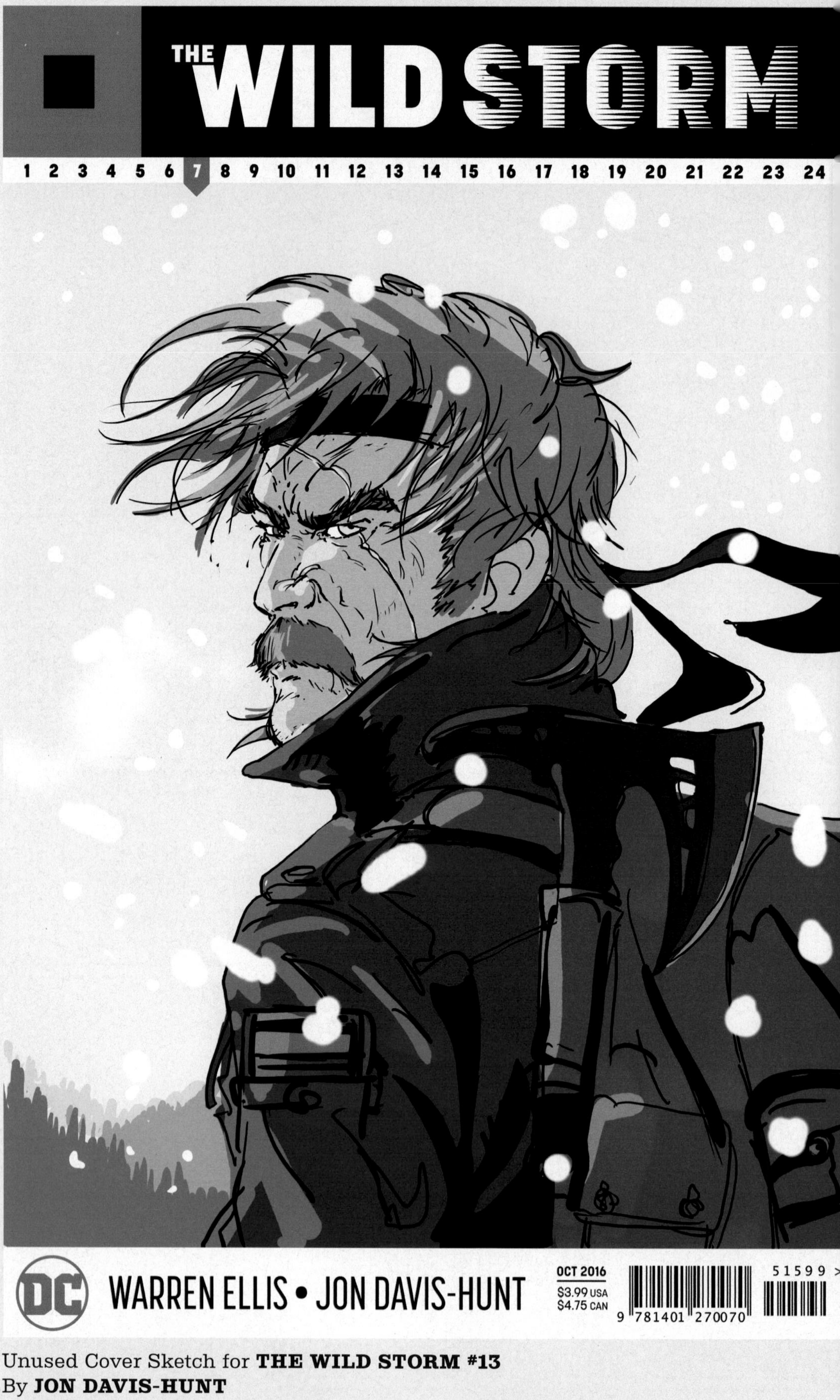
THE WILD STORM
1 2 3 4 5 6 7 8 9 10 11 12 13 14 15 16 17 18 19 20 21 22 23 24
DC
WARREN ELLIS • JON DAVIS-HUNT
OCT 2016
$3.99 USA
$4.75 CAN

Unused Cover Sketch for **THE WILD STORM #13**
By **JON DAVIS-HUNT**

Layouts for **THE WILD STORM #13**
By **JON DAVIS-HUNT**

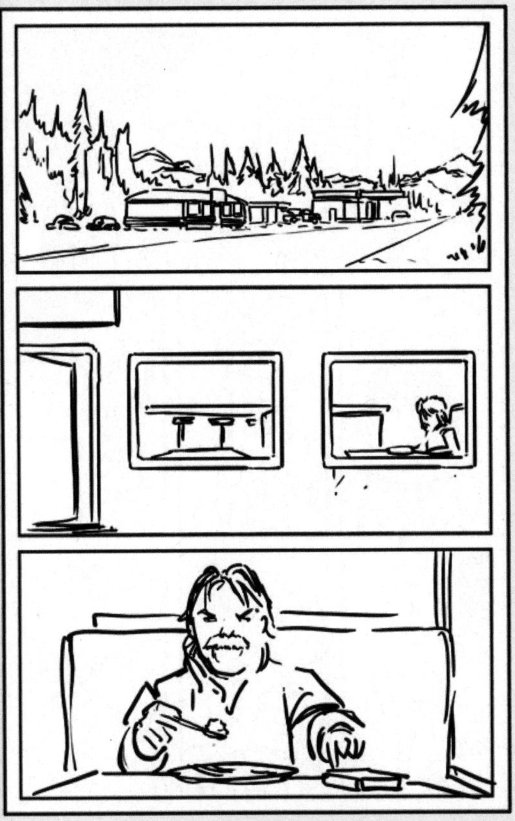

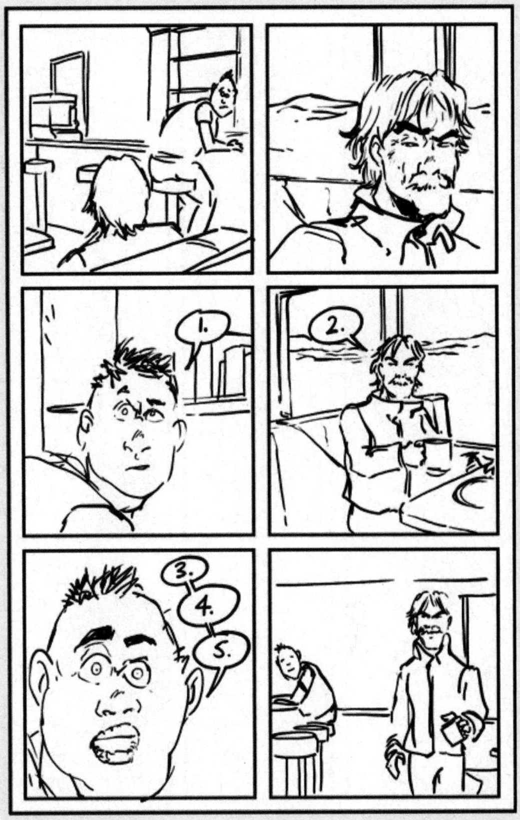
1.
2.
3.
4.
5.

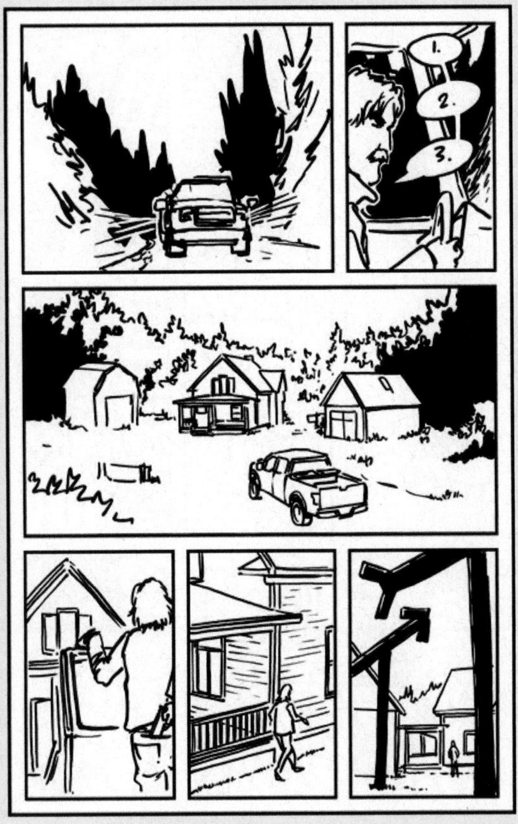
1.
2.
3.

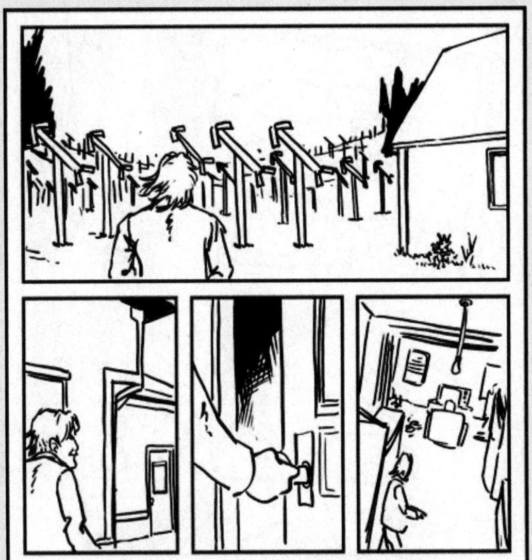
1.
CHALLENGERS OF THE UNKNOWN
2.
3.
4.

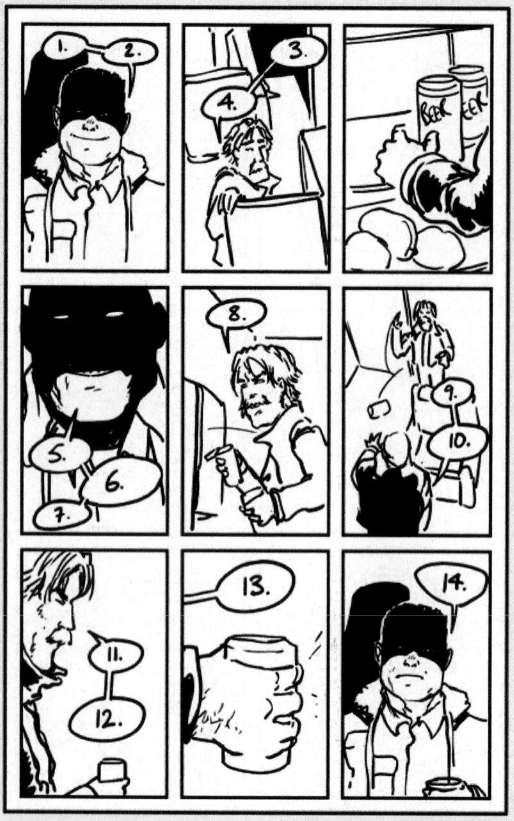
1.
2.
3.
4.
BEER
BEER
5.
6.
7.
8.
9.
10.
11.
12.
13.
14.

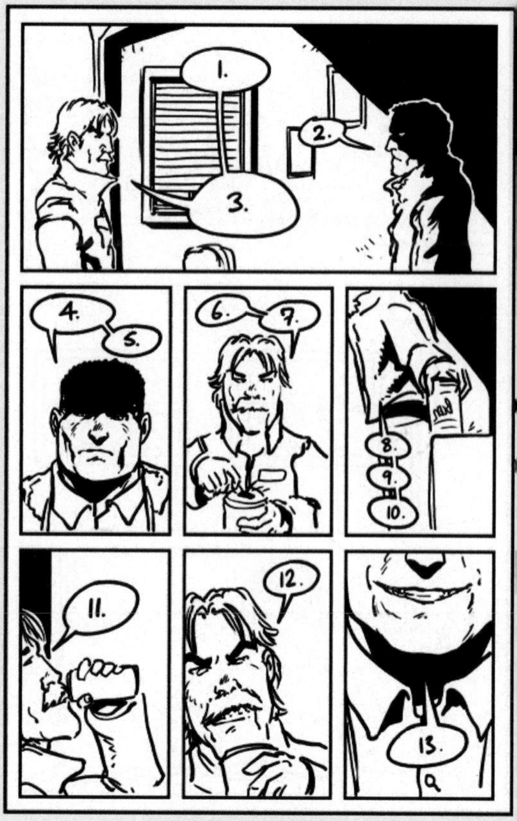
1.
2.
3.
4.
5.
6.
7.
8.
9.
10.
11.
12.
13.

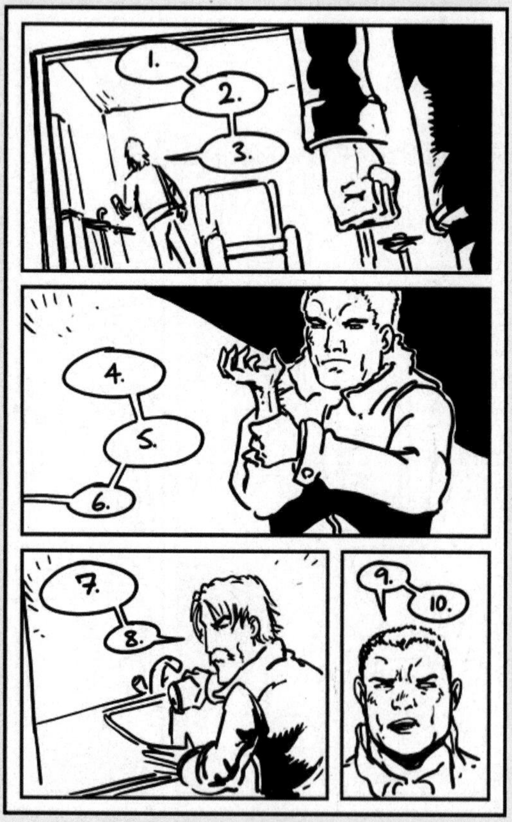
1.
2.
3.
4.
5.
6.
7.
8.
9.
10.

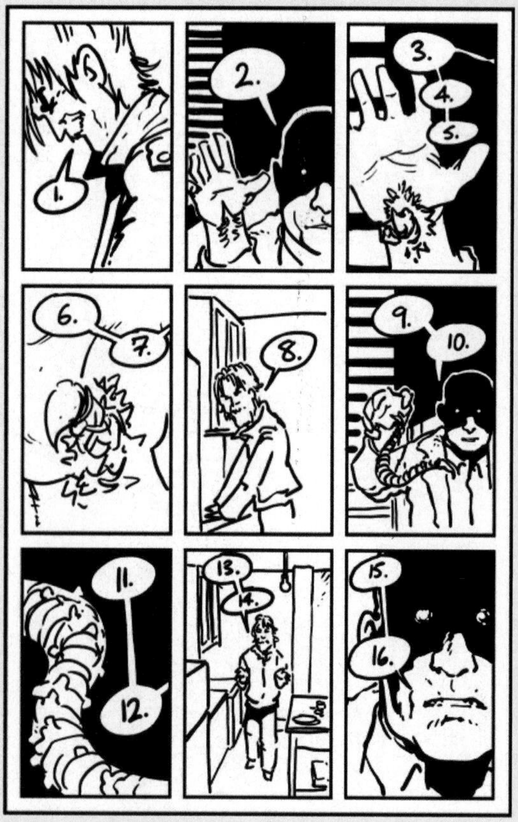
1.
2.
3.
4.
5.
6.
7.
8.
9.
10.
11.
12.
13.
14.
15.
16.

WHIP BREAKS TABLE, NOT DOOR AS WE ALREADY ESTABLISHED DOOR POSITION ON PREVIOUS PAGE. ALSO, TABLE HAS PLATES/PANS/ETC TO MAKE MORE EPIC DESTRUCTION.
(N.B. I'LL GO BACK AND ADD PLATES TO THIS TABLE ON PREVIOUS PANELS WHERE NEEDED.)

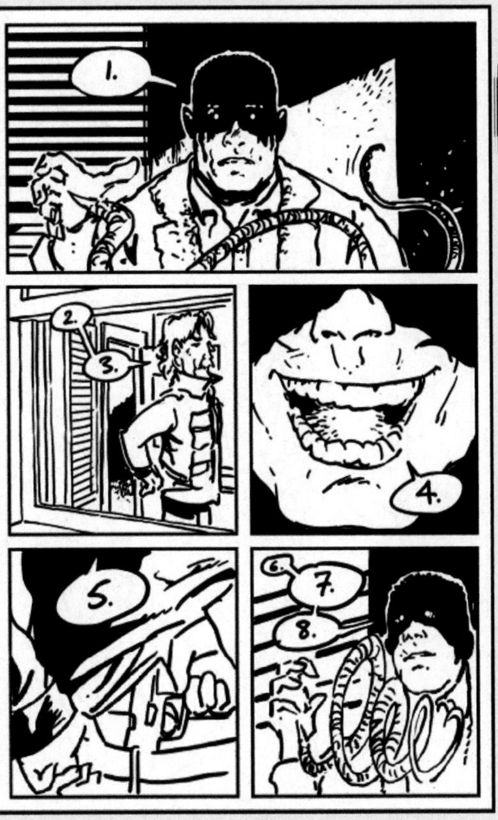

1.
2.
3.
4.
5.
6.
7.
8.

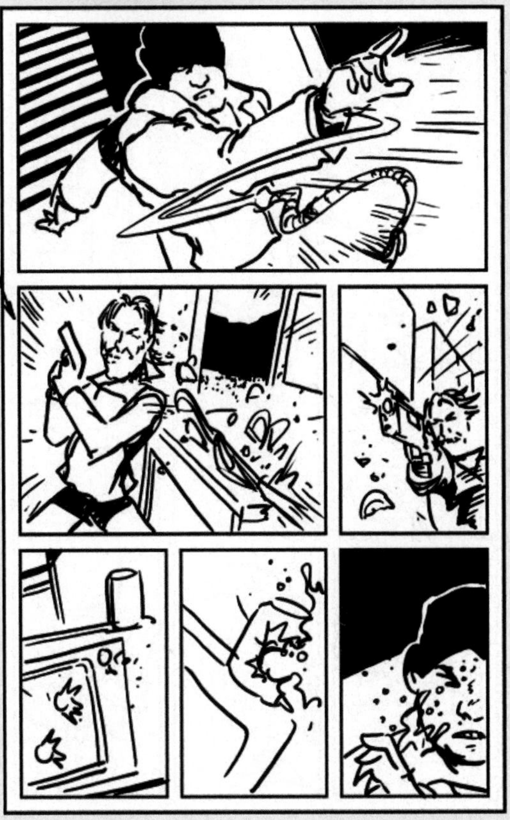

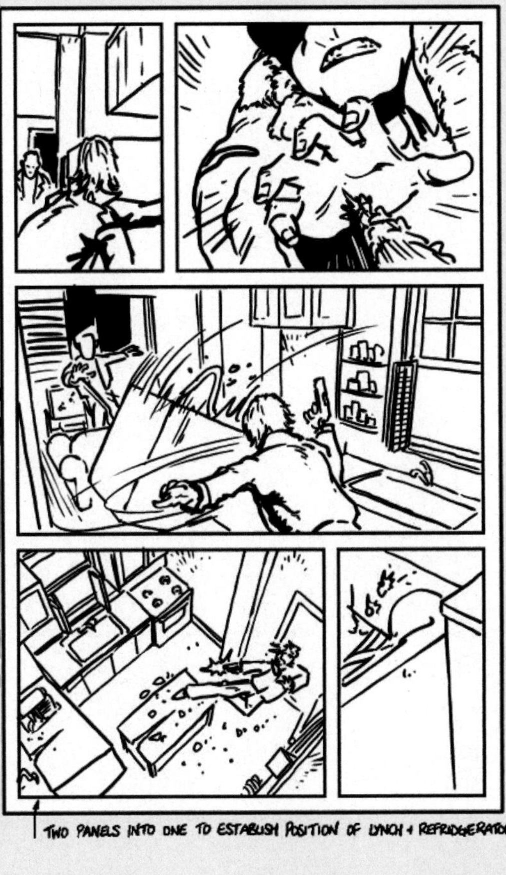

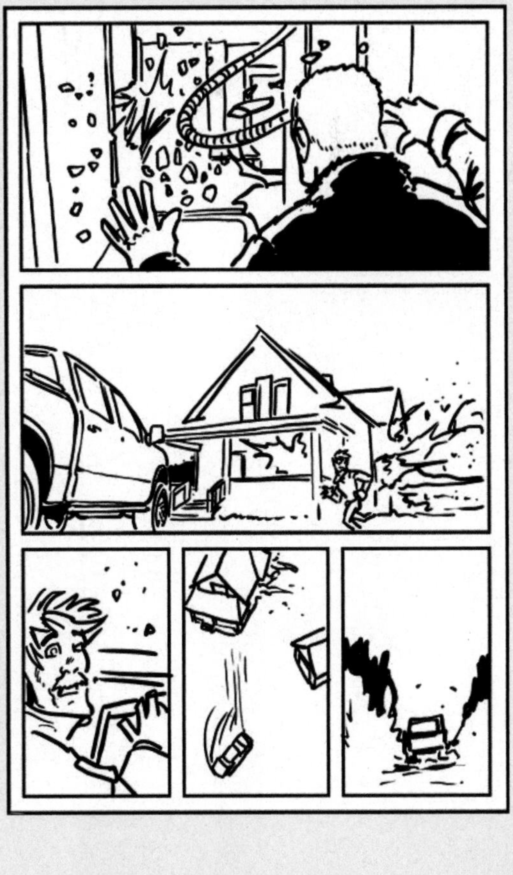

TWO PANELS INTO ONE TO ESTABLISH POSITION OF LYNCH + REFRIDGERATOR

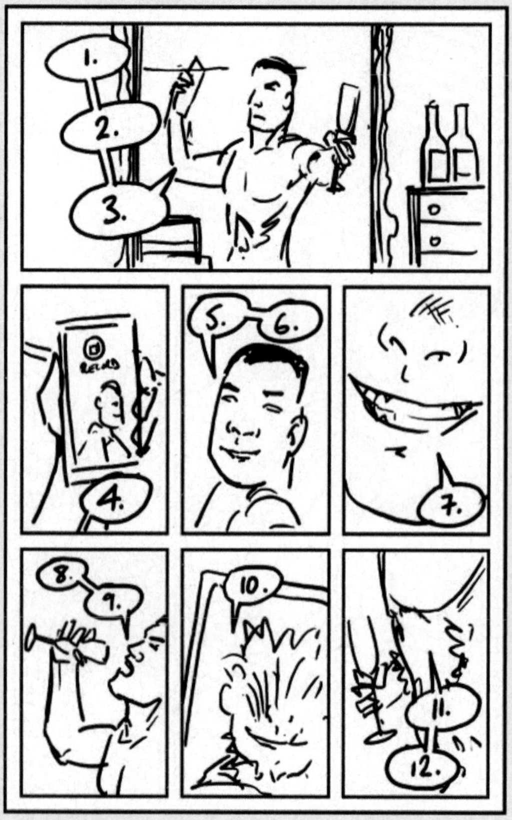
1.
2.
3.
RECORD
4.
5.
6.
7.
8.
9.
10.
11.
12.

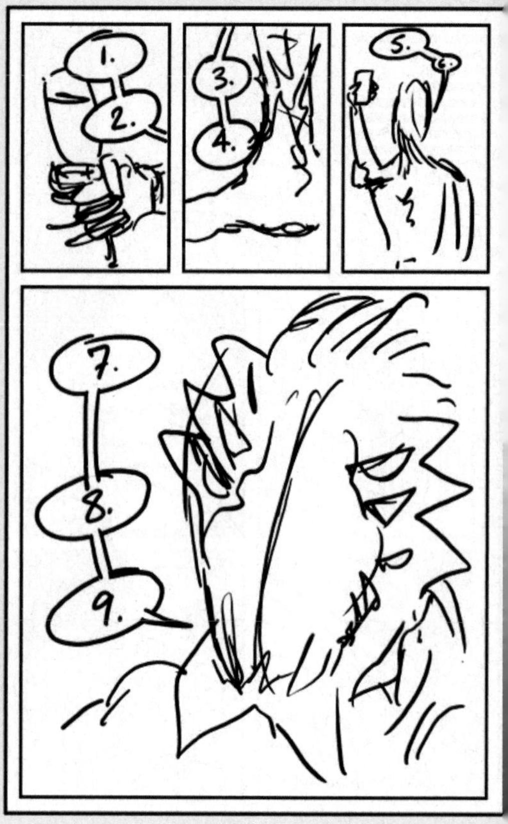
1.
2.
3.
4.
5.
7.
8.
9.

TWS
*03